LEARN THE WORD™

Revelation for Teens

LEARN THE WORD • LEARN THE WORD • LEARN THE WORD • L ARN

DAYMOND R. DUCK

STARBURST PUBLISHERS®

P. O. Box 4123, Lancaster, Pennsylvania 17604

www.starburstpublishers.com

Revelation for Teens: Learn the Word™ is an adaptation of *Revelation: God's Word for the Biblically-Inept*™.

If you don't know the Word, you can't live it!™

CREDITS:
Written by Daymond R. Duck
Adapted for teens by Frieda Nossaman
Cover design by Richmond & Williams
Text design and composition by John Reinhardt Book Design
Illustrations by Bruce Burkhart and Melissa A. Burkhart
Cartoons by Randy Glasbergen

Unless otherwise indicated all Scripture was taken from the HOLY BIBLE: NEW INTERNATIONAL VERSION®. NIV®. Copyright © 1973, 1978, 1984 by International Bible Society. Used by permission of Zondervan Publishing House.

First printing, April 2002
ISBN: 1-892016-55-9
Library of Congress Catalog Number 2001096269
Printed in the United States of America

WHAT'S IN THIS BOOK?

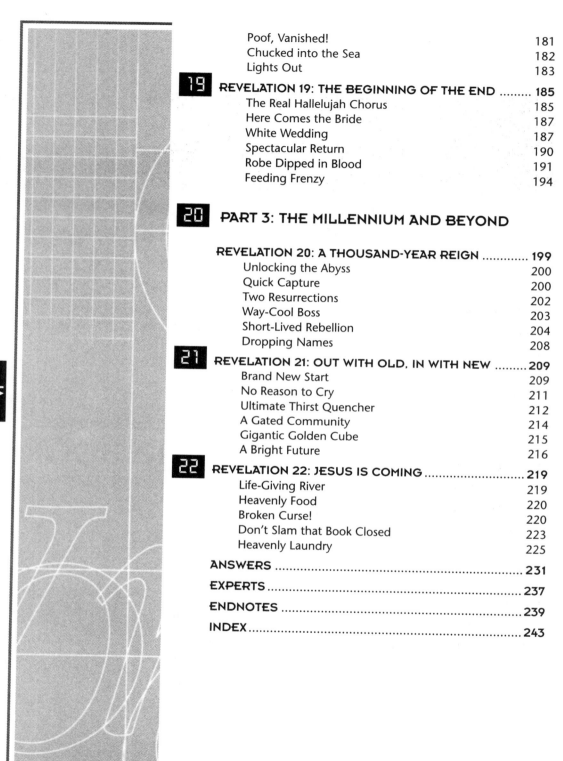

ILLUSTRATIONS, MAPS, AND TIMELINES

ILLUSTRATIONS

vii

MAPS

TIMELINES

HOW TO USE THIS BOOK

The chapter divisions in this book correspond to the chapter divisions in the Bible. There are twenty-two chapters in Revelation and twenty-two chapters in this book. First, you will find each verse of Revelation, and then the author's thoughts, and lots of icons and other information to help you. Here's what you will see:

What?

When you see a word in boldface, you'll find its definition in the sidebar.

Bible Quote

This is a verse or verses of Scripture.

Key Symbols

This feature highlights certain symbols and tells you what they mean.

Go!

When you see something underlined, the sidebar lists other places you can look in the Bible to find information about the underlined word or phrase.

⟫⟫ THE PROLOGUE: GET READY

"Revelation" means unveiling or exposing what was hidden. You likely have things you wouldn't want revealed in front of the whole school or even things that your friends know about you that you'd hate to have your parents find out! The Book of Revelation uncovers secrets about Jesus Christ, but they aren't things he's tried to keep hidden because he messed up like we sometimes do. Rather these are things that are going to happen that were kept secret for a time. God didn't want us to be clueless about the future, so he gave the message to his Son, Jesus, who gave it to an **angel** who gave it to John, who gave it to us. (Reminds me of the way a baton is passed in a relay race.)

angel: *heavenly being that serves God*

OUTSIDE CONNECTION

Kevin Johnson: You have a life to live—you hope. Will the world have time for you? One answer is to say, "Fret not. The world won't ever end." Another answer is what you'll hear more and more: "The world will end today. Or tomorrow." Maybe there's a different answer. Your reaction can take extremes. "This is a crock." Or you might think, "this message rocks." ¹

KEY SYMBOLS

Seven Golden Lampstands

Seven churches/periods of the Church Age
- Ephesus
- Smyrna
- Pergamum
- Thyatira
- Sardis
- Philadelphia
- Laodicea

Revelation 1:3
Blessed is the one who reads the words of this prophecy, and blessed are those who hear it and take to heart what is written in it, because the time is near.

⟫⟫ HELLO TO ALL!

John originally wrote this book to seven churches in Asia (check out the map on page 9), but it is meant for all Christians. It was common for letter writers in John's day to begin by saying, "Grace and peace to you" much the way some of you might say, "Hey, what's up?" or "Yo!"

The seven spirits before God's throne sounds like a posse of ghosts. But it refers to the Holy Spirit and the seven virtues that make up his nature.

Revelation is also *"from Jesus Christ."* This is our letter from Jesus, who loved us so much he chose to die so we could live

GO!
Isaiah 11:2
(seven spirits)

Your Move

Here's where you can have a say! Write your answers on the lines provided.

Notice that John calls himself "Servant John." Here's a guy who had every right to call himself "Jesus' best bud," "great gospel writer," "superapostle," or "Mega-Saint John," but he was interested in only one title: Servant. Are we as interested in being called servants? Why or why not? _____

_____

What might you have to give up or change to act like a servant? _____

_____

_____

 Jesus was the greatest servant of all! Even though he was the king of the universe, he stooped down to wash his disciples' feet. John's role model for servanthood was Jesus; Jesus should be our role model too.

Get Real

Listen to straight talk about the Bible and stuff that matters in everyday life.

forever with him. Proof of Jesus' love is in his actions. He allowed himself to be **crucified**, paying the penalty for our **sins** with his own blood. (Read more about Jesus in LWBI, chapters 12–16.) Some day Jesus will bring his kingdom to earth, and it will <u>never end</u>. That is a way cool concept!

 Jesus will judge us by what the Bible says. We should listen up whenever the Bible is read.

GO!
John 19:16–30 (crucified)
Luke 1:29–33 (never end)

crucified: executed on a Roman cross

Stop!

God wants to protect us so he warns us about danger. When you see this icon, stop and read God's message.

_F. F. Bruce: John's Revelation belongs to the literary genre called "apocalyptic." "Apocalyptic" literature is so called because it deals with the revealing or "unveiling" of things normally inaccessible to human knowledge, such as the course of future events or the secrets of outer space.[1]

OUTSIDE CONNECTION

The Chinese army has tested its "Taiwan rocket gun," a new weapon with a range of over 200 miles. According to a report translated from the _Wen Hui Bao_ newspaper, "China has tested a newly developed rocket gun, named the WS-1B, which claims to have a range of 360 kilometers, the longest range in the world of a

HAPPENINGS

Outside Connection

This feature gives you relevant quotes from other people.

Happenings

When you see this icon, you'll discover historical information or recent news that points toward the end times.

JOHN GOES DREAMING • ONE

ix

5

LEARN THE WORD • REVELATION FOR TEENS

INTRODUCTION

Welcome to *Revelation for Teens: Learn the Word™*! This is the second book in a new series that takes you deep into God's Word without boring you. Books in this series are designed to make studying Scripture simple, rewarding, and fun! So grab your favorite chair and let's *Learn the Word™*!

WHY STUDY REVELATION?

Wouldn't it be great to know the future? Revelation is God's message to all of us who are concerned about the future. Some people pay psychics to tell them things they *think* will happen. God gave us a whole book to tell us about what he *knows* will happen, and it's free!

Sometimes scary things occur—wars, terrorist bombings, environmental disasters, school shootings, divorce, even tests. We can feel lost—like no one's in charge. Revelation shows that God is the one who is in control no matter how bad things look. Reading Revelation will strengthen your faith. It urges believers to "hang in there!" It also warns against making certain mistakes and tells how to gain eternal life.

Here are seven reasons you'll want to be in the know:

1. Revelation is the Word of God—that means it's important.
2. Jesus told us to watch for signs of things to come.
3. If we do not study Revelation, our understanding of the entire Bible will remain biblically inept.
4. Revelation reveals God's plan for the future.
5. A special blessing is promised to readers of Revelation.
6. Revelation can change lives.
7. Revelation gives us a reason to be concerned about those who haven't made up their minds about believing Jesus.

HOW TO STUDY REVELATION

Keep in mind that the Bible is the best teacher available. That is why we have included other verses of Scripture from the Bible to explain difficult areas of Revelation.

As you study Revelation remember its three main divisions:

1. Part One is called **The Church Age** (chapters 1–3). We are now living in the Church Age, and it is almost over.
2. Part Two is called **From the Rapture to the Second Coming** (chapters 4–19). It will be a terrible time in which to live. Many prophetic signs indicate that this time is coming closer. We need to learn what to watch for and what to do so we can avoid terror.
3. Part Three is called **The Millennium and Beyond** (chapters 20–22). Some of the most special verses in the Bible are found in these chapters. They are filled with inspiration and hope for the future.

Also keep in mind four ways to interpret or understand Revelation:

1. It is a message to each one of us.
2. It is a message to the entire church.
3. It is a message to seven specific churches.
4. It is a message of prophecy about future events.

CODE LETTERS

Occasionally throughout this book I will give you a fast way to learn more about a topic by referring you to another book for teens. You'll see something like this: "(Check out LWBI, page 90.)" The letters *LWBI* refer to the other book in the *Learn the Word*™ series—*The Bible for Teens.* If you have that book, you can turn to page 90 to read about something discussed in *this* book.

WHO WROTE REVELATION?

John, one of the twelve disciples of Jesus, wrote Revelation under the guidance of its true author—the Holy Spirit, the third person of the Trinity. The word *trinity* is not found in the Bible, but it is used to explain the three different ways God reveals himself—as God the Father, his Son Jesus, and the Holy

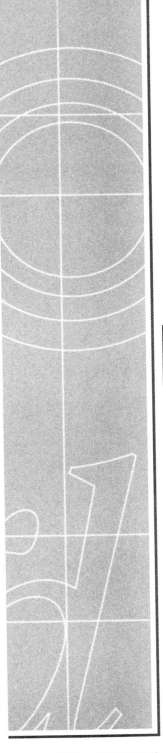

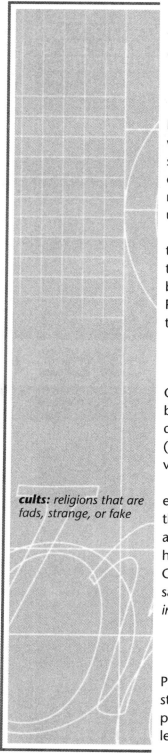

Spirit. These are three different expressions of God, just as thoughts, spoken words, and written words are three different expressions of every person.

SYMBOLS, SYMBOLS, AND MORE SYMBOLS

Revelation is filled with symbols. John was in prison when he wrote the book, and some believe he used symbols so he could smuggle his message to the outside world. Perhaps he had to convince prison authorities that these were the writings of a madman. Others believe God had John use symbols to make us study the entire Bible to understand its meaning.

Whatever the reason, the symbols make some people think they need a Ph.D. to understand Revelation. No one can deny the value of a good education, but people of all educational backgrounds (including teenagers) do enjoy learning about Revelation. If you like science fiction novels, you'll love Revelation. The best news is that this book is true.

SO MANY DIFFERENT VIEWPOINTS

Obviously, with so many different symbols there are bound to be many different explanations. One of the biggest areas of disagreement has to do with when the church will go to heaven (aka the Rapture). This book uses the most widely accepted viewpoint—Pre-Tribulation.

cults: *religions that are fads, strange, or fake*

Many people are tempted to date the events found in Revelation. Don't do it! Various **cults** have set dates for the end of the world and have looked stupid or killed themselves in an attempt to make their predictions come true. Forget it! Do your homework. Finish your chores. Apply for that job. And trust God to take care of the future in his time. Believe what the Bible says, *"No man knows about that day or hour, not even the angels in heaven, nor the Son, but only the Father"* (Matthew 24:26).

ONE FINAL TIP

Prayer and meditation are valuable. God wants you to understand the Bible, and the Holy Spirit can open your mind. So pray and think as you read. It is surprising how much you can learn and remember when you put your mind to it.

PART 1

THE CHURCH AGE

John Goes Dreaming

 LET'S DIVE IN

Imagine. You walk to your mailbox and pull out a crusty, dirty, rotting letter from a friend who moved years ago to a distant island. Get this, your friend tells you God has shown him the future and that "the end of the world is near!" Whadda ya do? Crumple up the letter and toss it? Write him back? Call the tabloids and make some money off his crazy notion? Believe him?

John sent just such a letter to his friends, but they knew better than to call him a weirdo. John was an apostle, one of the twelve men Jesus chose to begin a revolutionary movement of which John's **correspondents** were now an important part. (To learn more about John's life, check out the map on page 4.) John's readers would have been riveted, although they, too, might have had a hard time believing his message.

correspondents: people John is writing to; the seven churches in Asia (Turkey)

> **Revelation 1:1–2**
> The revelation of Jesus Christ, which God gave him to show his servants what must soon take place. He made it known by sending his angel to his servant John, who testifies to everything he saw—that is, the word of God and the testimony of Jesus Christ.

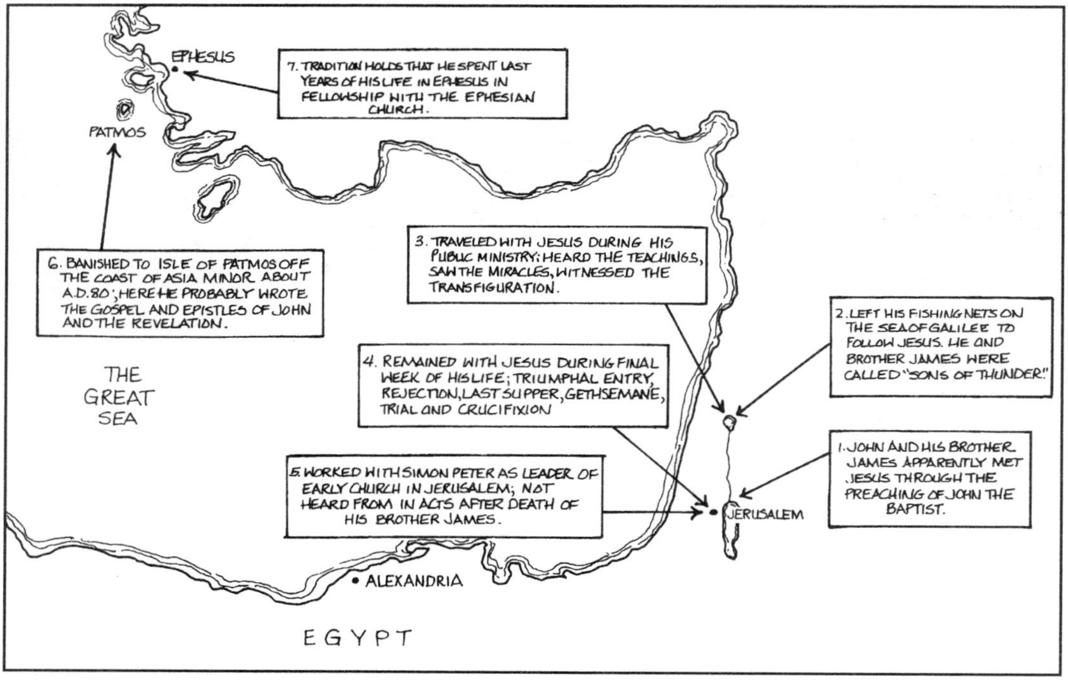
EPHESUS
7. TRADITION HOLDS THAT HE SPENT LAST YEARS OF HIS LIFE IN EPHESUS IN FELLOWSHIP WITH THE EPHESIAN CHURCH.
PATMOS
6. BANISHED TO ISLE OF PATMOS OFF THE COAST OF ASIA MINOR ABOUT A.D. 80; HERE HE PROBABLY WROTE THE GOSPEL AND EPISTLES OF JOHN AND THE REVELATION.
3. TRAVELED WITH JESUS DURING HIS PUBLIC MINISTRY; HEARD THE TEACHINGS, SAW THE MIRACLES, WITNESSED THE TRANSFIGURATION.
2. LEFT HIS FISHING NETS ON THE SEA OF GALILEE TO FOLLOW JESUS. HE AND BROTHER JAMES WERE CALLED "SONS OF THUNDER."
THE GREAT SEA
4. REMAINED WITH JESUS DURING FINAL WEEK OF HIS LIFE; TRIUMPHAL ENTRY, REJECTION, LAST SUPPER, GETHSEMANE, TRIAL AND CRUCIFIXION
1. JOHN AND HIS BROTHER JAMES APPARENTLY MET JESUS THROUGH THE PREACHING OF JOHN THE BAPTIST.
5. WORKED WITH SIMON PETER AS LEADER OF EARLY CHURCH IN JERUSALEM; NOT HEARD FROM IN ACTS AFTER DEATH OF HIS BROTHER JAMES.
JERUSALEM
ALEXANDRIA
EGYPT

The Life of John

This map shows where major events occurred in John's life. The events are numbered chronologically.

THE PROLOGUE: GET READY

"Revelation" means unveiling or exposing what was hidden. You likely have things you wouldn't want revealed in front of the whole school or even things that your friends know about you that you'd hate to have your parents find out! The Book of Revelation uncovers secrets about Jesus Christ, but they aren't things he's tried to keep hidden because he messed up like we sometimes do. Rather these are things that are going to happen that were kept secret for a time. God didn't want us to be clueless about the future, so he gave the message to his Son, Jesus, who gave it to an **angel**, who gave it to John, who gave it to us. (Reminds me of the way a baton is passed in a relay race.)

angel: *heavenly being that serves God*

Christians disagree about how to understand Revelation. Some think the events described are **symbolic** and have already happened. Others think events are not described in chronological order but rather in seven parallels throughout the book. Most believe Revelation explains Christ's plans from the time he left earth until the end of the world. They understand

symbolic: *something that stands for or represents something else*

Notice that John calls himself "Servant John." Here's a guy who had every right to call himself "Jesus' best bud," "great gospel writer," "super apostle," or "Mega-Saint John," but he was interested in only one title: Servant. Are we as interested in being called servants? Why or why not?_____

_____

What might you have to give up or change to act like a servant?_____

_____

_____

Jesus was the greatest servant of all! Even though he was the king of the universe, he stooped down to <u>wash</u> his disciples' feet. John's role model for servanthood was Jesus; Jesus should be our role model too.

Be a servant this week by offering to help a young kid with his homework; volunteering for a chore you know your mom or dad hates (like pooper-scooping the yard); driving your sisters or brothers to one of their activities; or mowing an elderly neighbor's lawn for free. Gold crowns of reward won't fall out of heaven as a result, but your efforts will be noticed by the most important Person of all, Jesus.

the events literally and see chapters 4 to 22 as future events because *"what must soon take place"* means the future. This book was written around A.D. 96 by the <u>apostle John</u>, one of the original **disciples** of Jesus (see LWBI, page 131, for a list of their names), so some of what was future stuff then is history now!

GO!
John 13:3–5 (wash)
Acts 1:21–26
 (apostle John)

disciples: followers

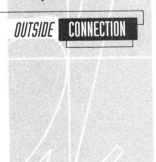

Kevin Johnson: *You have a life to live—you hope. Will the world have time for you? One answer is to say, "Fret not. The world won't ever end." Another answer is what you'll hear more and more: "The world will end today. Or tomorrow." Maybe there's a different answer. Your reaction can take extremes. "This is a crock." Or you might think, "this message rocks."*[1]

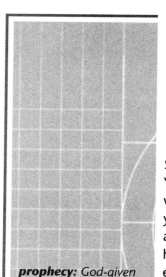

> ### Revelation 1:3
> Blessed is the one who reads the words of this prophecy, and blessed are those who hear it and take to heart what is written in it, because the time is near.

Prophetic Promise

So, you've decided to tackle this tough topic. Good for you! You're about to undertake an excellent adventure, one that will leave you a bit dazed and confused at times, but will make you spiritually richer in the end. God wants us to read, hear, and apply what we learn from this book. As we do our part, he'll help us understand what we've read. The author of Revelation calls his book a **prophecy**, a message of what will happen in the future. Also, this is the only book of Scripture that promises a blessing just for reading it! Did your English teacher promise blessings for reading Shakespeare or Dostoyevsky?

prophecy: God-given news about future happenings

> ### Revelation 1:4–6
> John, To the seven churches in the province of Asia: Grace and peace to you from him who is, and who was, and who is to come, and from the seven spirits before his throne, and from Jesus Christ, who is the faithful witness, the firstborn from the dead, and the ruler of the kings of the earth. To him who loves us and has freed us from our sins by his blood, and has made us to be a kingdom and priests to serve his God and Father—to him be glory and power for ever and ever! Amen.

 HELLO TO ALL!

John originally wrote this book to seven churches in Asia (check out the map on page 9), but it is meant for all Christians. It was common for letter writers in John's day to begin by saying, "Grace and peace to you" much the way some of you might say, "Hey, what's up?" or "Yo!"

The <u>seven spirits</u> before God's throne sounds like a posse of ghosts. But it refers to the Holy Spirit and the seven **virtues** that make up his nature:

GO!
Isaiah 11:2
  (seven spirits)

virtues: characteristics or traits

- *The spirit of the Lord*—the nature of Jesus
- *The spirit of wisdom*—the ability to make the right decision
- *The spirit of understanding*—the ability to understand everything
- *The spirit of counsel*—the ability to give good advice
- *The spirit of might*—the power to do what God wants
- *The spirit of knowledge*—the ability to know beyond human understanding
- *The spirit of the fear of the Lord*—the ability to respect God's will

Revelation is also *"from Jesus Christ."* This is our letter from Jesus, who loved us so much he chose to die so we could live forever with him. Proof of Jesus' love is in his actions. He allowed himself to be **crucified**, paying the penalty for our **sins** with his own blood. (Read more about Jesus in LWBI, chapters 12–16.) Some day Jesus will bring his kingdom to earth, and it will <u>never end</u>. That is a way cool concept!

F. F. Bruce: *John's Revelation belongs to the literary* **genre** *called "apocalyptic." "Apocalyptic" literature is so called because it deals with the revealing or "unveiling" of things normally inaccessible to human knowledge, such as the course of future events or the secrets of outer space.*[2]

> **Revelation 1:7**
> Look, he is coming with the clouds, and every eye will see him, even those who pierced him; and all the peoples of the earth will **mourn** because of him. So shall it be! Amen.

Everyone's Gonna Know

Have you ever said something bad about someone and found out that he or she heard everything you said? Oops! It's hard to regain a friend's trust after you've been caught gossiping, isn't it? (Not to mention way embarrassing!)

When Jesus returns to the earth, every eye will see him—even those who <u>pierced</u>, or killed, him! Unbelievers will realize that they've been bad-mouthing the Son of God—the ruler

GO!
John 19:16–30 (crucified)
Luke 1:29–33 (never end)

crucified: *executed on a Roman cross*

sins: *thoughts, deeds, and omissions that are against God's will*

genre: *category*

mourn: *grieve, be sad or depressed, cry out in sorrow*

GO!
Psalm 22:16; Isaiah 53:5 (pierced)

7

and king of the universe. The hugeness of unbelievers' sins will overwhelm them, but there won't be any way out. It will be too late. They will be losers in the truest sense of the word.

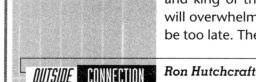

Ron Hutchcraft: Before this generation, most people at least knew what **morality** was, knew the basic outlines of the Gospel, and had heard John 3:16. Today, that is no longer true.[3]

> **Revelation 1:8**
> "I am the Alpha and the Omega," says the Lord God, "who is, and who was, and who is to come, the Almighty."

Not Gen X or Y, but Gen A to Z!

Being labeled isn't fun, especially if you're a teenager. Marketing experts have divided the generations into manageable marketing groups and labeled them with a letter of the alphabet. Generation X is the people in their twenties. Generation Y is today's teens, and soon Generation Z will run the teenage world. (We're talking about babies who are in diapers now.)

Jesus is larger than any block of time or space. He can't be stuffed into a generation and labeled. Jesus says he is the **Alpha** and the **Omega**, the beginning and the end. He's Generation A to Z! In Revelation 1:4 John says that Jesus is, was, and is to come. That just about sums it up, yet Jesus tries to get us to understand how much larger than life he is. He's a never-ending Being who is equal to Almighty God. Jesus is all-powerful, everlasting, and forever all at the same time.

Alpha: first letter of the Greek alphabet, much like "A" in English alphabet

Omega: last letter of the Greek alphabet, much like "Z" in English alphabet

> **Revelation 1:9**
> I, John, your brother and companion in the suffering and kingdom and patient endurance that are ours in Jesus, was on the island of Patmos because of the word of God and the testimony of Jesus.

 REAL ISLAND LIVING?

John explains to his audience where he is—on a small island in the Mediterranean Sea (see illustration, page 9) where the Roman emperor Domitian imprisoned him. Do you think John was lounging on the beach, brushing sand out of his slurpy? No, he was suffering for his Lord. He was living in this desolate spot, imprisoned and guarded because of his faith in Jesus. John was willing to be thrown in prison, even killed, rather than **deny** his Savior.

deny: *reject, turn away from*

Revelation 1:10–11
On the Lord's Day I was in the Spirit, and I heard behind me a loud voice like a trumpet, which said: "Write on a scroll what you see and send it to the seven churches: to Ephesus, Smyrna, Pergamum, Thyatira, Sardis, Philadelphia, and Laodicea."

SEVEN HAPPENIN' CHURCHES

When friends are engrossed in listening to music or playing video games it's hard to get their attention. John was tuned in to God and what he was saying. It was Sunday, and John was meditating in prayer when the Holy Spirit began to have power over him. As he drew <u>near to God</u>, John heard an unusual voice—a voice that blasted out at him like a trumpet.

GO!
Hebrews 10:22
(near to God)

6

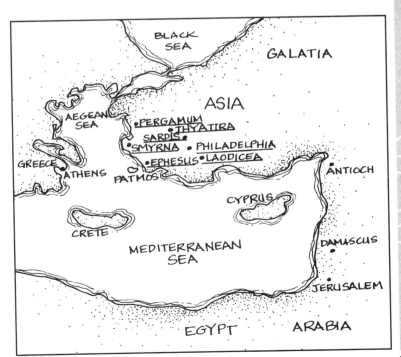

Map of Seven Churches

John wrote his letter to the churches located in the cities that are underlined on this map. He was imprisoned on the island of Patmos when he wrote Revelation.

John heard the names of seven churches. The church in Philadelphia isn't where cream cheese is made or steak sandwiches are eaten. All seven churches were in Asia (see illustration, page 9). Jesus had a good reason why he listed them in the order that he did. We can learn from these churches that had good and bad qualities, much like churches of today. (Unless, of course, your church is perfect.) Each church represents a period of time in the **Church Age**.

OUTSIDE CONNECTION

George Barna: *The research we have conducted among teens reveals that they are unusually well connected to churches. Indisputably, the Christian Church in America is ailing, but that condition is not attributable to a widespread rejection by teenagers. In some respects, the Church retains a greater measure of potential and hope for the future because of the dogged spirituality of teenagers.*[4]

> **Revelation 1:12**
> I turned around to see the voice that was speaking to me. And when I turned I saw seven golden lampstands, . . .

Seven Haven

As you study Revelation, you'll see the number seven reoccurring. (Okay, that's an understatement. You will probably get sick and tired of the seven thing!) In the verse above, when he heard the voice, John turned around and saw seven golden lampstands. Later, in Revelation 1:20 we'll learn that these seven golden **lampstands** represent the seven churches. And the seven churches stand for seven different periods of the Church Age (see timeline 1, page 46).

Don't get confused about the different aspects of these seven churches. Instead, imagine how bright and shiny this vision must have been. John must have felt like a Hollywood celebrity on Academy Award night—dazzled by shimmery gold and photographers' flashbulbs!

> **Revelation 1:13**
> . . . and among the lampstands was someone "like a son of man," dressed in a robe reaching down to his feet and with a golden sash around his chest.

lampstands: *stands made to hold pots of burning oil*

KEY SYMBOLS

Seven Golden Lampstands

Seven churches/periods of the Church Age
- Ephesus
- Smyrna
- Pergamum
- Thyatira
- Sardis
- Philadelphia
- Laodicea

Hi-ya Priest

After searching for the person behind the voice, John came face-to-face with Someone who looked like the Son of man standing in the middle of the seven churches. This Being wore a long robe that went down to his feet and had a golden sash around his chest. (Okay, get the picture out of your mind of your dad coming down for breakfast in his bathrobe.) This image of the Son of man is way mind-boggling and would take your breath away if you saw it.

Who was this Son of man? This was Jesus dressed as a high priest (see illustration below). This vision means that Jesus is the center of the church during the Church Age. He replaced the high priests who conducted worship ceremonies for the people of Israel. Jesus is always with believers as a spiritual priest to **intercede** for us. What a great feeling to know that Jesus prays for us in much the same way that we pray for others.

intercede: work or pray in our place

High Priest

The high priest of Israel is shown here dressed in official attire. Twelve stones on his breastplate represent the twelve tribes of Israel. Today Jesus is our high priest.

> ### Revelation 1:14
> His head and hair were white like wool, as white as snow, and his eyes were like blazing fire.

Eyes of Fire

Like a teacher whose piercing blue eyes glare over the top of her glasses and catch every movement and note you try to pass to a friend, the Son of man has eyes that blaze like fire, seeing everything. As Jesus looked over the seven churches mentioned in Revelation 1:14, he saw every good and bad deed of all the generations to come. (That includes the sins and bad things you have done and will continue to do, too!)

> ### Revelation 1:15–16
> His feet were like bronze glowing in a furnace, and his voice was like the sound of rushing waters. In his right hand he held seven stars, and out of his mouth came a sharp double-edged sword. His face was like the sun shining in all its brilliance.

Seriously Powerful Surf Sounds

Ever stand on the beach during a storm? It's hard to talk to the person beside you, and nothing can withstand the damage of the pounding surf. In Revelation 1:15 Jesus' voice was so loud that it was like crashing waves. Jesus' voice was so powerful it spoke everything into existence (creation), it raised the dead, and it had authority over nature. Imagine if you could speak your homework into appearing on your desk! That would be a big help on those days when you left it at home.

In addition to creating with his voice, Jesus will judge the universe, and no one will be able to overpower him. Jesus' feet glowed like a burning fire or furnace, which symbolizes that Jesus will **judge** everyone.

The seven stars are the seven angels of the seven churches. (I warned you there would be lots of "sevens," didn't I!) It was the responsibility of these seven angels to look after the churches.

Jesus is known as the sun of righteousness and the light of the world. No brighter light has been seen than the light that reflects from Christ's face.

GO!

Genesis 1:2–26
(creation)
John 11:43–44
(raised the dead)
Mark 4:39
(over nature)
John 8:12
(light of the world)

judge: decide our future place and the rewards we will get

Jesus will judge us by what the Bible says. We should listen up whenever the Bible is read.

> **Revelation 1:17–18**
> When I saw him, I fell at his feet as though dead. Then he placed his right hand on me and said: "Do not be afraid. I am the First and the Last. I am the Living One; I was dead, and behold I am alive for ever and ever! And I hold the keys of death and **Hades**."

John Loses It

What would you do if you came face-to-face with the actor or musician you most admire? Jump all over him or her, wanting autographs and gushing, "I'm your biggest fan!"

What if you saw Jesus in all of his glory? John collapsed on the ground in front of Jesus when he saw him. Jesus didn't leave him there but gently placed his right hand on John and said, *"Do not be afraid. I am the First and the Last."* John must have been comforted.

Jesus said this about himself:

- *"I am the Living One"*—I always existed and will always exist.
- *"I was dead"*—Jesus paid the penalty for our sin.
- *"I am alive for ever and ever"*—He has <u>risen</u> from the dead and is in total control of death and hell. Because of what Jesus did, John and other Christians don't need to be afraid of dying or going to hell.

> **Revelation 1:19**
> "Write, therefore, what you have seen, what is now and what will take place later."

How It Is

Unlike the bizarre special effects or creatures that Hollywood moviemakers enjoy creating, John didn't make these things up. Instead, he wrote things down just as they were. *"What you have seen"* refers to the events we have covered so far in

Hades: *temporary hell*

GO!
Luke 24:6 (risen)

13

KEY SYMBOLS

Jesus
White head and hair
- has brightness and purity of heaven

Eyes like blazing fire
- sees everything

Feet like glowing bronze
- will judge everything

Voice like rushing waters
- has power to create

Seven stars in his right hand
- seven angels of seven churches

Mouth a double-edged sword
- the Bible

Face like the sun
- glory of God

Tribulation: *seven years when God displays his anger*

Millennium: *thousand-year rule of Christ on earth*

Rapture: *when believers are taken to heaven at Christ's return*

KEY SYMBOLS

Seven Stars
Angels of the seven churches

Seven Lampstands
Seven churches

this chapter. Notice that several of the verses in this chapter are written in the past tense. *"What is now"* refers to happenings of the present Church Age. *"What will take place later"* refers to future events that will take place after the Church Age is over. They reveal what will happen during the **Tribulation** plus what will happen during the **Millennium** and beyond. That is why this book is divided into three sections: (1) the Church Age—chapters 1–3; (2) the **Rapture** to the Second Coming—chapters 4–18; and (3) the Millennium and beyond—chapters 20–22. (See timelines 1, 2, and 3, page 46.)

> **Revelation 1:20**
> "The mystery of the seven stars that you saw in my right hand and of the seven golden lampstands is this: The seven stars are the angels of the seven churches, and the seven lampstands are the seven churches."

 THE UNKNOWN BECOMES KNOWN— THAT'S REVELATION

Jesus clearly identified the seven stars (there's that number again!) in his right hand as the angels of the seven churches. Whether they were real angels or great spiritual leaders can be argued. They had, however, clearly been given authority over their respective churches. Their authority wasn't to be questioned or messed with. The seven lampstands stand for the seven churches. They also foretold the history of the church from Pentecost to the Rapture.

CHAPTER CHECKUP

1. In what way did Jesus get John's attention to tell him great things?
2. Why are people afraid of the Book of Revelation? Why shouldn't believers be afraid?
3. Who will see Jesus when he returns to earth?
4. Why are these seven churches important today?
5. Who is the high priest (or Son of man)? Why is he such an important character in this chapter?

CRASH COURSE

▶ God promises a blessing to those who read, hear, and keep the Word of God. (Revelation 1:3)

▶ Christ is the ruler of all rulers, and the day will come when he will rule over all the nations of the earth. (Revelation 1:5)

▶ Jesus is the Alpha and the Omega. He is everything from the beginning to the end. (Revelation 1:8)

▶ The seven lampstands symbolize seven churches and seven church periods. Each church represents one of the seven periods of the Church Age. (Revelation 1:12, 20)

▶ Jesus is the great high priest of the church. Our intercessor, he works in our place to bring us back into a relationship with God that has been damaged by sin. (Revelation 1:13)

▶ Jesus holds the keys to death and hell since he conquered both through his death and resurrection. (Revelation 1:18)

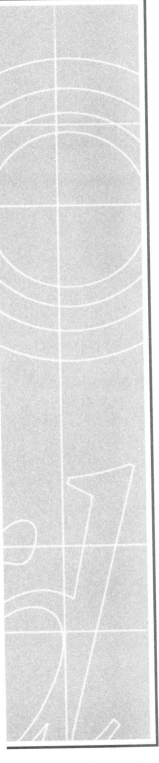

A Real Need for Jesus

▶▶ LET'S DIVE IN

When you were in elementary school, were you excited about Valentine's Day? Did you prepare for the day by making a holder for your valentines? Did you buy valentines, or did you make your own out of construction paper and frilly doilies? Did you ever agonize over what to write to a "special friend," or did the words just flow? How did you feel on February 14th when you opened your valentines and read what people had written to you?

The second chapter of Revelation begins with a similar buzz in the air. Seven incredible letters were written to seven specific churches, and they represent seven periods of time. Although these letters were written to people who lived two thousand years ago, they have messages for us today! (And the messages are way more important than those Valentine's Day notes we received years ago.) These letters are **inspired** by the Holy Spirit. They are prophecy, giving a glimpse at church history from **Pentecost** to the Rapture.

GO!
Revelation 1:3
 (prophecy)
Acts 2:1–4
 (Pentecost)

inspired: *thoughts or words that came from God*

Pentecost: *day Christians first received the Holy Spirit*

> **Revelation 2:1**
> "To the angel of the church in Ephesus write: These are the words of him who holds the seven stars in his right hand and walks among the seven golden lampstands:"

17

Angel Power

GO!

Revelation 1:16, 20
(seven stars)

Revelation 1:12–13, 20
(seven golden
lampstands)

Like we said in chapter 1, the number seven is here to stay. The <u>seven stars</u> stand for seven angels and <u>seven golden lampstands</u> stand for seven churches. Jesus told John to write this letter. Jesus holds seven angels in his right hand and walks in the midst of the seven churches. The picture this verse should conjure up in your mind is one of extreme power.

In most Bible stories when humans encounter an angel, the first words out of the angel's mouth are, "Fear not!" Why? Because the human is facedown, shaking in his boots! Jesus is not afraid of angels like most humans are. Instead, Jesus rules over the angels and controls them.

The message that follows is for the church at Ephesus about what we call the Ephesus period. Bible scholars disagree about some of the dates of the seven periods as the table below shows.

The Church Age

Author	Ephesus Period	Smyrna Period	Pergamum Period	Thyatira Period	Sardis Period	Philadelphia Period	Laodicea Period
Tim LaHaye[1]	A.D. 30 to A.D. 100	A.D. 100 to A.D. 312	A.D. 312 to A.D. 606	A.D. 606 to Trib. Per.*	A.D. 1520 to Trib. Per.*	A.D. 1750 to Trib. Per.*	A.D. 1900 to Trib. Per.*
Hal Lindsey[2]	A.D. 33 to A.D. 100	A.D. 100 to A.D. 312	A.D. 312 to A.D. 590	A.D. 590 to A.D. 1517	A.D. 1517 to A.D. 1750	A.D. 1750 to A.D. 1925	A.D. 1900 to Trib. Per.
J. Vernon McGee[3]	Pentecost to A.D. 100	A.D. 100 to A.D. 314	A.D. 314 to A.D. 590	A.D. 590 to A.D. 1000	A.D. 1517 to A.D. 1800	A.D. 1800 to Rapture	Does not say
Daymond R. Duck	Pentecost to A.D. 100	A.D. 100 to A.D. 312	A.D. 312 to A.D. 590	A.D. 590 to A.D. 1517	A.D. 1517 to A.D. 1750	A.D. 1750 to A.D. 1900	A.D. 1900 to Trib. Mid-Point

*Tim LaHaye believes these four church periods all end with the Tribulation Period.

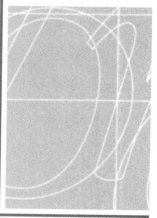

Revelation 2:2–3

"I know your deeds, your hard work and your perseverance. I know that you cannot tolerate wicked men, that you have tested those who claim to be apostles but are not, and have found them false. You have persevered and have endured hardships for my name, and have not grown weary."

JESUS: A KNOW-IT-ALL

Know-it-alls are usually unpopular, but that's because they *think* they know everything (and tend to be annoying as a result). Can you imagine how popular people would be if they truly knew everything? How awesome it would be to know somebody like that. Jesus is that somebody. Jesus knows your deeds, hard work, and **perseverance**. Jesus knew about the struggles of the church in Ephesus. He realized they had been faithful to God even though they were surrounded by **immorality** and **pagan** beliefs.

> **Revelation 2:4–5**
> "Yet I hold this against you: You have forsaken your first love. Remember the height from which you have fallen! Repent and do the things you did at first. If you do not repent, I will come to you and remove your lampstand from its place."

 ## FALLING AWAY FROM GOD

Although this church was on the right track, the people in it had one mucho problemo! They weren't as close to Jesus as they had been, because they had stopped loving him like they did as new Christians.

Jesus wanted the people of this church to take a good, hard look at how far they'd <u>fallen away</u> from him and to return to him immediately. He warned them that if they didn't stop **backsliding**, he would take away their right to exist as a church.

> **Revelation 2:6**
> "But you have this in your favor: You hate the practices of the Nicolaitans, which I also hate."

Digging the Dude, Not the Deed

We aren't certain who the Nicolaitans were. Most Bible experts think their teachings promoted compromise with sin. What we do know is that whatever these people were doing was wrong, and the church in Ephesus made it no secret that they hated whatever it was. Jesus hated it too. Keep in mind

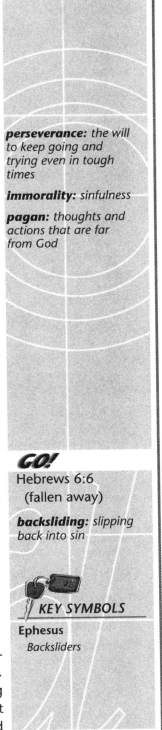

perseverance: *the will to keep going and trying even in tough times*

immorality: *sinfulness*

pagan: *thoughts and actions that are far from God*

19

GO!
Hebrews 6:6
(fallen away)

backsliding: *slipping back into sin*

KEY SYMBOLS

Ephesus
Backsliders

Amos 5:15; John
15:12 (didn't hate)

that Jesus <u>didn't hate</u> the sinner, but he hated the sin. We can learn from this example that it's okay to voice our anger at *things* that are wrong but we should do this in a way that still shows love and concern for the person involved in the wrong-doing.

Dr. Emory Griffin: *Give some thought to these five proven techniques for loving the person not the sin: 1) Don't try to change the person—change the situation. 2) Don't tell him what to do—show him. 3) Don't knock down his present actions—attribute (or show) to him the response you desire. 4) Don't speak in generalities—get specific as to what he should do. 5) Don't expect too much change at one time—request minor behavior shifts.*[4]

> **Revelation 2:7**
> "He who has an ear, let him hear what the Spirit says to the churches. To him who overcomes, I will give the right to eat from the tree of life, which is in the paradise of God."

Listen Up

As we might say today, "Word up!" This is *real* important stuff! It's easy to hear or read words without allowing important truths to sink into our brains. A study of Revelation, however, isn't the place to sleep. Even Jesus wanted to make sure all who read this Book listened carefully.

Jesus promises a blessing for those <u>who **overcome**</u>. Remember the tree of life? When Adam and Eve sinned in the <u>Garden of Eden</u>, we lost our chance to live forever. What Jesus is saying here is that we can regain that right. We can experience eternal life in **paradise** if we trust Jesus Christ as our Savior. Keep in mind these do's and a don't to help you overcome sin:

1 John 5:4
  (who overcome)
Genesis 3:3–22
  (Garden of Eden)

overcome: *win over sin through faith in Jesus*

paradise: *heaven*

- Do ignite the feelings you had for your first love (Jesus).
- Don't lie about slipping away (backsliding) from God.
- Do the good things (deeds) you once did.

> ### Revelation 2:8
> "To the angel of the church in Smyrna write: These are the words of him who is the First and the Last, who died and came to life again."

Mega-Tough Times

When the going gets tough, the tough don't go shopping. The church in Smyrna that John was writing to had been through some really difficult stuff. They had been persecuted because of their faith in Jesus. Jesus wanted to remind them that he is the First and the Last. He is the Alpha and the Omega (the Greek letters *A* and *Z*). Jesus was there <u>in the beginning</u>, and he's also going to be there at the very end.

Jesus also knows about tough times. He <u>sweat blood</u> as he anguished in the Garden of Gethsemane. The soldiers drove nails through his hands and into a cross to crucify him. He was <u>forsaken</u> by his Father, God. Things don't get any tougher than that.

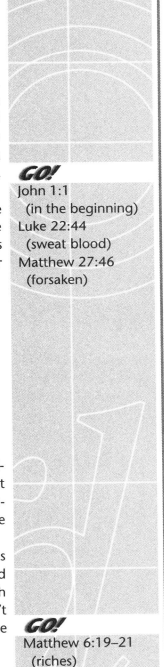

GO!
John 1:1
  (in the beginning)
Luke 22:44
  (sweat blood)
Matthew 27:46
  (forsaken)

> ### Revelation 2:9
> "I know your afflictions and your poverty—yet you are rich! I know the slander of those who say they are Jews and are not, but are a synagogue of Satan."

Get-Rich-Quick Syndrome

In this age of dot-coms, mega-lottery prizes, and million dollar sports contracts, it's easy to think we'll strike it rich (or at least play in the NFL). Then reality sets in, and we get depressed. Money doesn't flow into our hands, so we forget we are children of a powerful God.

The people of Smyrna felt similar to the way we sometimes feel—poor. They had lost their jobs and their property had been taken away from them. Jesus reminded them through John's letter that they really weren't poor. Their riches weren't earthly possessions. They had <u>riches</u> in heaven's bank because they were living for God.

GO!
Matthew 6:19–21
  (riches)

Jesus also knew about a group in Smyrna who falsely called themselves Jews. Even though their place of worship was called a **synagogue**, Jesus saw right through them. They were hypocrites. He called their church a synagogue of Satan.

synagogue: *Jewish place of worship*

 OUTSIDE CONNECTION

George Barna: Earlier than ever before, today's segment of teenagers realizes that their decisions today will shape significant aspects of their life from here on. And although it conflicts with the popular notion of modern teens, our research has discovered that teens believe that you reap what you sow. Consequently, they believe that they alone are responsible for what they ultimately get from life and they must, therefore, strive to make something worthwhile out of life.[5]

Revelation 2:10

"Do not be afraid of what you are about to suffer. I tell you, the devil will put some of you in prison to test you, and you will suffer persecution for ten days. Be faithful, even to the point of death, and I will give you the crown of life."

If you could get inside someone's heart to know what he or she was thinking and feeling, what would you want to know? _____

_____

When you look good on the outside but are scared or sinful on the inside, are others fooled? Why or why not?_____

_____

How do you think Jesus feels when he looks inside your heart?_____

_____

_____

Jesus not only sees what is in your heart, but he can also read you like a book. This should be a reminder always to be up front with God. Honesty is the best policy.

Be Faithful, Not Fearful

Suffering is not on our "must have" list. We all like creature comforts: high speed internet access, surround sound, drive-through windows, and remote controls. Forget suffering and being persecuted—we want our food supersized and our allowances on time!

Revelation isn't shy about revealing the suffering that is going to take place as this world draws to an end. Jesus told the church of Smyrna that they would be persecuted for ten days. It is not certain if those were chunks of time or twenty-four-hour days. History, however, reveals that there were ten periods of really bad persecution during the Smyrna period. Christians were jailed, beaten, tortured, and killed. Jesus urged them to be faithful.

We can look forward to these rewards in heaven:

- Incorruptible or indestructible crown (1 Corinthians 9:24–27)
- Crown of rejoicing (1 Thessalonians 2:19–20)
- **Crown of life** (James 1:12; Revelation 2:10)
- Crown of righteousness (2 Timothy 4:8)
- Crown of glory (1 Peter 5:2–4)

> **Revelation 2:11**
> "He who has an ear, let him hear what the Spirit says to the churches. He who overcomes will not be hurt at all by the second death."

crown of life: reward of eternal life

Word Up!

"Listen up!" Jesus calls out. He also uses that word *overcome* again. This time, however, it comes with a promise. Through Jesus Christ we can not only overcome the things of this world, but also we can gain assurance that we can overcome death. The Bible teaches that there are two deaths: physical death and spiritual death. A person would be better off if physical death were the end of everything than to die a second, spiritual, death—being thrown into the **Lake of Fire** and being separated from God forever.

Lake of Fire: hell; place devil will be thrown

GO!
Numbers 22–31
(Balaam)

martyred: killed for
certain beliefs

> **Revelation 2:12–13**
>
> "To the angel of the church in Pergamum write: These are the words of him who has the sharp, double-edged sword. I know where you live—where Satan has his throne. Yet you remain true to my name. You did not renounce your faith in me, even in the days of Antipas, my faithful witness, who was put to death in your city—where Satan lives."

True Blue

Jesus carries a sword called the Word of God. This sword is razor sharp on both sides. Watch out! Jesus reminds this church in Pergamum that he will deal with them through the Word of God. God's Word cuts away our cover-up attempts and shows our attitudes and actions for what they are. No makeup or hat can cover up our inner pimples or sins.

Jesus knew the church of Pergamum was in a city full of idols. People worshiped Athena, Caesar Augustus, Dionysus, Asklepios, Hadrian, and Zeus. Satan was busy in this city. Yet good Christians lived there too. They were faithful to God and did not give up their faith even when Antipas, a fellow-believer and servant of God, was **martyred**.

> **Revelation 2:14–15**
>
> "Nevertheless, I have a few things against you: You have people there who hold to the teaching of Balaam, who taught Balak to entice the Israelites to sin by eating food sacrificed to idols and by committing sexual immorality. Likewise you also have those who hold to the teaching of the Nicolaitans."

A Whopper Deal

The church of Pergamum had a problem. They had two groups of people who called themselves Christians but who did not stick to the truth. One group within the church acted like Balaam. The other followed the teachings of the Nicolaitans.

In the Old Testament, Balaam, a prophet, was to receive money from a king named Balak in exchange for cursing Israel. God intervened and stopped Balaam. Balaam wanted the money, so he told Balak to have the women in his country seduce the Jews and **intermarry** with them. That way these women could talk their husbands into doing things that were against God. Balak didn't defeat Israel in battle, but he used ungodly women to lead Jewish men away from God. (A pretty smart strategy based on the fact that most men do what their wives ask them to in an attempt to keep them happy.)

The group who followed the teachings of the Nicolaitans believed that they could live sinful lives because the **flesh** and the **spirit** had no connection with each other. They didn't care what they did on earth because they didn't think it would matter in eternity. You probably have friends that live this way too—who think their actions will never catch up with them.

> **Revelation 2:16**
> "Repent therefore! Otherwise, I will soon come to you and will fight against them with the sword of my mouth."

Throw the Book at Them

Jesus throws the book at the church in Pergamum by warning them to repent. The book he throws isn't a book of laws; it's the Word of God, the Bible. The Bible is an effective weapon because it **convicts** us of sin.

Here are some ways that the Bible is a spiritual sword:

- It shows us all things that relate to life and godliness (2 Peter 1:3).
- It shines the light of God on our hidden mistakes and failures (John 3:20).
- It reveals the true will of God (1 Thessalonians 4:3).
- It convicts us of our sin (John 8:7).
- It shows us the love of God (John 3:16).
- It shows us the judgment of God (Romans 14:10).
- It calls for us to repent and change our behavior (Acts 2:38).

Nicky Gumbel: The Bible is God's revelation of His will for His people. The more we discover His will and put it into practice, the freer we shall be. God has spoken. We need to hear what He has said.[6]

KEY POINT

Hold fast to the truth. Don't compromise your beliefs.

convicts: *brings to awareness sins in our lives*

KEY SYMBOLS

Pergamum
Compromising beliefs

OUTSIDE **CONNECTION**

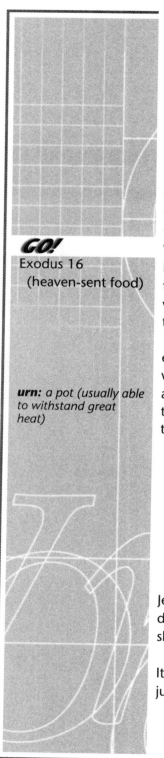

GO!

Exodus 16
(heaven-sent food)

urn: *a pot (usually able to withstand great heat)*

Revelation 2:17

"He who has an ear, let him hear what the Spirit says to the churches. To him who overcomes, I will give some of the hidden manna. I will also give him a white stone with a new name written on it, known only to him who receives it."

 TOTALLY TAKEN CARE OF

Remember manna? It was white food that God sent down from heaven to feed the Israelites in the desert. To our mega-variety tastes today it might sound gross, but for the Israelites who were in the wilderness it was a happy meal from on high. What was cool about this <u>heaven-sent food</u> was that it couldn't be stockpiled. God sent only enough for each day. Those who tried to keep the stuff got a rotten, smelly surprise. It was God's way of showing the Israelites they could count on him to meet their daily needs.

The white stone mentioned in the verse above is a reference to the way people voted in John's day. When a person was tried for a crime, the jurors voted by dropping stones into an **urn**: black for guilty or white for innocent. Jesus promises that believers will be found innocent when God judges everything.

Revelation 2:18

"To the angel of the church in Thyatira write: These are the words of the Son of God, whose eyes are like blazing fire and whose feet are like burnished bronze."

One Tough Dude

Jesus identifies himself here as the Son of God. He goes on to describe what he looks like, eyes blazing like fire and feet like shiny bronze.

This isn't a comforting picture for the church of Thyatira. It's an image of Jesus as a mighty judge. Why did Jesus need to judge this church? Stay tuned.

 **A DONE DEAL**

Before he hit them with the rap sheet, Jesus gave them some praise. The Bible teaches that all believers will appear before the judgment seat of Christ. We will have to give an account for all we've said and done. If we haven't lived up to our name as Christians, we will probably feel sad. (This judgment seat isn't the same place that the non-Christians will stand. That place is called the **Great White Throne Judgment**.) The judgment seat of Christ is where the heavenly crowns will be given. Being a perfect, righteous judge, Jesus knows how we lived.

Concerning this church, Jesus knew about the following:

1. *Their deeds.* If you're a Christian you will live like one. People who don't do the works of God are not Christian. In other words, what you do in this life shows where you will spend eternity.
2. *Their love.* When people turn to God, they receive the Holy Spirit. The first <u>fruit</u> of the Holy Spirit is love. Christians should be full of God's <u>love</u>.
3. *Their service.* Service is a ministry. Christians aren't Christians because of all the great things they can get out of church. They choose to follow Christ because he forgave them. Thankful for that, Christians now serve God by serving others.
4. *Their faith.* Real faith can be seen. It produces good character and deeds. This is how the unbelieving world sees Jesus in Christians.
5. *Their perseverance.* This is the fourth fruit of the Holy Spirit, often called long-suffering. Many in this church suffered for long periods of time for Jesus.
6. *Their last works.* This church never stopped doing. This should be the goal of every church: to grow, to do more, to reach more people, and to increase in good works.

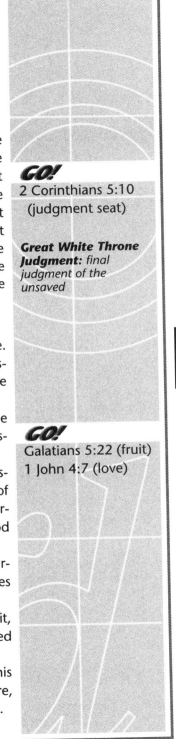

GO!
2 Corinthians 5:10 (judgment seat)

Great White Throne Judgment: *final judgment of the unsaved*

27

GO!
Galatians 5:22 (fruit)
1 John 4:7 (love)

KEY SYMBOLS

Thyatira
*Committing spiritual
adultery*

occult: *satanic
practices*

forerunner: *one who
goes before*

harlot: *prostitute*

adulterous: *one who is
unfaithful, a cheater*

> ### Revelation 2:20–21
> "Nevertheless, I have this against you: You tolerate that woman Jezebel, who calls herself a prophetess. By her teaching she misleads my servants into sexual immorality and the eating of food sacrificed to idols. I have given her time to repent of her immorality, but she is unwilling."

WILD WOMAN JEZEBEL

Jezebel was a priestess at a pagan temple. She was also deeply involved in fortune-telling and the **occult** but was passing herself off as a prophetess of God. Instead of teaching people to be faithful to God, she was telling them to two-time or cheat on God.

Jesus was patient with this wild woman Jezebel. Jesus gave the Thyatira church about one thousand years to change. Those who mess with the things of the occult can find it difficult to change. Such was the case with Jezebel. Some people call this period the Devil's Millennium.

All who bring evil and sin into the church while pretending it's part of Jesus or Christianity are begging to be judged by God.

> ### Revelation 2:22
> "So I will cast her on a bed of suffering, and I will make those who commit adultery with her suffer intensely, unless they repent of her ways."

Playing with Fire

The church of Thyatira is a **forerunner** to the **harlot** church in chapter 17. When we reach that chapter, we will study events that will occur during the Tribulation and learn that world leaders will turn on the harlot church and destroy it. She'll be toast!

Harlots are known for committing sexual sins, so Jesus warns this church that he will make a bed for Jezebel and her **adulterous** followers. He will put them together and cause them to experience intense suffering. If a church wants to play with fire, Jesus will let it play.

> **Revelation 2:23**
> "I will strike her children dead. Then all the churches will know that I am he who searches hearts and minds, and I will repay each of you according to your deeds."

You Got It Coming to You

In today's age of tolerance and no absolutes, it's hard for us to understand that God will judge people for not following his rules. It's important to remember two of God's attributes: (1) He is good, and (2) he is just, righteous. Although God is good, he will be no more tolerant of **spiritual adultery** in our day than he was in Jezebel's day.

Jesus is the one *"who searches our hearts and minds."* This means he sees right through us into our real motives, thoughts, and wants. There will be degrees of reward in heaven and degrees of punishment in hell. Everyone will receive according to what he or she did on earth.

> **Revelation 2:24–25**
> "Now I say to the rest of you in Thyatira, to you who do not hold to her teaching and have not learned Satan's so-called deep secrets (I will not impose any other burden on you): Only hold on to what you have until I come."

Hang On

Jesus is talking to those in Thyatira who either rejected Jezebel's teachings or were not aware of what she was saying and doing. They were already serving God under tough circumstances, so he would not ask anything more of them. "Hang on until I return," Jesus said, referring to the Rapture.

> **Revelation 2:26–28**
> "To him who overcomes and does my will to the end, I will give authority over the nations—He will rule them with an iron scepter; he will dash them to pieces like pottery—just as I have received authority from my Father. I will also give him the morning star."

KEY POINT

If you want to play with fire, Jesus will let you play with fire and get burned.

GO!
Romans 11:22
(attributes)

spiritual adultery: saying you are a Christian but not acting Christlike

29

OVERCOMERS RULE

If you persist in following Jesus until either your death or Jesus' return, you will receive a position over the nations. In other words, you'll rule! You will receive power and authority from Jesus in the same way he received power and authority from God the Father. You will break those who don't obey your authority like a potter breaks pieces of clay.

The <u>Bright and Morning Star</u> is one of the names of Jesus. Jesus will <u>never leave</u> the believer, and he will guide the believer during dark or difficult times of life.

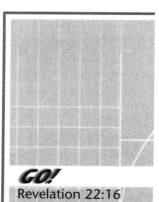

GO!
Revelation 22:16
(Bright and
Morning Star)
Hebrews 13:5
(never leave)

> **Revelation 2:29**
> "He who has an ear, let him hear what the Spirit says to the churches."

Be Prepared

Teachers always repeat things! "We will have pop quizzes. Be prepared for a pop quiz. Quizzes will not be announced ahead of time." In Revelation there is some repeating going on too. The statement about listening has already appeared four times. It's gotta be really important!

Before the Tribulation begins, Jesus will remove his faithful from the earth. True believers will not suffer the terrible events found later in Revelation, but instead will be removed from this earth in what we know as the Rapture. In Revelation 13:9 we read, *"He who has an ear, let him hear."* Notice that sentence is missing its usual ending as stated above: *"what the Spirit says to the churches."* The words in the gray box above occur seven times before Revelation 13:9, and then suddenly they are shortened. Why? Could it be that the church is no longer on earth? I think so.

CHAPTER CHECKUP

1. How did the church in Ephesus mess up?
2. Why was the church in Smyrna rich?
3. What did the church in Pergamum have going for it?

4. Why was God angry with the church in Thyatira?
5. What is the main message that Christians should take to heart after reading these letters?

▶ The first four church letters come to Ephesus, Smyrna, Pergamum, and Thyatira. Each letter does two things: It explains the churches' problems and offers a solution.

▶ Getting right with God and getting out of sin is the only way we can overcome the second death. Through faith in Jesus Christ we can live forever with God. (Revelation 2:11)

▶ Jesus Christ is described as having eyes of fire and feet of bronze. His blazing eyes show us that he has the ability to see everything that we do. His feet of bronze refer to his position as judge over all of creation. (Revelation 2:18)

▶ Jezebel, a false priestess in Thyatira, was leading people away from God. God told this church to rid themselves of her or face punishment. (Revelation 2:20–23)

▶ When Christ promises to give the Bright and Morning Star to overcomers, he is promising himself. (Revelation 2:28)

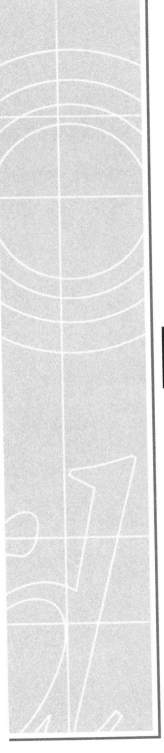

31

3

You're Either Hot or Not

CHAPTER CAPTURE

- Get Booked
- Open and Shut Case
- Where Satan Hangs Out
- Don't Get Spit Out!
- I Stand and Knock

 LET'S DIVE IN

This chapter deals with some stuff that's hard for most people to hear. Jesus calls on believers to be either hot or not. (And he's not talking about looks!) In other words, be either for God or against him. Don't hang out in the middle and try to ride every wave that comes your way. You won't catch God's wave to heaven.

> **Revelation 3:1**
> "To the angel of the church in Sardis write: These are the words of him who holds the seven spirits of God and the seven stars. I know your deeds; you have a reputation of being alive, but you are dead."

Forever Phonies

Jesus controls everything, even the angels. Jesus knew the ins and outs of all the churches we've read about so far. This church at Sardis was on a downward slope. Instead of doing more and more good deeds, their works were becoming less and less. When people looked at Sardis, they saw a church that was alive, but Jesus knew this church was actually dead.

HAPPENINGS

Ninety-Five Theses:
*statements challenging
Catholic Church beliefs
and errors*

Reformation: *religious
movement that split the
church into two groups:
Catholic and Protestant*

34

Christian historians believe that the Sardis church period began when Martin Luther nailed his **Ninety-Five Theses** to the church door in Wittenburg, Germany. This began what is commonly called the **Reformation**. Before long, however, the Reformation stalled, people quit caring, and the church started living off of its reputation instead of growing in love and good deeds.

> **Revelation 3:2–3**
>
> "Wake up! Strengthen what remains and is about to die, for I have not found your deeds complete in the sight of my God. Remember, therefore, what you have received and heard; obey it, and repent. But if you do not wake up, I will come like a thief, and you will not know at what time I will come to you."

Be Prepared!

The church of Sardis was phony and had failed in many areas. Jesus said, "Quit playing church and get real." There were some areas of this church's faith that were strong, but other areas were weak. God wanted this church to have a relationship with him instead of just going through the motions of holding services and running programs. (Sound familiar?)

Thieves don't phone ahead to tell you they're coming. But Jesus is sending out an advance memo with a warning. Get ready or else! He's warning them to be ready for the Rapture and judgment.

Don't put off changing your attitude or relationship with God. If you do, you may be surprised when the Rapture occurs and it's too late to change.

Greg Johnson: *God cares who you spend time with. He knows the joys of having close friends who help to take you in the right direction, and he realizes the hazards of spending your time with those who do not have a mind for God. So must you.*[1]

> **Revelation 3:4–6**
>
> "Yet you have a few people in Sardis who have not soiled their clothes. They will walk with me, dressed in white, for they are worthy. He who overcomes will, like them, be dressed in white. I will never blot out his name from the book of life, but will acknowledge his name before my Father and his angels. He who has an ear, let him hear what the Spirit says to the churches."

 GET BOOKED

Some of the people of Sardis had managed to keep clean, so to speak, from all of the sin around them. Jesus promised that these people would walk with him and wear robes of white. Why were these people honored this way? Because they had sincerely accepted Jesus as their Savior and, by the power of the Holy Spirit, had lived holy lives.

Everyone who is born twice (born physically and born again spiritually) has his or her name entered into the **Lamb**'s Book of Life. This is an assurance that the saved will not be forgotten.

Jesus promised that he would acknowledge believers' names before his Father and his angels. Imagine that roll call—hearing your name called out by Jesus, in front of God and all of the angels in heaven. That's one attendance chart that you won't want to be left off of, that's for sure.

Michael W. Smith: Be brave. Live for God. Don't waste a minute of your life. Realize that this is your time.[2]

> **Revelation 3:7–8**
>
> "To the angel of the church in Philadelphia write: These are the words of him who is holy and true, who holds the key of David. What he opens no one can shut, and what he shuts no one can open. I know your deeds. See, I have placed before you an open door that no one can shut. I know that you have little strength, yet you have kept my word and have not denied my name."

GO!
Revelation 21:27
(Lamb's Book of Life)

Lamb: name for Jesus

OUTSIDE CONNECTION

OPEN AND SHUT CASE

holy: *different or separate*

true: *real or genuine*

evangelistic: *preaching the gospel of Jesus Christ*

KEY POINT

No matter what door it is, if Jesus opens it, no one can close it. If he closes it, no one can open it.

Jesus is **holy** and **true**. He is the real deal. The phrase *"who holds the key of David"* is a way of saying that Jesus is the ultimate key holder. He is the authority over everything. His decisions are final.

The church in Philadelphia was more like what churches should be. It was an **evangelistic**, Bible-believing church. Jesus is in control of the doors of opportunity that are opened and shut. We are dependent on him, and he knows our weaknesses. We can't save people by ourselves, no matter how well we preach the gospel or how persistent we are with unbelievers. God is the one who saves people. All we can do is point them to him.

> **Revelation 3:9**
> "I will make those who are of the synagogue of Satan, who claim to be Jews though they are not, but are liars—I will make them come and fall down at your feet and acknowledge that I have loved you."

 WHERE SATAN HANGS OUT

Some people from the church of Philadelphia rejected the name of Jesus and tried to get others to follow them. These people claimed to be more godly than other people because they were Jews. Jesus called them fakes and their place of worship a *"synagogue of Satan."* He promised they would pay for their sins and that some day they would be forced to bow down and worship at the true believers' feet, acknowledging that Jesus is Lord.

 **OUTSIDE CONNECTION**

George Barna: *Most Americans (more than four out of five) consider themselves to be "Christian." Over the last several decades, that faith label has taken on a pale image of its past meaning."*[3]

Have you ever been with "Christians" who did things that were contrary to Christ? Explain the situation here._____

_____

_____

_____

How did you feel about their actions?_____

_____

_____

What did you do?_____

_____

GET REAL

Not everyone who claims to be a **child of God** really is. Perhaps some of your so-called Christian friends are hanging where Satan hangs. Don't take it lightly. Jesus knows who his real children are.

Revelation 3:10–11

"Since you have kept my commandment to endure patiently, I will also keep you from the hour of trial that is going to come upon the whole world to test those who live on the earth. I am coming soon. Hold on to what you have, so that no one will take your crown."

child of God: *true believer*

Hold on to Your Hat!

The hour of trial mentioned here refers to the Tribulation. Those who trust in Jesus won't have to endure this hard time. Jesus is coming soon. His coming will take many by surprise. Both the Rapture and the Second Coming will take place in the twinkling of an eye. That's about as fast as you can blink. Jesus says, "Hang in there!" Keep doing the right thing and you'll be rewarded.

GO!
1 Corinthians 15:52
(twinkling)

"Him who overcomes I will make a pillar in the temple of my God. Never again will he leave it. I will write on him the name of my God and the name of the city of my God, the new Jerusalem, which is coming down out of heaven from my God; and I will also write on him my new name. He who has an ear, let him hear what the Spirit says to the churches."

Promises from Jesus

Jesus promises this to those who overcome:

1. *"I will make you a pillar in the temple of my God"*—Jesus will make his followers strong, long lasting, and stable in the house of God.
2. *"Never again will he leave it"*—Jesus will make his followers secure and safe. They will want to stay forever, and no one will move them.
3. *"I will write on him"*—Jesus will write three things upon the foreheads of his followers:

   - The <u>Seal</u> (name) of God to make them stand out as a child of God
   - The name of his eternal home, which is **new Jerusalem**
   - A new <u>name of Jesus</u> that confirms their personal relationship to the Lord of lords and King of kings. Those who overcome will belong to God. They will be citizens of the new Jerusalem and will have a special relationship with Jesus.

GO!
Revelation 9:4 (Seal)
Revelation 21:9–22:6 (new Jerusalem)
Revelation 22:4 (name of Jesus)

new Jerusalem:
heaven

38

Revelation 3:14
"To the angel of the church in Laodicea write: These are the words of the Amen, the faithful and true witness, the ruler of God's creation."

Da Ruler of All

Laodicea is the last of the seven churches. Finally! What has been revealed through these seven churches is incredible truth of how Jesus feels about not only these churches, but also about things believers are doing today. The Laodicea period is the last of the Church Age. In other words, this letter is a prophecy about what the church will be like just before the Rapture. We are living in the Laodicea church period today. That gets your attention, doesn't it?

> **Revelation 3:15–16**
> "I know your deeds, that you are neither cold nor hot. I wish you were either one or the other! So, because you are lukewarm—neither hot nor cold—I am about to spit you out of my mouth."

DON'T GET SPIT OUT!

Have you ever put a cold soda in the sun and forgotten about it? Hours later you remember and take a sip. Yuck! It's warm, so you spit it out. This is what Jesus is saying here. He'll see right away who doesn't belong to him, and he'll spit that person out of his heavenly kingdom. It sounds harsh, but only those who are true believers of Jesus Christ will go to heaven. The church members mentioned here were lukewarm, indifferent toward God.

Indifference is the worst state of all. It would be easier to take steps to help a cold or dead church and easier to bless a hot or spiritual church. The question is, what do you do with a church that doesn't care—that claims Christ, but doesn't live by his words. Jesus will reject it. This applies to us today as well.

> **Revelation 3:17**
> "You say, 'I am rich; I have acquired wealth and do not need a thing.' But you do not realize that you are wretched, pitiful, poor, blind and naked."

First Cocky Church of Christ

This church was cocky. A reality check by Jesus told them that they weren't all they had talked themselves into being. They had lost sight of Jesus and were caught up in grabbing wealth and stuff. They thought they were rich, but in reality they were spiritually **wretched**, pitiful, poor, blind, and naked.

wretched: worthless, hopeless, lost

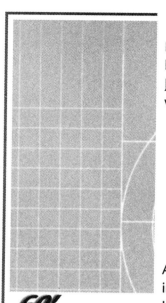

Many churches today think they are great because of how large their sanctuary is, how many programs they have, and how many important people in town attend their services. Jesus doesn't care about that. He cares about how obedient we are and how many people we are winning to Christ.

> **Revelation 3:18**
> "I counsel you to buy from me gold refined in the fire, so you can become rich; and white clothes to wear, so you can cover your shameful nakedness; and salve to put on your eyes, so you can see."

Like Pure Gold

After gold is mined it is put in a red-hot furnace. All of the impure things in it are melted away. All that is left is pure gold. In a similar way, we are <u>refined</u> by God's fiery furnace of trials. He takes our lives and purifies them by sending hard times to make us stronger. When we come out of these difficulties, we are like pure gold. We can shine for him because we are literally glowing from within!

This church was naked because their sin was showing and blind because they couldn't see their problem. The white clothes Jesus offers symbolize the **righteousness** of Christ. When we are at the judgment throne, the only thing that will hide our spiritual nakedness and shame is what Jesus has done for us on the cross.

> **Revelation 3:19–22**
> "Those whom I love I rebuke and discipline. So be earnest, and repent. Here I am! I stand at the door and knock. If anyone hears my voice and opens the door, I will come in and eat with him, and he with me. To him who overcomes, I will give the right to sit with me on my throne, just as I overcame and sat down with my Father on his throne. He who has an ear, let him hear what the Spirit says to the churches."

GO!
1 Peter 1:7 (refined)

righteousness: nature or qualities of Christ— purity, love, kindness

KEY POINT
The overcomer will sit on the throne of Jesus and reign with him.

 **I STAND AND KNOCK**

Remember when your parents said, "I'm only punishing you because I love you," or "This hurts me more than it hurts you"?

At that time you probably thought, *Yeah, right!* Hopefully by now you appreciate some of the <u>discipline</u> you received.

Jesus corrects and disciplines those he loves. Usually growth hurts. God's discipline helps us to be honest about our sins, to **repent**, and to change our behavior.

Jesus didn't wait around for the church of Laodicea to come to him. No, Jesus went to them and knocked on their door. Just as Jesus overcame Satan by living a life of obedience to God, we can overcome sin by believing in Jesus Christ and what he accomplished on the cross. As a reward we will reign with Christ.

GO!
Hebrews 12:5–8
(discipline)

repent: *confess and turn from sin*

OUTSIDE CONNECTION

Greg Johnson: A basketball coach once said, "Don't worry when I'm yelling at you. Worry when I stop yelling." He was saying that his voice level communicated his concern for the player. So when he quit yelling, he quit caring.

God's not a yeller, but if you want him to bless you, expect to be disciplined.[4]

CHAPTER CHECKUP

1. What was wrong with the church of Sardis?
2. What weakness did the church at Philadelphia have?
3. Why did Jesus "chew out" the church at Laodicea?
4. Which of these letters probably applies to today's church?
5. What can you do to keep from being a lukewarm Christian?

CRASH COURSE

▶ The last three church letters are to Sardis, Philadelphia, and Laodicea. Each of these letters explains further problems for the church and offers solutions.

▶ Jesus gives us his word that he'll keep the names of overcomers in the Lamb's Book of Life and will acknowledge the believers' names before God. (Revelation 3:4–5)

▶ Jesus Christ holds the key to our lives. When he opens or shuts a door, no one can mess with what he's done. (Revelation 3:7)

▶ For a Christian, the worst state we can be in is to be

41

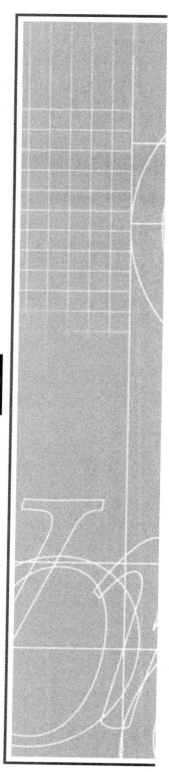

lukewarm—neither on fire for God nor ignorant of him. Being indifferent leads to Christ's anger. He will spit these kinds of people out of his mouth. (Revelation 3:15–16)

▶ Jesus comes to us (our door) and knocks to be let in. Those who fellowship with him are winners. (Revelation 3:20)

FROM THE RAPTURE TO THE SECOND COMING

IF ONE PAIR OF LIPS LEAVES AT 8:45 AND TRAVELS 2.3 MILES AT 3.3 MPH AND ANOTHER PAIR OF LIPS LEAVES AT 8:53 AND TRAVELS AN EQUAL DISTANCE IN THE OPPOSITE DIRECTION AT 3.7 MPH, HOW LONG WILL IT TAKE FOR THEM TO KISS?

GLASBERGEN

Allen gets a love letter from the president of the Math Club.

4

How It's Gonna Be

CHAPTER CAPTURE
- A Glimpse into Heaven
- Out-of-Spirit Experience
- Elders around God, 24/7
- Freaky Looking Creatures
- Creator of All

45

 LET'S DIVE IN

Now, things turn toward the future. Chapters 1–3 dealt with John's vision of Jesus and the Church Age. Most of these events are now past, and the Church Age will soon be over. The true mystery of this book—the future—is about to be revealed.

Revelation goes in chronological order. Revelation 4:1 reveals the Rapture (when blink, wink, Christians are taken out of the world). Revelation 6:2 reveals the appearance of the **Antichrist**, the ultimate bad guy. Revelation 6:17 reveals the beginning of the Tribulation. The order of these events indicates a period of time between Revelation 4:1 (the Rapture) and Revelation 6:17 (the Tribulation). The Bible does not tell us how long that time will be, so patience is key. All we know is that the Antichrist will become powerful, will rise to power in Europe, take over the entire government of the world, and negotiate a covenant to protect Israel. There are also three separate theories about the timing of these events: pre-tribulation Rapture, mid-tribulation Rapture, and post-tribulation Rapture theories. The timelines on page 46 show the order of events for each theory.

After the Rapture and the Tribulation take place, the Millennium will occur.

Antichrist: *powerful ruler who is against Christ*

Timelines of Three Rapture Theories

Pre-Tribulation Theory—*The belief that the church is taken out of the world before the Tribulation*

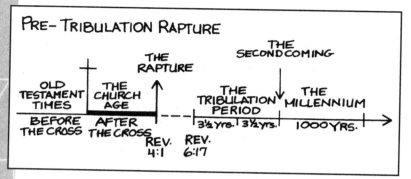

Mid-Tribulation Theory—*The belief that the church is taken out of the world in the middle of the Tribulation*

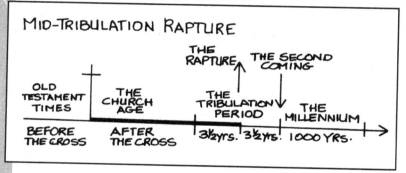

Post-Tribulation Theory—*The belief that the church is taken out of the world after the Tribulation*

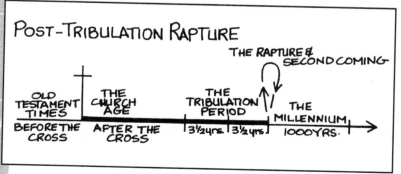

Do you worry about things that could take place in your future? Explain._____

_____

If you knew the future, would you worry less or more? Why or why not?_____

_____

_____

Revelation takes a good deal of the guessing out of the world's future. Instead of wondering what might happen, people can read the Book of Revelation and study what will take place. Take a moment to pray to God and give any worries you might have about your future over to him. It's great to know that God is in control of the future.

A Mega-Long Theory—7,000 Years to Be Exact!

Many Christians believe Christ will set up a kingdom on earth for 1,000 years—called the Millennium. They believe this will happen soon, and they arrive at that conclusion because of the 7,000-Year Theory. This theory dates from the earliest days of the church. Here's the scoop:

- The Millennium is spoken of as a day of rest (Hebrews 4:4–11).
- One day with the Lord is 1,000 years (2 Peter 3:8).
- The Millennium will be 1,000 years in our time scheme (Revelation 20:1–9).
- God will deal with the human race for six of his days (6,000 of our years) and rest on the seventh day (the Millennium).
- According to the Jewish calendar, the time between creation and the beginning of the Christian Era is 3,760 years. That is almost four of God's days.
- Since A.D. 1, the **Christian Era** has lasted 2,000 years, or two more of God's days.
- This means that the human race is approaching the seventh of God's days (the Millennium).

Christian Era: *another name for Church Age*

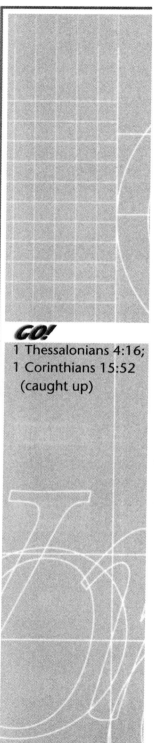

GO!

1 Thessalonians 4:16;
1 Corinthians 15:52
(caught up)

 Revelation 4:1

After this I looked, and there before me was a door standing open in heaven. And the voice I had first heard speaking to me like a trumpet said, "Come up here, and I will show you what must take place after this."

A GLIMPSE INTO HEAVEN

John was chosen to see future events and to get a glimpse of heaven. (Lucky guy!) First, John looked up and saw a door standing open to heaven. Then, he heard a loud voice like a trumpet blast that said, "Come up to heaven and I'll show you the future." Unimaginable! If this happened to you, would you go up there and find out how the world was gonna end? Must say, John was one brave dude.

Many prophecy experts believe that John represents the whole church, and his going up to heaven is symbolic of the Rapture when believers will be <u>caught up</u> in the clouds. They believe this, in part, because the voice John heard was like a trumpet and is the same kind of voice the Bible says will rapture the church. When the Rapture occurs, all believers will go up into heaven at the sound of a trumpet, just like John did.

Although the actual word *rapture* is never found in the Bible, the truth of this concept is clearly conveyed. Here are some examples from the Bible of people who "raptured," so to speak:

1. *Enoch* (Genesis 5:24; Hebrews 11:5)—Enoch was taken from this life and did not experience death.
2. *Elijah* (2 Kings 2:11)—Elijah was walking on earth when he was suddenly taken up into heaven.
3. *Jesus* (Acts 1:9)—Jesus was taken up into the clouds to heaven.
4. *Philip* (Acts 8:39)—Philip was taken away, but then reappeared in another location.
5. *Paul* (2 Corinthians 12:1–4)—Paul was caught up into heaven, and then later returned to earth.
6. *Two Witnesses* (Revelation 11:3–12)—After being killed, they will rise from the dead and ascend into heaven.

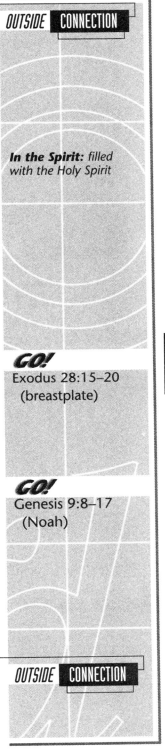

Revelation 4:2–3

At once I was **in the Spirit,** and there before me was a throne in heaven with someone sitting on it. And the one who sat there had the appearance of jasper and carnelian. A rainbow, resembling an emerald, encircled the throne.

In the Spirit: *filled with the Holy Spirit*

OUT-OF-SPIRIT EXPERIENCE

John saw Jesus on the throne in heaven surrounded by something like a laser light show without all the loud music. Around Jesus were bright colors of white and red flashing off of two precious stones, jasper and carnelian. These are the first and the last stones in the breastplate of the Israelite high priest (see illustration, page 11). Jasper, which flashes a white light, is similar to a diamond and stands for the purity and holiness of Jesus. Carnelian, which flashes fiery red, symbolizes the blood that Jesus shed on the cross. These stones remind us of Jesus' majesty and splendor and that we have access to God through Jesus, our forever high priest.

The first rainbow was given to Noah as a sign that God would never again destroy the earth in a flood. When the church enters heaven, there will be a rainbow surrounding God's throne, showing that God won't destroy the earth during the Tribulation. The rainbow is a reminder to us that he keeps his promises. The emerald mentioned here symbolizes eternal life that comes only from God. If you have trusted Jesus as your Savior, you can be confident that he will keep his promise of eternal life to you!

GO!
Exodus 28:15–20
(breastplate)

GO!
Genesis 9:8–17
(Noah)

49

ELDERS AROUND GOD, 24/7

The number twenty-four occurs six times in the Old Testament. In each case it is associated with the priests of Israel. At one time <u>twenty-four</u> priests ministered in the Temple and represented the entire nation of Israel.

In the same way, twenty-four elders will one day represent all believers from Pentecost to the Rapture. They will surround the throne of God and represent a nation of kings and priests. They will stand for all overcomers. Their white robes represent the <u>righteousness of God</u>. Notice that these elders have their robes and crowns *before* the Tribulation begins. There can be no doubt that God is showing us the *pre-tribulation* Rapture.

KaBam and KaBoom!

There are few things more memorable than a hot, summer night's thunderstorm. Crashes of lightning followed by booming roars shake the ground. John describes a thunderstorm in verse 5. The storm that John foresees, however, is a storm of judgment. God's patience with those on earth is just about through. He's had it! The Tribulation is approaching—the time when God will bring forth his judgment on the earth. Following the Rapture, the Holy Spirit will occupy a place in the presence of God. He will no longer be needed on earth to help believers because they will be gone. Yippee for them! Not so great for those left behind.

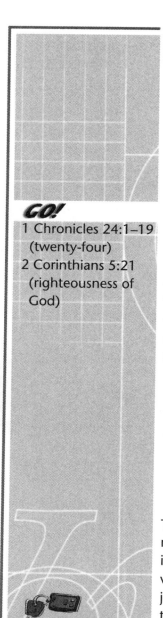

GO!
1 Chronicles 24:1–19 (twenty-four)
2 Corinthians 5:21 (righteousness of God)

KEY SYMBOLS
Seven Lamps
Seven spirits of God
Seven virtues of the Holy Spirit

50

> **Revelation 4:6**
>
> Also before the throne there was what looked like a sea of glass, clear as crystal. In the center, around the throne, were four living creatures, and they were covered with eyes, in front and in back.

FREAKY LOOKING CREATURES

Did you know that dragonflies seem to have eyes in the back of their heads? In reality they have two huge bulging eyes made up of approximately 20,000 to 25,000 tinier eyes, allowing them to zero in on the flying insects that are their daily meals. Their many eyes also make it really hard for them to get caught by predators because they can always see what is approaching.

In this verse, there are four creatures, covered with eyes, in front and in back. In reality, these beings aren't freaky at all. They are unusual, for sure, but they serve an important purpose. These creatures are angelic beings who possess characteristics of the **seraphim** and the **cherubim**. Their many eyes indicate they can see all that is happening in every direction. They could be the highest and greatest of all heavenly beings.

When John looked before the throne, he saw these beings and a sea of crystal-clear glass. Prophecy experts suggest this sea of glass might be (1) the church, because the sea is a biblical symbol for all humankind; (2) the water of the Word; or (3) the water of baptism. Whatever it is, it shows us that all is calm around the throne of God. Nothing is present that would cause even a ripple. The church will be at peace with God when it goes before him.

> **Revelation 4:7–8**
>
> The first living creature was like a lion, the second was like an ox, the third had a face like a man, the fourth was like a flying eagle. Each of the four living creatures had six wings and was covered with eyes all around, even under his wings. Day and night they never stop saying: "Holy, holy, holy is the Lord God Almighty, who was, and is, and is to come."

KEY POINT

The Holy Spirit is everywhere, even in the presence of God.

 GO!

Isaiah 6:1–3 (seraphim)
Revelation 17:15 (sea)
Ephesians 5:26 (water)

seraphim: *angels that worship God, also associated with God's judgment*

cherubim: *angels that guarded the tree of life in the Garden of Eden and guard God's throne*

51

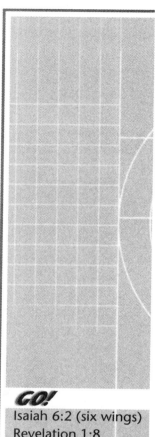

Animals, Animals, Everywhere!

The powerful display John sees in heaven isn't really about animals. The animals are symbolic descriptions of Jesus as the king of earth, a servant, a human, and the king of the skies. Here's what's up:

- *Lion*—Jesus is called the Lion of the tribe of Judah (Revelation 5:5). The lion rules the jungle and Jesus rules the world (Matthew 2:2; 21:5). Jesus is also called the King of the Jews (Matthew 27:11).
- *Ox*—Jesus came to this earth to serve (Mark 10:45). In a similar way that an ox carries its burden, Jesus carried our sins. Jesus also carried his own cross on his shoulders (John 19:17).
- *Man*—Jesus was human, the Son of man (Luke 5:24; 6:5; 7:34). His human side helped him experience everything that we experience, with the exception of sin, and allows him to empathize with our needs.
- *Eagle*—Just as an eagle rules the skies, Jesus rules the heavens and controls all things (John 1:1–3).

GO!

Isaiah 6:2 (six wings)
Revelation 1:8 (who was)

These creatures are wild looking. They have <u>six wings</u>, characteristic of the seraphim. They have eyes everywhere, see everything, and never stop praising God. They don't sleep a wink and keep all of their eyes open all the time! Way cool! Their whole purpose is to give glory to the one who is *"Holy, Holy, Holy,"* the God *"<u>who was</u>, and is, and is to come."*

> **Revelation 4:9–11**
> Whenever the living creatures give glory, honor, and thanks to him who sits on the throne and who lives for ever and ever, the twenty-four elders fall down before him who sits on the throne, and worship him who lives for ever and ever. They lay their crowns before the throne and say: "You are worthy, our Lord and God, to receive glory and honor and power, for you created all things, and by your will they were created and have their being."

 **CREATOR OF ALL**

The twenty-four elders worship God by laying their crowns before his throne. The twenty-four elders acknowledge that God is the creator of all things. He existed <u>in the beginning</u>. He will exist forever and ever. He holds all of the earth in his hands, even little us, and we can only marvel at his magnificent power as we, too, fall before the throne and praise him for his greatness.

GO!
Genesis 1:1
(in the beginning)

CHApTeR cHECKUp

1. What are the three views of the Rapture or Tribulation?
2. What did the trumpet-like voice say to John, and what happened to John's spirit after this?
3. What color will the twenty-four elders wear in heaven, and what does this color symbolize?
4. What did the elders lay before the throne, and what attribute did they acknowledge about God?

CRASH COURSE

▶ When John goes to heaven in the spirit, it is symbolic of the Rapture of the church. (Revelation 4:1–2)
▶ God's throne is surrounded by a rainbow, twenty-four elders, seven lamps, a sea of glass, and four living creatures. (Revelation 4:2–6)
▶ The flashes of lightning, rumblings, and peals of thunder coming from the throne of God are symbols of the approaching storm called the Tribulation. (Revelation 4:5)
▶ The four living creatures have six wings and are covered with eyes. Each creature looks like a different animal: lion, ox, man, and eagle. (Revelation 4:7–8)
▶ When the four living creatures glorify God, the twenty-four elders lay their crowns before the throne and proclaim that God is worthy. (Revelation 4:9–11)

53

Totally Worthy

 **LET'S DIVE IN**

Imagine that you finally got your driver's license, but you don't have a car. You walk to the BMW car dealership near your house to drool over the latest models. When the salesman approaches, you show him your license and explain that you're checking out your dream car. He smiles and tells you that he just inherited a million dollars and nothing would make him happier than to make your dream come true. An hour later after all the paperwork is completed, a brand new, sparkling BMW is yours. Free! You drive home singing all the way!

"Yeah right!" you say. This wouldn't happen in a trillion years. It would be nice, though, wouldn't it, if this happened to you? Well, something like this *did* happen! Only what you were given has far greater value than a BMW. Jesus Christ has given you eternal life. If that doesn't make you break out singing, at least you can say thank you now and then.

> **Revelation 5:1–2**
> Then I saw in the right hand of him who sat on the throne a scroll with writing on both sides and sealed with seven seals. And I saw a mighty angel proclaiming in a loud voice, "Who is worthy to break the seals and open the scroll?"

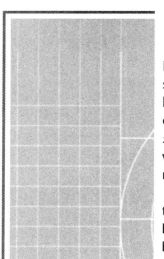

⚡⚡ A MYSTERIOUS SCROLL

In Revelation 5 we find a scroll that's sealed up with seven seals—not just lightly sealed like an envelope someone licked, but superglued shut by a supernatural force. No one is able to open it up. A mighty angel yells, *"Who is worthy to break the seals and open the scroll?"* In other words, "Will we ever know what this scroll says? If no one is able to open it, it might be a mystery forever."

Whatever this scroll is, there is no doubt that it is important. Why would God reveal this scroll to his church? Could it be that he has the destiny of humankind in his hands? Could it be that he is in charge of all that happens on earth? We know God did not allow the Flood to destroy the earth until Noah and his family were safely inside the ark (see LWBI, page 9). We also know God didn't allow the cities of Sodom and Gomorrah to be destroyed until Lot and his family were safely out of the city. Could it be that God would not allow this scroll to be opened until his church is safely in heaven?

GO!
Genesis 6–7
(the Flood)
Genesis 18:16; 19:29
(Sodom and Gomorrah)

OUTSIDE CONNECTION

procure: *get or obtain*

parchment: *for writing, similar to paper*

Hal Lindsey: Sealing a scroll was a common and important practice in biblical times. The wills of both Emperor Vespasian and Caesar Augustus, for example, were secured with seven seals. For such a document, a scribe would **procure** *a long roll of* **parchment** *and begin writing. After a period of writing he would stop, roll the parchment enough to cover his words, and seal the scroll at that point with wax. Then he would resume writing, stop again, roll the scroll, and add another seal. By the time he was finished, he would have sealed the scroll seven times. The scroll would be read a section at a time, after each seal was opened.*[1]

Revelation 5:3–5
But no one in heaven or on earth or under the earth could open the scroll or even look inside it. I wept and wept because no one was found who was worthy to open the scroll or look inside. Then one of the elders said to me, "Do not weep! See, the Lion of the tribe of Judah, the Root of David, has triumphed. He is able to open the scroll and its seven seals."

The Only Guy for the Job: Jesus Christ

John is totally bummed out. Perhaps the scroll holds the secret to solving all of the earth's problems. How is he ever going to know what the scroll says? He is so disappointed he can't stop crying.

Wait! One of the twenty-four elders tells John someone worthy to open the scroll has been found. The one worthy is called the <u>Lion</u> of the tribe of Judah, the <u>Root of David</u>. These are two Old Testament names for Jesus.

GO!
Genesis 49:9 (Lion)
Isaiah 11:1; Revelation 22:16
(Root of David)

> ### Revelation 5:6
> Then I saw a Lamb, looking as if it had been slain, standing in the center of the throne, encircled by the four living creatures and the elders. He had seven horns and seven eyes, which are the seven spirits of God sent out into all the earth.

THE SUPER SACRIFICE

When <u>John the Baptist</u> first introduced Jesus to his followers he said, *"Look, the lamb of God, who takes away the sin of the world"* (John 1:29). When a different John (the John who wrote Revelation) saw Jesus in heaven he described Jesus as a Lamb, *"looking as if it had been slain."* Jesus is our sacrificed lamb. Long before Jesus was born, the Old Testament prophet Isaiah said Jesus would be as a lamb <u>led to slaughter</u>.

The seven horns described here mean that Jesus is all-powerful. He may look gentle, like a lamb, but he has the power of God Almighty. His looks really can kill. After being raised from the dead, Jesus said, *"All authority in heaven and on earth has been given to me"* (Matthew 28:18).

GO!
Matthew 3:1–17
(John the Baptist)
Isaiah 53:7
(led to slaughter)

KEY SYMBOLS

Seven Horns
All powerful

Seven Eyes
All knowing

> ### Revelation 5:7–8
> He came and took the scroll from the right hand of him who sat on the throne. And when he had taken it, the four living creatures and the twenty-four elders fell down before the Lamb. Each one had a harp and they were holding golden bowls full of incense, which are the prayers of the saints.

57

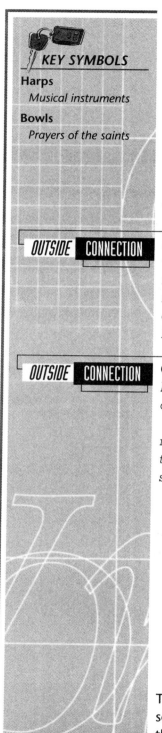

KEY SYMBOLS

Harps
Musical instruments

Bowls
Prayers of the saints

Roaring Lion

When Jesus took the scroll, the four living creatures and the twenty-four elders fell down and worshiped him. Each creature had a harp and a golden bowl. The harps are musical instruments that will be played along with the singing in heaven. The golden bowls hold the prayers of the saints. Who and what will believers be praying for? Believers will be praying for loved ones on earth who are being persecuted, for the defeat of Satan, the Antichrist, and the False Prophet, and for the Second Coming and reign of Jesus Christ.

OUTSIDE CONNECTION

Kevin Johnson: While Christians argue over the details of what will take place when the world dies, they agree on the main points: Jesus will appear a second time—and this time not as a helpless baby but as all powerful Lord of all. He will crush evildoers. He will establish his eternal kingdom. And he will take Christians home to live with him forever.[2]

OUTSIDE CONNECTION

Charles R. Swindoll: One day Jesus Christ will come for us. His coming is sure, and He will keep His promise. Since he conquered death, He will get us beyond those jaws as well.

If you are ready, the thought of his coming is a comfort. If not, it's a dread. The secret of escape is being sure you know the One who can get us out of the grave. His coming is sure . . . are you?[3]

> **Revelation 5:9–10**
> And they sang a new song: "You are worthy to take the scroll and to open its seals, because you were slain, and with your blood you purchased men from God from every tribe and language and people and nation. You have made them to be a kingdom and priests to serve our God, and they will reign on the earth."

 SINGING A NEW SONG!

The Irish band U2 has a song that says, "I will sing, sing a new song." Well, the song talked about in Revelation 5:9 is one that was sung for the first time when Jesus was found to be

Do you know for sure that you're going to go to heaven? How can you have assurance of your salvation?_____

_____

_____

If you're sure of your salvation, how can you help bring assurance of salvation to others who are unsure about their faith?_____

_____

_____

Jesus Christ gave his life so that we can have eternal life. Jesus is the only one who is able to open up the scrolls. He's worthy because he lived a perfect life, died in our place, and then rose again. He died so we could live eternally. If you know someone who hasn't accepted this truth, commit to praying for, and talking to, this person right away. The truth may set him or her free.

worthy. Those in heaven will sing this new song for a very long time.

Jesus paid the penalty for our sin. He died for everyone—every tribe, language, people, and nation—because he <u>loved the world</u>. As our high priest, he made us a royal priesthood to serve and rule with him. He **commissioned** us to go and make <u>disciples</u> of all nations. When he returns at his Second Coming at the end of the Tribulation, believers will <u>reign with him</u> on earth for one thousand years (the Millennium).

Jim Petersen: God is creating an inheritance for His Son consisting of people out of every tribe and nation in the world. These people, His church, are being adopted into God's family. They will share in all that is His. He will even give them the Kingdom![4]

GO!
John 3:16
 (loved the world)
Matthew 28:19
 (disciples)
Revelation 20:6
 (reign with him)

commissioned:
appointed, assigned, authorized

ten thousand times
ten thousand: too
many to count

Revelation 5:11–14

Then I looked and heard the voice of many angels, numbering thousands upon thousands, and **ten thousand times ten thousand**. They encircled the throne and the living creatures and the elders. In a loud voice they sang: "Worthy is the Lamb, who was slain, to receive power and wealth and wisdom and strength and honor and glory and praise." Then I heard every creature in heaven and on earth and under the earth and on the sea, and all that is in them, singing: "To him who sits on the throne and to the Lamb be praise and honor and glory and power, for ever and ever!" The four living creatures said, "Amen," and the elders fell down and worshiped.

 PRAISE FEST

When John looked, he saw more angels than he could count or describe. (Hark, the herald angels are many!) He heard them singing and declaring the worthiness of Christ.

What would it sound like to hear every creature praising God? Deafening! Wonderful! Scary! Awesome! If you've ever been with thousands of other Christians in a huge auditorium, convention center, or arena, you may have felt chills up and down your spine while you were all singing or praying. If so, you've had a taste of how John felt here.

CHAPTER CHECKUP

1. Why is this scroll so important?
2. Describe the difference between Jesus the Lamb and Jesus the Lion?
3. What do the angels around the throne say about Jesus?
4. The church is described as a kingdom and priests (Revelation 5:10). What significance does this have for believers today?
5. According to Revelation 5:11–14, how do we know Jesus is more than a good man or a prophet?

- God holds a seven-sealed scroll in his right hand as an angel asks for someone worthy to open it. John cries when no one steps forward. (Revelation 5:1–4)
- Jesus is the Lion of Judah, and he is the only one worthy to open the scroll. He is worthy because he was slain for the sins of the world. (Revelation 5:5–7)
- Once Jesus takes the scroll, the four living creatures and twenty-four elders sing a new song; the angels also join in proclaiming Christ's worthiness. (Revelation 5:8–12)
- When heaven sings to Jesus, all creatures on earth and under the sea also sing praises to him. (Revelation 5:13)

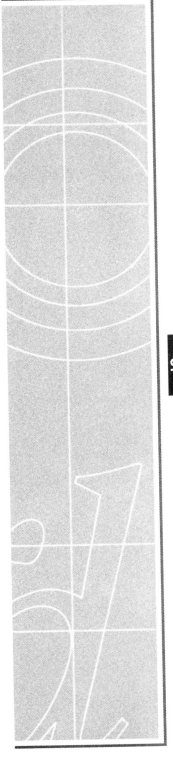

Horses, Despair, Gore, and More

6

 LET'S DIVE IN

In chapter 6 the scene shifts from future events in heaven to future events on earth. We've already seen what will happen in heaven between the Rapture and the Tribulation. Now we'll see what will happen on earth in this same time period. (And it won't be pretty!) Bible experts disagree about how long this period will last, but three years is a good possibility.

The Tribulation is a time when Jesus will start to deal with Satan and humankind's rebellion on earth. God will pour down his wrath from heaven onto earth. The events in this chapter and the following chapters can be divided into three sets of seven: *seven seal judgments*, *seven trumpet judgments*, and *seven bowl judgments*. It would be easy to say that twenty-one judgments will happen, but that isn't the case. The first six seals are broken one at a time, and each seal will produce one judgment each for a total of six judgments. The seventh seal will not produce a seventh judgment, but rather the seven trumpets.

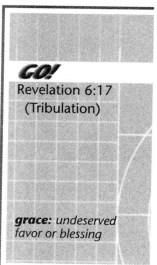

GO!
Revelation 6:17
(Tribulation)

grace: *undeserved favor or blessing*

The first six trumpets produce one judgment each for a total of six. But the seventh trumpet will produce the seven bowls. (See the chart below for help in understanding this.) Once the seventh bowl is poured out, the Tribulation will be over.

In each of the first four seal judgments, a horse and rider are released by one of the four living creatures mentioned in chapter 4. Each horse waits in its stall ready to charge, as if in a race, when the command is given. They won't all race at once like they do at the Kentucky Derby. God restrains each horse until its turn so that only one bad thing will happen at a time. This shows the **grace** of God.

Chart of God's Judgments

Seven Seal Judgments *Revelation 6*	Seven Trumpet Judgments *Revelation 8–9*	Seven Bowl Judgments *Revelation 12:12; 16*
1st seal: Antichrist appears	1st trumpet: One-third earth burned	1st bowl: Sores
2nd seal: Wars	2nd trumpet: One-third sea polluted	2nd bowl: All seas polluted
3rd seal: Economic collapse and famine	3rd trumpet: One-third freshwater polluted	3rd bowl: All freshwater polluted
4th seal: Death	4th trumpet: One-third sunlight dimmed	4th bowl: All sunlight scorches
5th seal: Martyrdom	5th trumpet: People tortured (woe)	5th bowl: Darkness everywhere
6th seal: Earthquakes	6th trumpet: People killed (woe)	6th bowl: Euphrates dried up
7th seal: Seven trumpet judgments (Rev. 8–9)	7th trumpet: Satan and the Seven bowl judgments (woe) [Rev. 12:12; 16]	7th bowl: Mass destruction

Revelation 6:1–2

I watched as the Lamb opened the first of the seven seals. Then I heard one of the four living creatures say in a voice like thunder, "Come!" I looked, and there before me was a white horse! Its rider held a bow, and he was given a crown, and he rode out as a conqueror bent on conquest.

WHITE HORSE—FAKE RULE

The judgments of the Tribulation will not begin like a nuclear explosion, but rather like a tiny snowball rolling down a hill, gathering speed and growing in size as it rolls. All who are in its way should be prepared to be run over! Christ opens the first of the seven seals. A voice like thunder is heard and then a white horse and a rider appear. The rider isn't out for a peaceful trot in the country. He's holding a bow, symbolizing military power. He is also carrying his crown, which implies that it was given as a <u>gift</u>, not earned or inherited.

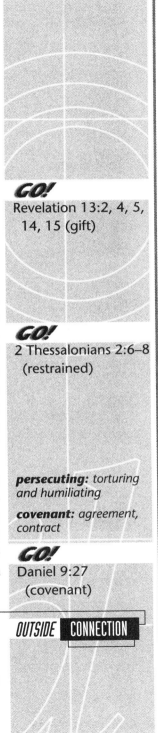

GO!
Revelation 13:2, 4, 5, 14, 15 (gift)

Revelation chapter 19 also speaks of a rider on a white horse—Jesus. For this reason a few experts suggest that the rider here is Jesus. But most experts believe this rider is the counterfeit Christ, or Antichrist.

Over the centuries people have tried to figure out who the Antichrist is since he will probably be alive when the church is raptured. His identity will be hard to guess because he will be <u>restrained</u> until the proper time. When the true church is raptured, it will be time to start watching for the Antichrist. If you're a believer you won't have to worry about what he looks like because you won't be around to catch his wrath! But those who are still on earth should know that he will not stand out at first, so the best characteristics for them to look for will be a popular and powerful person. When he signs a seven-year treaty to protect Israel, his identity will be known.

GO!
2 Thessalonians 2:6–8 (restrained)

The world will be looking for a ruler who can put an end to nuclear weapons, environmental problems, poverty, and economic troubles. At first this man will gain power by being charming. Then he will gain more power by **persecuting** and killing all who oppose him. He won't protect people. The earth will have a leader who negotiates a **<u>covenant</u>** that is a fake.

persecuting: *torturing and humiliating*

covenant: *agreement, contract*

GO!
Daniel 9:27 (covenant)

John Hagee: *The Antichrist will be a man who makes his debut upon the stage of world history with hypnotic charm and charisma. He will probably come from the European Union or a country or confederation that was once part of the Roman Empire, which stretched from Ireland to Egypt and included Turkey, Iran, and Iraq.*[1]

OUTSIDE **CONNECTION**

KEY SYMBOLS

First Four Seal Judgments
Four living creatures
Four horses and riders

First Seal
First horse (white)
• Antichrist

Second Seal
Second horse (fiery red)
• wars

communism:
government system where property and goods are held in common, such as former Soviet Union, modern-day China, and North Korea

Ezekiel 38–39
(attack Israel)
Ezekiel 38:21–23
(against brother)

HAPPENINGS

Revelation 6:3–4

When the Lamb opened the second seal, I heard the second living creature say, "Come!" Then another horse came out, a fiery red one. Its rider was given power to take peace from the earth and to make men slay each other. To him was given a large sword.

 RED HORSE—CHAOS

Just when people think life will be peaceful as a result of the Antichrist's plan, things will go berserk. When Jesus breaks the second seal, the second living creature will shout, "Come!" This red horse will have an unusual power. He will cause men to kill each other. The sword in his hand signifies great weapons of war.

Some experts associate this rider with **communism**. The prophet Ezekiel predicts the rise of a dictator from the far north (possibly Russia) who will <u>attack Israel</u> in the last days. This dictator will advance with a great army, carrying swords and riding horses, but will meet defeat when many of his own soldiers kill each other because God will turn each man <u>against brother</u> so that God's glory may be shown.

The Antichrist will be a false prince of peace. He will plot to wipe out Israel as a way to gain world peace. God will show the world he is a fake by causing his phony peace programs to fail. Jesus is the true Prince of Peace. When world leaders reject Jesus, they reject the only solution to their problems.

In spite of all the emphasis on peace, the past century has given us World War 1, World War 2, the Korean War, Vietnam War, and the Persian Gulf War and the war on terrorism. Civil wars and armed conflicts are raging all over the world even as you read this. True peace on this earth won't happen until Jesus Christ returns to earth to reign.

 Wars are nasty, but don't get scared. God is working behind the scenes to bring glory to himself.

66

BLACK HORSE—MASSIVE INFLATION

When Jesus opens the third seal, the third living creature will give the same command the first two gave, *"Come!"* This horse will be black, symbolizing grief and mourning. Its rider will hold a pair of scales (or weights) that symbolize economic disaster and starvation. The scales will be used to weigh food that will be sold for outrageous prices.

Wars kill farmers, destroy land and crops, and cause the fall of societies and governments. After the Rapture things will go from bad to way worse! Wicked men will ruin, steal, and hoard food supplies, creating great despair, poverty, and eventually death. People will spend all their money on a little bit of food and won't be able to buy other things they'll need, like housing, clothing, or cars. The rich, however, will still be able to afford items like oil and wine.

John Hagee: People ask, "Why would God allow a financial collapse in America?" I'll tell you why. Because the First Commandment says, Thou shalt have no other gods before me (Exodus 20:3 KJV). And in America, money is god.[2]

KEY SYMBOLS

Third Seal
Third horse (black)
- famine

OUTSIDE CONNECTION

plague: *natural disasters or diseases that hurt crops and people*

imposters: *fakes*

HAPPENINGS

KEY SYMBOLS

Fourth Seal
Fourth horse (pale)
• death

inhabitants: *those who live in a certain area*

GO!
Matthew 10:28
(cannot be killed)

 ## PALE HORSE—TERRIBLE TIMES

The pale horse and its rider bring even worse things than the horses and riders before it. This verse contradicts those who say that the church will eventually bring in a perfect society. The Bible says, *"There will be terrible times in the last days. . . . evil men and **imposters** will go from bad to worse"* (2 Timothy 3:1, 13).

This horse will stun everyone with its creepy pale color. His rider and the creature following him represent death and hell.

Hiroshi Nakajima, Director General of the World Health Organization, says, *"We are standing on the brink of a global crisis in infectious diseases. . . . During the past 20 years, at least 30 new diseases have emerged to threaten the health of hundreds of millions of people. For many of these diseases there is no treatment, cure, or vaccine."*[3] The AIDS crisis and Ebola virus outbreaks in Africa are evidence of the truth of Hiroshi's words.

> **Revelation 6:9–10**
> When he opened the fifth seal, I saw under the altar the souls of those who had been slain because of the word of God and the testimony they had maintained. They called out in a loud voice, "How long, Sovereign Lord, holy and true, until you judge the **inhabitants** of the earth and avenge our blood?"

 ## A CRY FOR JUSTICE

The opening of the fifth seal switches attention from the death of unbelievers to the death of believers, from hell to God's altar. The four living creatures will not call for any more horses. The last three seals will be different from the first four.

When the Rapture happens, multitudes of people that are left behind will accept Jesus. These people are usually called the tribulation saints. They will be extremely unpopular, and entire governments will turn against these new believers. These believers will be courageous, unafraid of physical death because they know their souls <u>cannot be killed</u>.

The souls of the tribulation saints are under the altar crying

68

out instead of rejoicing and praising God around the throne with the rest of the church. Unlike earlier believers who received their **glorified bodies** in the Rapture, these saints will have to wait until later for theirs. Because of this, they will be fully conscious and able to think about their persecution, torture, and murder. They cry to God, asking for justice and to be raised, avenged, and given glorified bodies.

glorified bodies: *new bodies believers receive in heaven*

> **Revelation 6:11–12**
>
> Then each of them was given a white robe, and they were told to wait a little longer, until the number of their fellow servants and brothers who were to be killed as they had been was completed. I watched as he opened the sixth seal. There was a great earthquake. The sun turned black like sackcloth made of goat hair, the whole moon turned blood red, . . .

YOU AIN'T SEEN NOTHIN' YET

The tribulation saints will be told to wait until other believers are killed, indicating that Jesus has a specific plan for the rest of the world.

When Jesus opens the sixth seal, the whole earth will shake. John calls this shaking a great earthquake, but the description sounds more like a nuclear explosion. Whatever it is, it will be massive. Possibly one or more nuclear explosions will take place. The resulting pollution will cause darkness to cover the land and the moon to appear red. Reminds me of what the prophet Joel said, *"The sun will be turned to darkness and the moon to blood before the coming of the great and dreadful day of the Lord"* (Joel 2:31).

> **Revelation 6:13–15**
>
> . . . and the stars in the sky fell to earth, as late figs drop from a fig tree when shaken by a strong wind. The sky receded like a scroll, rolling up, and every mountain and island was removed from its place. Then the kings of the earth, the princes, the generals, the rich, the mighty, and every slave and every free man hid in caves and among the rocks of the mountains.

KEY SYMBOLS

Fifth Seal
Souls under the altar
 • martyrs

KEY SYMBOLS

Sixth Seal
Earthquakes

How do you feel when you think about the horses, riders, and terror the earth will experience?_____

_____

When you try to warn your friends about God's coming judgment, how do they react?_____

_____

When you think about God telling the tribulation saints to wait a little longer to be avenged, how does that make you feel about God?_____

_____

_____

Christians have assurance that they won't suffer through these horrible end times. What's hard is knowing non-Christians who either don't believe they'll face God's wrath, or don't care if they do. Unbelievers may think it's cool to shrug off the gloom and doom of future destruction, especially when life around them is going great. Regardless of their response, we can thank God for his mercy in giving the people in the world more time to turn to him.

GO!
Isaiah 34:1–10
(sky rolls up)
Isaiah 24:1–13
(panic)

🎬🎬 STAR WARS

The world as we know it will be no more. Stars will fall. Mountains and islands will collapse. All peoples—from the rich to the poorest slave—will run and hide from the Lord. It sounds like a bad asteroid movie, but the reality of it will be chilling.

Since the word for *"stars"* in the original Greek could also be translated "meteors," this could indicate a meteor shower or a missile attack. Modern-day cruise missiles and laser-guided bombs could have looked like stars to someone living two thousand years ago.

"The sky receded like a scroll, rolling up" is another indication of a nuclear war. During a nuclear blast the wind is rapidly pushed out for several miles, creating a vacuum at the center of the blast site. Suddenly, this wind, like a giant tidal wave, rushes violently back into the vacuum. The sky rolls up on itself. Massive panic will result. People will rush into caves and bomb shelters.

> **Revelation 6:16–17**
> They called to the mountains and the rocks, "Fall on us and hide us from the face of him who sits on the throne and from the wrath of the Lamb! For the great day of their wrath has come, and who can stand?"

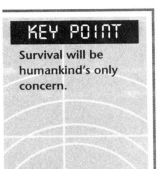

KEY POINT

Survival will be humankind's only concern.

 ## NOBODY ESCAPES GOD'S WRATH

You would think that by now, these people would be like, "Duh, I can't run away from God!" But no, these people don't <u>call</u> on Jesus. Instead, they call out to nature to save them. They call out to the rocks and mountains to fall on them, so they don't have to face God.

    The <u>Day of Wrath</u> is another name for the Tribulation. Although people recognize the Tribulation has come, we don't read about these people repenting and accepting Jesus. And there is the question: *"Who can stand?"* The answer is in Revelation 7:3–8 when God will choose some to be saved. We'll get to this in the next chapter.

GO!

Acts 4:12 (call)
Zephaniah 1:14–16 (Day of Wrath)

David Hocking: Our present generation has no desire to hear of these things or to believe them. We want to be stroked and reminded of our self-worth and potential for success. The real issue has not changed—heaven and hell, life and death. Where will you spend eternity? [4]

OUTSIDE **CONNECTION**

CHAPTER CHECKUP

1. Who is the person riding the white horse, and what weapon did the rider carry?
2. What power was given to the rider on the red horse?
3. How much will a quart of wheat cost during the Tribulation?
4. What was the name of the rider on the pale horse, and what was following him?

CRASH COURSE

▶ The judgments of the Tribulation begin when Christ opens the first of seven seals. (Revelation 6:1)

▶ The four horsemen will bring about the Antichrist, war, economic ruin, famine, and death. (Revelation 6:2–8)

▶ During the Tribulation people will still turn to Christ and be killed for their faith. These people will be known as the tribulation saints, and they will ask God to avenge their deaths. (Revelation 6:9–10)

▶ An earthquake will strike the earth affecting the sun, moon, sky, land, and sea. (Revelation 6:12–14)

▶ Following the sixth seal, fear will grip everyone on earth as they try to hide from the wrath of God. (Revelation 6:15–17)

Marked Messengers

 LET'S DIVE IN

God's Word has been translated into almost every language, and our means of communicating it has multiplied because of the internet, television, cable, and radio. (Notice, I left out cell phones because you shouldn't talk and drive!) The world won't end until the gospel has been preached <u>in the whole world</u>. Everyone will hear about Jesus and have an opportunity to accept salvation before they die or take the <u>mark</u> of the beast.

GO!

Matthew 24:14
  (in the whole world)
Revelation 13:17
  (mark)

> **Revelation 7:1–2**
> After this I saw four angels standing at the four corners of the earth, holding back the four winds of the earth to prevent any wind from blowing on the land or on the sea or on any tree. Then I saw another angel coming up from the east, having the seal of the living God. He called out in a loud voice to the four angels who had been given power to harm the land and the sea:

 THE WIND KNOCKED OUT OF 'EM

Angels are divided into different ranks; some have higher ranks than others. Some serve Satan while others serve God. We aren't told who this angel from the east is, but we are told that

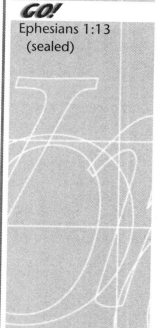
he will have authority (or rule over) the other four angels who are preventing the wind from blowing. This angel will use his loud voice and the seal of the living God to stop the other angels from harming the earth and sea. He will **mark** a group of special messengers.

> **Revelation 7:3**
> "Do not harm the land or the sea or the trees until we put a seal on the foreheads of the servants of our God."

 GOOD MARKINGS

When animals are bred for show, breeders often promote the sale of the animal by saying that it has "good markings." Usually this means that the animal's face is all one color or the color of its fur is the perfect shade or mixture of colors for that particular breed. When people hear of markings in Revelation, they usually think negatively of the mark of the beast. That is different than the mark (or seal) of protection mentioned here for God's people.

The four angels will be commanded not to harm the land or sea or trees until God's servants can be <u>sealed</u>. The Bible doesn't say what this seal will be, only that believers will be protected by some kind of mark. It will appear on their foreheads and will show others that they belong to God. It will be a heavenly tattoo created for the believers' protection. This is one tattoo your mom will want you to have!

> **Revelation 7:4–8**
> Then I heard the number of those who were sealed: 144,000 from all the tribes of Israel. From the tribe of Judah 12,000 were sealed, from the tribe of Reuben 12,000, from the tribe of Gad 12,000, from the tribe of Asher 12,000, from the tribe of Naphtali 12,000, from the tribe of Manasseh 12,000, from the tribe of Simeon 12,000, from the tribe of Levi 12,000, from the tribe of Issachar 12,000, from the tribe of Zebulun 12,000, from the tribe of Joseph 12,000, from the tribe of Benjamin 12,000.

74

 144,000

Who are these people who will be sealed? They will come from the twelve tribes of Israel—the Jews. Two of the original tribes—Dan and Ephraim—will be left out, and the tribes of Levi and Joseph will take their place. Most experts believe the first two tribes mentioned will be skipped because they were both guilty of worshiping false gods and idols. Levi wasn't counted among the original twelve tribes because it was made up of priests. Joseph wasn't originally counted, but will now be counted instead of his son's tribe, Ephraim, that worshiped idols.

 Even though these verses state clearly that the 144,000 come from Israel, the Jehovah's Witness cult uses this passage to refer to 144,000 of its members. All **Gentiles** are excluded from this number. The 144,000 referred to here will be Jews. It's best to ignore any and all speculation and take this passage to mean just what it says.

> **Revelation 7:9**
> After this I looked up and there before me was a great multitude that no one could count, from every nation, tribe, people and language, standing before the throne and in front of the Lamb. They were wearing white robes and were holding palm branches in their hands.

 MULTIPLE MURDERS AND MARTYRS

Once God has sealed 144,000 Jews, the entire world will hear his message, and multitudes of people will be saved. The Antichrist and his prophets will be really mad and try to stop the revival before it gets out of hand. They will take food and medicine from people, and they will kill many new Christians. The number of martyrs will be more than anyone can count.

These martyrs will be given white robes to symbolize the righteousness of Christ. They will also receive palm branches, symbolizing their triumphant entry into heaven, just like Jesus was given palm branches when he <u>entered Jerusalem</u> before his death.

KEY SYMBOLS

144,000
Marked from Israel's twelve tribes

Gentiles: *people who aren't Jews*

75

KEY SYMBOLS

Multitude before the Throne
Martyrs (tribulation saints)

GO!
John 12:12–13
(entered Jerusalem)

What do you think God has called you, personally, to do to proclaim the good news of Jesus before the end times begin? Has he called you to missions? To friends and neighbors? To family?

_____

_____

Since God wants everyone to hear about Jesus, how does that make you feel about his coming judgment?_____

_____

_____

Jesus commanded us to go into all the world and preach the gospel (Matthew 28:19–20). This commandment wasn't *just* given so all people would have a chance to believe in Jesus, but it was given so that the things in Revelation could be fulfilled.

OUTSIDE CONNECTION | **Greg Stier:** *When I was a teenager, I couldn't imagine doing street evangelism. As I plunged into my first "witnessing" experience, my heart was pounding, my palms were sweaty, and my knees were knocking. But somehow I managed to sputter out the gospel message to five senior highers I'd met. I was sick. I was scared. I was nervous. I was hooked. Now I lead thousands of kids on street-evangelism outreaches every year.*[1]

Revelation 7:10–11
And they cried out in a loud voice: "Salvation belongs to our God, who sits on the throne, and to the **Lamb**." All the angels were standing around the throne and around the elders and the four living creatures. They fell down on their faces before the throne and worshiped God . . .

Lamb: *Jesus*

KEY POINT

God, the author of salvation, has given us only one way to heaven—his Son.

 FALLING FLAT BEFORE GOD

This will be one of the greatest worship times ever known to humankind. All of these martyrs (tribulation saints), angels, elders, and living creatures will praise God for providing salvation through his Son, Jesus, the Lamb. Everyone in heaven is going to want to take part in this service!

> **Revelation 7:12–14**
>
> . . . saying, "Amen! Praise and glory and wisdom and thanks and honor and power and strength be to our God for ever and ever. Amen!" Then one of the elders asked me, "These in white robes—who are they, and where did they come from?" I answered, "Sir, you know." And he said, "These are they who have come out of the great tribulation; they have washed their robes and made them white in the blood of the Lamb."

 ## THANKS TO THE LAMB!

After praise has been given to God, the twenty-four elders ask two questions: *"Who are they, and where did they come from?"* The elders know the answer, but they want everyone else to know as well. This great multitude before the Lamb of God will come out of the Tribulation. When most prophecy experts talk about the Great Tribulation, they are talking about the last three and one-half years of the seven-year period. But in this verse, the term refers to all those who have been saved over the entire seven-year Tribulation.

> **Revelation 7:15–17**
>
> "Therefore, 'they are before the throne of God and serve him day and night in his temple; and he who sits on the throne will spread his tent over them. Never again will they hunger; never again will they thirst. The sun will not beat upon them, nor any scorching heat. For the Lamb at the center of the throne will be their shepherd; he will lead them to springs of living water. And God will wipe away every tear from their eyes.'"

 ## THE GOOD SHEPHERD

Those who have suffered at the hands of the Antichrist have been given an awesome promise. Once they get to heaven they will be <u>protected by God</u> and be with Jesus, surrounded by angels similar to how a mother hen covers her baby chicks with her wing. They will no longer have to run for their lives or hide from those who hate Christians.

GO!
Psalm 91:1–16;
46:1–11
(protected by God)

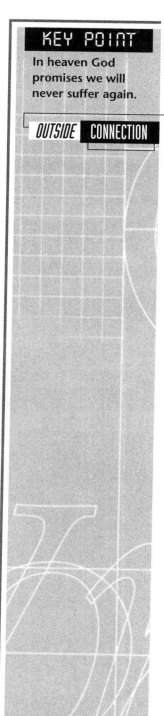

OUTSIDE **CONNECTION**

The Lamb will be their shepherd. He will lead them to springs of living water, and they won't ever thirst again. God will wipe away every single tear from their eyes, and all of the suffering that they've been through will be over forever.

Max Lucado: *The King of Kings will raise his pierced hand and proclaim, "No more." The angels will stand and the Father will speak, "No more." Every person who lives and who ever lived will turn toward the sky and hear God announce, "No more." No more loneliness. No more tears. No more death. No more sadness. No more crying. No more pain.*[2]

CHAPTER CHECKUP

1. What did the four angels do to the wind? What might this have prevented?
2. What did the 144,000 cry out? Why is their message so important?
3. Who are those in the white robes, and where did they come from?
4. Describe life in heaven according to Revelation 7:15–17.

CRASH COURSE

▶ An angel will place the mark of God on the foreheads of God's servants so that his judgments do not harm them. (Revelation 7:2–3)

▶ God is not finished with Israel. He will seal 144,000 Israelites with his mark of protection. Twelve thousand will come from each of the twelve tribes of Israel. (Revelation 7:4–8)

▶ During the Tribulation multitudes of Christians will be killed on earth. These martyrs will find themselves in heaven standing before Jesus. (Revelation 7:9)

▶ A great worship service will start in heaven when the tribulation saints, followed by the rest of those in heaven, start worshiping God for being the provider of their salvation. (Revelation 7:10–11)

▶ God promises that the martyrs will never again endure the hardships they suffered on earth, and he promises to wipe their tears away. (Revelation 7:15–17)

Trumpets of Doom

79

 LET'S DIVE IN

We got through a lot of things in chapter 6, some of which you already might want to forget, but we never got to that seventh seal. Finally, we get to see what happens when the seventh seal is opened. The opening of the seventh seal reveals the appearance of seven angels with seven trumpets (see chart on page 64 or Timeline #2, page 46).

Here's how it works. The seven seals can be divided into two sets: (1) four horsemen (not headless, but terrible nonetheless), and (2) three new judgments (in other words, more bad news). In a similar way, the seven trumpet judgments can be divided into two sets: (1) four judgments called "judgments of one-third," and three other judgments called "woes"—as in "woe is me!" The first four judgments are called judgments of one-third because only one-third of the grass burns, one-third of the water is polluted, and so on. This shows the grace of God. He doesn't destroy everything at once. He gives people the chance to change. Refer to the chart in chapter 6, page 64 for more help understanding the events in this chapter.

> **Revelation 8:1–2**
> When he opened the seventh seal, there was silence for about half an hour. And I saw the seven angels who stand before God, and to them were given seven trumpets.

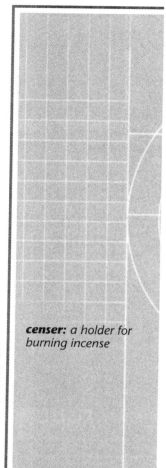

SILENCE—SOON TO BE BROKEN

Have you ever been quiet for thirty minutes straight? Sure, you might say, in church or class when you're supposed to be listening. How about when no one is talking, or even moving, and the only thing you can hear is the sound of your own breath or heartbeat? Have you ever been *that* quiet? It's really pretty hard to do!

That's how still it will be in heaven when this seal is opened. Even the rumblings and flashes of lightning around the throne will stop. The four living creatures, who up until this moment haven't stopped praising God, will be silent. All of heaven knows what's going down. It's going to be huge!

Then the seven angels who stand before God will be handed seven trumpets. It looks as though the silence will be broken.

censer: *a holder for burning incense*

80

> **Revelation 8:3–4**
>
> Another angel, who had a golden **censer**, came and stood at the altar. He was given much incense to offer, with the prayers of all the saints, on the golden altar before the throne. The smoke of the incense, together with the prayers of the saints, went up before God from the angel's hand.

AROMA OF PRAYER

Some experts believe this eighth angel is Jesus, but he is probably just another powerful angel. This angel has a special position of service before the golden altar (see illustration, page 77) of God. He holds a censer of gold (see illustration, page 77) similar to the one used in the Old Testament Temple. That censer contained charcoal that was burned under a layer of incense. When the hot charcoal warmed the incense, a sweet smell was created similar to chestnuts roasting on an open fire. When the incense mentioned in the verse above mixes with the prayers of the saints, an incredible aroma of prayer drifts up towards God. Our prayers are precious to God.

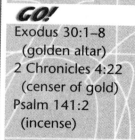

GO!
Exodus 30:1–8
(golden altar)
2 Chronicles 4:22
(censer of gold)
Psalm 141:2
(incense)

When you burn a scented candle, what happens to the aroma in the room?_____

_____

Describe a time of prayer you had that was especially meaningful. What made it significant?_____

_____

Prayer is a strange thing. After all, if God knows your thoughts and needs, why pray? Well, even Jesus Christ prayed, and he was God. If Jesus thought it was important to spend time in prayer, then we should too. Instead of trying to handle things on his own, Jesus prayed when his soul was anguished in the Garden of Gethsemane. (See Matthew 26:36–46; Mark 14:32–42; Luke 22:40–46; John 18:1). Do you have a concern or need to lift up to God right now? He's listening and he cares about you! Your prayers are a sweet smell to him.

Golden Censer

The golden censer mentioned in Revelation reminds us of the censer, shown here, used for burning incense in Jewish worship during Old Testament times.

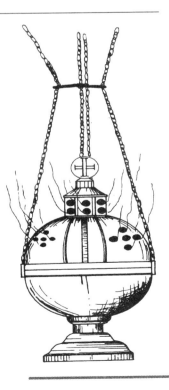

Golden Altar

The golden altar was made by King Solomon for God's Temple in Jerusalem. It symbolizes the altar of God in heaven where an angel will mix incense with the prayers of the tribulation saints.

OUTSIDE CONNECTION

Mark Littleton and Jeanette Gardner Littleton: Only Jesus, of all the powerful leaders in the world, had the power to overcome death. Because he did, he lives. And because his power can even overcome death, you can be sure that he has the power to handle whatever you are facing in life. Don't be afraid to ask for his death-revolting, life-changing power to help you today![1]

> **Revelation 8:5**
> Then the angel took the censer, filled it with fire from the altar, and hurled it on the earth; and there came peals of thunder, rumblings, flashes of lightning, and an earthquake.

 HURLING FIREBALL

When the prayers of the saints have been consumed in the censer, the angel will take the empty censer, go back to the altar, fill it with fire, and hurl it down on the earth. A sure-fire way to get everyone's attention! The prayers of the martyred believers will go up to heaven, and the answer will come down to earth. God will avenge the death of the tribulation saints. The hurling fireball will be followed by thunder, lightning, and an earthquake.

OUTSIDE CONNECTION

David Breese: One person who had just been in an earthquake told me, "When the ground begins to shake beneath your feet, you lose faith in everything!" I was able to say, "Perhaps that's the way God intended [it]."[2]

HAPPENINGS

In the summer of 2000, over 70,000 earthquakes were felt in Japan. The people of Japan also encountered erupting volcanoes, sulfur dioxide in the air, and unprecedented flooding in September when over twenty-three inches of rain fell in one day![3]

This is just one example of natural phenomena. All over the earth nature seems to have gone berserk. Wildfires. Earthquakes. Tornadoes. Drought. Floods. Mudslides. Could it be that God is trying to get our attention while there is still time for repentance?

> **Revelation 8:6–7**
>
> Then the seven angels who had the seven trumpets prepared to sound them. The first angel sounded his trumpet, and there came hail and fire mixed with blood, and it was hurled down upon the earth. A third of the earth was burned up, a third of the trees were burned up, and all the green grass was burned up.

ENVIRONMENTAL NIGHTMARE

Can you imagine being in a storm where <u>hail, fire</u>, and blood rain down? Hollywood has never attempted such a scene! Not only will a storm like this cause immediate chaos, but also it will bring about many other terrible things. The trees used for lumber will be gone, as will the grain and other crops used for food. The entire balance of the earth will be messed up and many people will die.

Hal Lindsey: With this massive loss of vegetation will come soil erosion, floods, and mudslides. Air pollution will be immense; the smoke of the fire will fill the atmosphere, and the remaining vegetation will be unable to adequately absorb the hydrocarbons from automobiles and industry. Ecology will be thrown chaotically out of balance.[4]

> **Revelation 8:8–9**
>
> The second angel sounded his trumpet, and something like a huge mountain, all ablaze, was thrown into the sea. A third of the sea turned into blood, a third of the living creatures in the sea died, and a third of the ships were destroyed.

See Ya, Sea

The first trumpet will signal judgment on the earth. The second trumpet will signal judgment on the sea. Something huge (maybe an asteroid) will fall into the ocean. The impact of this object will turn the sea <u>to blood</u>. It will be like Moses' plagues all over again, only this time on a global scale! It will kill one-third of sea life and destroy one-third of the ships. Fish, dolphins, whales, sharks, and other sea creatures will die in great numbers. Much of the shipping industry will end. People will lose yet another source of food and income.

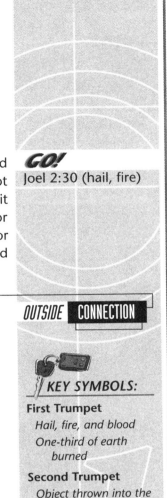

GO!
Joel 2:30 (hail, fire)

OUTSIDE **CONNECTION**

KEY SYMBOLS:

First Trumpet
Hail, fire, and blood
One-third of earth burned

Second Trumpet
Object thrown into the sea
One-third of sea polluted
One-third sea creatures and ships destroyed

GO!
Exodus 7:14–25 (to blood)

83

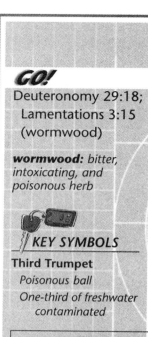

GO!
Deuteronomy 29:18;
Lamentations 3:15
(wormwood)

wormwood: *bitter,
intoxicating, and
poisonous herb*

KEY SYMBOLS

Third Trumpet
*Poisonous ball
One-third of freshwater
contaminated*

OUTSIDE CONNECTION

HAPPENINGS

Revelation 8:10–11

The third angel sounded his trumpet, and a great star, blazing like a torch, fell from the sky on a third of the rivers and on the springs of water—the name of the star is **Wormwood**. A third of the waters turned bitter, and many people died from the waters that had become bitter.

 CONTAMINATED WATER

Some believe this star *"blazing like a torch"* will be a meteor. Others say it could be a nuclear missile. Although people aren't sure what is described here, most agree about what it will do. It will contaminate one-third of the earth's freshwater supply, causing many people to drink the toxic water and die. Drinking bottled water and tap water will be risky. People will die from thirst, afraid to drink the bitter water.

Dr. William R. Goetz: *Mankind has never yet fashioned a weapon that hasn't been used. Indeed, both nuclear and chemical weapons have already been used in warfare, and many observers believe they will be used again.*[5]

"The Chinese army has tested its 'Taiwan rocket gun,' a new weapon with a range of over 200 miles. According to a report translated from the *Wen Hui Bao* newspaper, 'China has tested a newly developed rocket gun, named the WS-1B, which claims to have a range of 360 kilometers, the longest range in the world of a weapon of its kind.'

"'Various people have been working on this type of technology for some time,' said Frank Gaffney, noted defense analyst, president of the Center for Security Policy and a former assistant secretary of defense under President Reagan."[6]

If a weapon can target and shoot objects over 200 miles away, the missile would appear to be *"blazing like a torch"* falling from the sky.

84

LEARN THE WORD • REVELATION FOR TEENS

 PITCH DARK

The fourth trumpet judgment is going to affect everything in
the sky: sun, moon, and stars. Oftentimes when people choose
to believe false religions, they end up worshiping things of
nature. In this case, there won't be much in nature that people
will be able to depend upon.

It's possible that from this time forward, the light of the
sun, moon, and stars will be diminished by one-third. In that
case, the weather, climate, and temperature of the earth will
be totally altered. A nuclear war could hurl so much smoke,
dirt, and debris into the atmosphere that sunlight wouldn't
reach the earth. Temperatures would drop for months or years.
This kind of a deep freeze brought on by nuclear war is called
nuclear winter. It would cause a severe weather pattern
change that would halt farming and bring worldwide famine.

FROM BAD TO WORSE

Talk about a doomsday prophet! John must have done a double
take, hearing that the worst was yet to come.

What's up with this eagle? Some say it will be the raptured
church or an angel or a literal eagle. One thing is certain: God
can make animals talk, just as he did when he made Balaam's
donkey speak a warning. This eagle will call out three woes.
Some have called these the "trumpet woes." Believe it or not,
these woes will be much worse than anything we've seen so
far! Big bummer for everyone still on the earth.

KEY SYMBOLS

Fourth Trumpet
_One-third of sunlight
darkened_

nuclear winter:
_climate change after a
massive nuclear
explosion_

KEY POINT

The three trumpet
woes will be worse
than any prior
judgment.

Numbers 22:21–34
(Balaam's donkey)

85

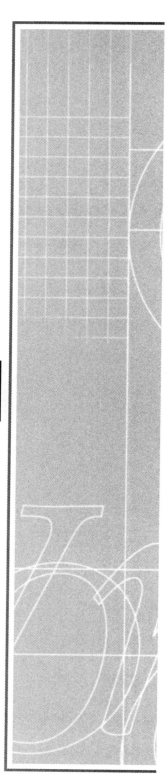

CHAPTER CHECKUP

1. Why was heaven silent for thirty minutes?
2. What is the golden censer? What does it symbolize?
3. What happened at each of the first four trumpet blasts?
4. What was the eagle saying?

CRASH COURSE

▶ Silence fills heaven for a half hour when the seventh seal is opened. (Revelation 8:1)
▶ The aroma coming from the incense mixed with the prayers of the saints will cause God to respond when the angel takes the golden censer filled with fire and hurls it to earth. (Revelation 8:3–5)
▶ The first four trumpet judgments will burn a third of the earth, turn a third of the seas to blood, pollute a third of all drinkable water, and darken a third of the light from the sky. (Revelation 8:7–12)
▶ After the first four trumpets have sounded, an eagle will fly through the air proclaiming three woes on the earth. These woes correspond to the last three trumpet blasts. (Revelation 8:13)

Tough Stuff

 LET'S DIVE IN

You probably learned about symbolism in English class (or at least you should have). Symbols can make things hard to understand. Even adults have trouble understanding some things in Revelation, so don't feel bad if you don't get it. John used symbols to describe events that will take place centuries after he lived. Some of these symbols are unusual, but that shouldn't keep us from trying to understand this chapter's prophecy. After all, it is the unusual stuff in Revelation that makes it so interesting! When you read, try to focus on the main points of what God wants us to learn.

> **Revelation 9:1–2**
> The fifth angel sounded his trumpet, and I saw a star that had fallen from the sky to the earth. The star was given the key to the shaft of the Abyss. When he opened the Abyss, smoke rose from it like the smoke from a gigantic furnace. The sun and sky were darkened by the smoke from the Abyss.

 SMOKIN' HOT!

Not another star! Didn't we just cover all of this in the other chapters? Well, this star isn't a literal star. It isn't even a star that *will* fall. This star is Satan, and he's already fallen. Revelation 9:2

morning star: Satan

Abyss: bottomless pit
where demons are kept

GO!
Luke 8:30–31 (Abyss)

KEY SYMBOLS

Fifth Trumpet
Satan opens the Abyss
People tortured by
insects

HAPPENINGS

refers to this star as a *he*. The prophet Isaiah said, "*How have you fallen from heaven, O **morning star**, son of the dawn! You have been cast down to the earth*" (Isaiah 14:12). Satan will be given the key to the **Abyss**. The Abyss is a place of torture and torment where the worst of Satan's demonic spirits are held and from where the Antichrist will come. Believe me, this is one place you really don't want to see.

OUTSIDE CONNECTION

David Jeremiah with C. C. Carlson: *The "pit" that has been the home of the demons is the Greek word for "abyss." We have a picture of a vast depth approached by a shaft, whose top is covered. It is a sobering thought to realize that many of the demons of hell are not free to hurt us in this present age. Satan is managing to do a good job of destruction today without his entire war corps to back him up.*[1]

> **Revelation 9:3**
> And out of the smoke locusts came down upon the earth and were given power like that of scorpions of the earth.

 SCI-FI GRASSHOPPERS

Locusts will come out of the smoke, but not locusts as we know them. They will not be the short-horned grasshoppers that have ruined crops around the world. Instead, they will be demon-possessed and have horrible features—part animal and part human.

These sci-fi-like creatures will be like scorpions that sting and poison people. Victims rarely die from these kinds of stings, but instead turn black and blue and go into convulsions. They suffer terribly.

Plagues of crop-destroying locusts have been known since ancient times. (Check out the Book of Joel and LWBI, page 79.) One swarm by the Red Sea was believed to cover an area of two thousand square miles. Swarms of migrating locusts are sometimes so large they block the sunlight. They interfere with railroad trains, airplanes, and make automobile travel dangerous.[2]

Agents of Torture

Even though these locusts will be sent by Satan, they will still be controlled by God and can only harm those that he allows. They will not harm those who have the seal of God on their foreheads—the 144,000 Jews. And these Jews will probably let out big sighs of relief knowing this!

Locusts typically eat plants, but God commands these locusts not to harm the grass, plants, or trees. God may have given this command to save what little is left of the earth's greenery. After all, the plagues and misfortunes before this have destroyed much of the earth, and human beings can't survive without oxygen, which plants produce.

These locusts will not kill and will *only* be able to torture humans for a period of five months, as if that isn't long enough!

elude: escape

No Way Out

Imagine being in so much pain you want to die! These people's nervous systems will be infected and their body parts that have been stung will swell up. Some people will suffer seizures and convulsions, and others will lose consciousness. No medicine will bring relief from the pain. Even when people try to kill themselves, they won't be able to die. God will not let them end their suffering in death.

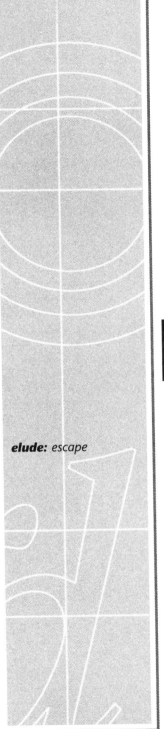

89

Revelation 9:7–10

The locusts looked like horses prepared for battle. On their heads they wore something like crowns of gold, and their faces resembled human faces. Their hair was like women's hair, and their teeth were like lion's teeth. They had breastplates like breastplates of iron, and the sound of their wings was like the thundering of many horses and chariots rushing into battle. They had tails and stings like scorpions, and in their tails they had power to torment people for five months.

 ## SERIOUS SYMBOLISM

John is using symbols and comparisons to describe what these demon-possessed locusts will look like. Their human-like faces will be wearing crowns. Their manes will resemble women's hair, and their teeth will be small and sharp like a lion's. Their tails will be like a scorpion's stinger, and their wings will sound like an army of chariots. Sounds a great deal like a character out of a horror movie, only this character isn't made up!

HAPPENINGS

It's possible this creature will be something like the female *heteropteryx dilatata* that's found in Malaysia. It's seven inches long and five inches wide and has about one hundred sharp spikes on its hard body. Check out a picture at www.buginabox.com/stickbugs.html and try matching John's description with this insect's appearance.

OUTSIDE CONNECTION

Oliver B. Greene: *In Italy and some other foreign countries locusts are called "little horses" and some of them resemble a horse.*[3]

Revelation 9:11

They had as king over them the angel of the Abyss, whose name in Hebrew is Abaddon, and in Greek, Apollyon.

 ## SATAN'S RIGHT-HAND DUDE

This angel must be one of Satan's leaders. His Hebrew name is *"Abaddon,"* meaning destruction, and his Greek name is

"*Apollyon,*" meaning destroyer. Destruction Destroyer—sounds like a WWF wrestler, doesn't it! Since his name is given in both Hebrew and Greek, it is likely that he will attack both Jews and Gentiles. His name is given two times, so it is a double warning of his dangerous powers.

> **Revelation 9:12–13**
> The first woe is past; two other woes are yet to come. The sixth angel sounded his trumpet, and I heard a voice coming from the horns of the golden altar that is before God.

Woes to Come!

Remember the eagle in chapter 8 that cried out about the woes to come? (C'mon, it isn't every day you hear a bird talk!) Well, like he said before, woes are here.

The altar mentioned above is the same altar where the angel mixes the incense with the prayers of the tribulation saints. The mixture rises to God, and he lets out his wrath. Although the prayers are sweet to him, the sins of the world are overwhelming to his perfect Being, and he brings judgment.

> **Revelation 9:14–15**
> It said to the sixth angel who had the trumpet, "Release the four angels who are bound at the great river Euphrates." And the four angels who had been kept ready for this very hour and day and month and year were released to kill a third of mankind.

Untie Those Angels

The voice tells the sixth angel to release the four angels bound (or tied up) by the Euphrates River. These angels have an awful job to do. Their job is to kill a third of all humans still alive on the earth.

Who were these four angels? Well, the fact that they were tied up indicates that they were fallen angels, although no real explanation is given.

✎ KEY SYMBOLS

Sixth Trumpet
Four fallen angels
- from the Euphrates River
- powerful workers of Satan

91

> ### Revelation 9:16–17
> The number of the mounted troops was two hundred million. I heard their number. The horses and riders I saw in my vision looked like this: Their breastplates were fiery red, dark blue, and yellow as sulfur. The heads of the horses resembled the heads of lions, and out of their mouths came fire, smoke, and sulfur.

DRAGON-LIKE ARMY

John repeats that he heard the number 200 million because in his day that many people didn't even live on the earth. Today only one nation has the capability of having an army of 200 million—China.

God will allow these evil angels to convince the army's leaders to go out and kill a third of all humans. Keep in mind, however, that God is permitting this. Without his permission, these angels would still be bound. Although you may struggle with why God would allow this, try to remember that plenty of opportunities for repentance have already been given.

 No matter how much you learn about Revelation, never think you know it all. John's use of the words *like* and *resembled* indicate he is using symbols to describe the future, so beware of anyone who says they know for certain when and how things will come to pass.

> ### Revelation 9:18–19
> A third of mankind was killed by the three plagues of fire, smoke and sulfur that came out of their mouths. The power of the horses was in their mouths and in their tails; for their tails were like snakes, having heads with which they **inflict** injury.

inflict: *cause, bring about*

Deadly Destruction

The Antichrist promised world peace, but he can't stop the destruction that God will allow to take place. This demon-possessed army of 200 million will do what the demon-possessed locusts couldn't do—kill, until a third of all humans are dead.

The horses (or machines) described here have some serious weaponry. A real arsenal for sure. These *"horses"* could be real horses or tanks, helicopters, or some futuristic weapon. Keep in mind that John was trying to describe things that he had never before seen. Our modern-day weaponry would have been impossible to describe over two thousand years ago.

> **Revelation 9:20–21**
>
> The rest of mankind that were not killed by these plagues still did not repent of the work of their hands; they did not stop worshiping demons, and idols of gold, silver, bronze, stone, and wood—idols that cannot see or hear or walk. Nor did they repent of their murders, their magic arts, their sexual immorality, or their thefts.

Get with the Program!

You would think the survivors would get it by now. How can they still worship false gods when it is so obvious that the world is crashing down on top of them? That's sin nature, I'm afraid. Instead of turning to God, these people will worship demons and create idols (likely replicas of the Antichrist).

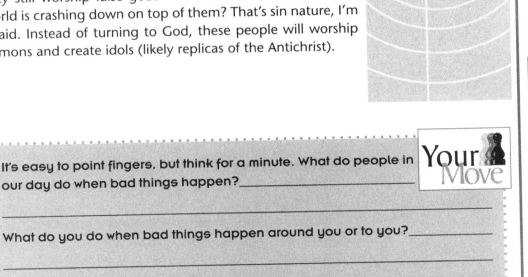

It's easy to point fingers, but think for a minute. What do people in **Your Move** our day do when bad things happen?_____

_____

What do you do when bad things happen around you or to you?_____

_____

GET REAL Astrology, horoscopes, New Age beliefs, ancestor worship, money, possessions, fame, drugs—people can use all of these things as substitutes or idols in place of God. It's easy to point fingers and think, *People are nuts not to see God at work in the world's disasters.* Whenever we point one finger, four fingers are pointing back at us. Take a moment to confess to God any idolatry that you might have, for example, wanting your friends' approval more than God's approval.

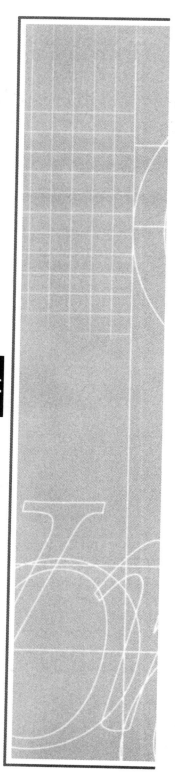

CHAPTER CHECKUP

1. Where did the locusts come from, and what will they do on the earth?
2. After being stung by locusts, what will the people wish?
3. Who asked for the release of the four angels at the river Euphrates?
4. What will these four angels do?
5. Describe some tribulation sins.

CRASH COURSE

▶ When the fifth trumpet is sounded, Satan will be given the key to the Abyss. The sun and sky will be darkened from the smoke pouring out of the Abyss. (Revelation 9:1–2)

▶ Demon-possessed locusts will come out of the Abyss to torment humankind for five months. The pain from the locusts will be so bad that people will seek death, but God will not let them find it. (Revelation 9:3–6)

▶ After the sixth trumpet is sounded, the four angels that have been bound at the Euphrates will be released to kill a third of all humans. (Revelation 9:13–15)

▶ An army of 200 million mounted troops will kill a third of all people through three plagues of fire, smoke, and sulfur that will come out of their horses' mouths. (Revelation 9:16–19)

▶ Those who are not killed by these plagues will still refuse to repent of their sins. Instead, they will cling to their idols and demon worship. (Revelation 9:20–21)

John Gets Involved

 LET'S DIVE IN

John did as he was told to do in chapter 1 and wrote down the stuff he saw. In chapter 10, John encounters a mighty angel and is told to *stop* writing. Even if we could figure out all the mysterious things in Revelation, God still has some surprises in store. John got a peek at them, but we will have to wait till they happen to get the scoop.

When the angel hands John a different book, he tells John to eat it. Gives a whole new meaning to the phrase "eat your words"—doesn't it?

Revelation 10:1
Then I saw another mighty angel coming down from heaven. He was robed in a cloud, with a rainbow above his head; his face was like the sun, and his legs were like fiery pillars.

 CLOUD-COVERED

This is the second mighty angel John encountered. The first mighty angel was in Revelation 5:2. We aren't told who this new angel is, but it's obvious that he has lots of power and authority. He is probably an archangel because he'll stand in front of God and speak for him—similar to how a presidential press secretary addresses reporters on the president's behalf.

What this angel is wearing, what's on his head, and how his face and feet look are important. He'll be wearing a designer cloud, much like a person wears a robe. Clouds in the Bible have been used to show God's presence, like when God used a <u>pillar</u> of cloud to lead the Israelites out of Egypt and through the wilderness. When Jesus went back <u>to heaven</u> from earth, he went in a cloud. The Bible tells us he will return <u>to earth</u> in a cloud. So this mighty angel's clothing may be a reminder that he is a messenger from God and that Jesus is returning soon.

This angel will also have a rainbow over his head. (Better than a rain cloud, right?) God used a <u>rainbow</u> when he promised Noah that he'd never again destroy the earth with a flood. The rainbow shows us God always keeps his promises.

This angel's face will shine like the sun. When John saw Jesus on the island of <u>Patmos</u>, Christ's face shone like the sun. Moses' face also <u>shone</u> after he was in God's presence on Mount Sinai. The awesome glory of God on this mighty angel's face will prove that he's been in God's presence. He'll glow and it'll show.

The angel's legs will be as pillars of fire. His legs will burn and it won't be because he's been working out! No, his burning legs will indicate God's plan to control the earth by his divine judgment.

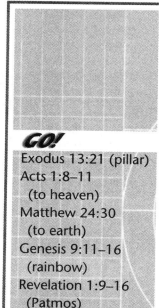

GO!

Exodus 13:21 (pillar)
Acts 1:8–11
(to heaven)
Matthew 24:30
(to earth)
Genesis 9:11–16
(rainbow)
Revelation 1:9–16
(Patmos)
Exodus 34:29–33
(shone)

OUTSIDE CONNECTION

David Hocking: *In the book of Revelation, angels are angels, not symbols of events, things, places, or persons.*[1]

Revelation 10:2–3

He was holding a little scroll, which lay open in his hand. He planted his right foot on the sea and his left foot on the land, and he gave a loud shout like the roar of a lion. When he shouted, the voices of the seven thunders spoke.

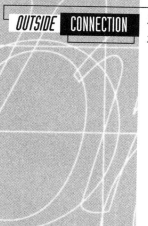

 **ROARING SHOUT!**

Like a conqueror claiming territory, this angel will put his right foot on the sea and his left foot on the land. He will shout with a loud voice *"like the roar of a lion"* to speak on behalf of the King of kings. At the same time he speaks, a voice in heaven will roar like the **seven <u>thunders</u>**. The Almighty God will make a strong statement when this angel speaks.

David Jeremiah with C. C. Carlson: This [thunder] is like a seven-gun salute in the skies.[2]

In 1969, when the U.S. astronauts landed on the moon, it was a tremendous moment for humankind. The astronauts celebrated their victory by staking the American flag into the moon's surface, claiming it. The angel does a similar thing in Revelation 10:2, indicating his claim of the sea and the land.

> **Revelation 10:4**
> And when the seven thunders spoke, I was about to write; but I heard a voice from heaven say, "Seal up what the seven thunders have said and do not write it down."

Pencils Down

God is pretty serious about John not sharing this information. This message is top-secret, classified, for John's eyes only! No one knows why John was prevented from recording what he heard, but remember that thunder also represents God's anger. Whatever was said probably had to do with how God will judge. It also might be too terrible for humans to understand.

> **Revelation 10:5–6**
> Then the angel I had seen standing on the sea and on the land raised his right hand to heaven. And he swore by him who lives for ever and ever, who created the heavens and all that is in them, the earth and all that is in it, and the sea and all that is in it, and said, "There will be no more delay!"

GO!
Psalm 29:3; Job 37:5 (thunders)

seven thunders:
symbol for God's voice

OUTSIDE CONNECTION

HAPPENINGS

KEY SYMBOLS
Mighty Angel
Robed in a cloud
 • God's messenger
Rainbow above his head
 • promises fulfilled
Face like the sun
 • glory
Legs like fiery pillars
 • judgment

97

No More Delay

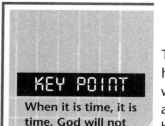

This angel will raise his right hand and take an oath, similar to how a court witness raises his right hand and swears to tell the whole truth. This angel's oath will emphasize that he has the authority and power of God behind him. The tribulation saints have been waiting to be avenged. Now time's up! Those on earth who have been running, hiding, and waiting for God to judge the wicked will also no longer have to wait. It's go-time for God and avenge-time for those who have been mistreated.

David Hocking: *Although at times we wonder if God knows or cares about what is taking place on earth, the Bible assures us that he does.*[3]

How does it make you feel to know that God will finally judge those who are wicked and seem to have gotten away with evil?_____

_____

_____

_____

How does knowing that God will judge the wicked make you feel toward those who have wronged you?_____

_____

If unbelievers could understand the reality of this message, how might they feel?_____

_____

GET REAL

One day all of the wrongs of this world will be righted by God! Unbelievers should tremble in their boots, knowing that no matter how long they have gotten away with their sins on this earth, at some point they will have to pay for them. Believers can be encouraged to know that they don't have to get revenge against people who have hurt them. God will avenge all of the earth's wrong, and only he can justly do so.

 **MYSTIFY ME!**

Jesus has now opened all seven seals, and six of the angels have sounded their trumpets. The last trumpet will bring the seven bowl judgments (see the chart on page 64). But before the seventh angel blows his trumpet, a voice from heaven declares that the mystery of God is about to be shown.

Here are some mysteries in the Bible that can't be fully understood:

- The mystery of the Rapture (1 Corinthians 15:51)
- The mystery of Israel's blindness (Romans 11:25)
- The mystery of God's wisdom (1 Corinthians 2:7)
- The mystery of Christ and the church (Ephesians 5:31–32)
- They mystery of Christ in us (Colossians 1:26–27)
- The mystery of the kingdom of heaven (Matthew 13)
- The mystery of godliness (1 Timothy 3:16)

The same voice of the seven thunders tells John to go and take the open book out of the mighty angel's hand. John has to get off his duff and do something. Serving God takes action, not just passive listening.

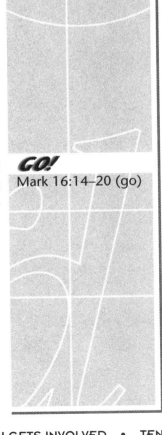

GO!

Mark 16:14–20 (go)

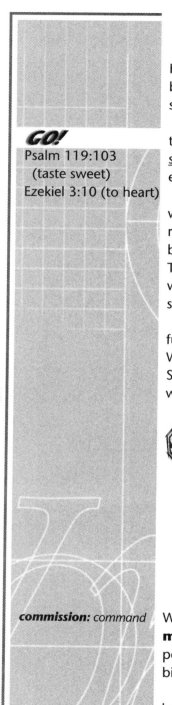

GO!
Psalm 119:103
(taste sweet)
Ezekiel 3:10 (to heart)

 PASS THE TUMS

Have you ever eaten something that tasted great, like a huge beef and bean burrito, only to find thirty minutes later, your stomach is killing you? That's sort of what happened to John.

The angel told John to do a crazy thing—eat the scroll. Then the angel warned John that although the scroll would <u>taste sweet</u> at first, it would eventually turn his stomach sour. Sure enough! John had a giant stomachache in no time!

So what's up with this? John went from being a spectator watching fantastic events to being a participant. The scroll represents God's Word. Eating it means the Word of God must be taken <u>to heart</u> (not left outside one's mind and actions). The Bible needs to become a part of us before we can apply its words. We not only need to read the Bible but also do what it says! In other words, eat up!

Why did the scroll turn sour? That was a warning. Once we fully understand the terrible judgments written about in God's Word, that reality will make us sick. It's sweet to know that Satan will be defeated but disheartening to know that people who are not saved will face awful punishment and suffering.

 The reality and horror of God's judgment will make us sick. Unbelievers will face terrible punishment.

> **Revelation 10:11**
> Then I was told, "You must prophesy again about many peoples, nations, languages, and kings."

 A GREAT COMMISSION

commission: command

When John was told to eat the book, he was also given a **commission** from God. He was told to prophesy "about many peoples, nations, languages, and kings." This was not only a big responsibility but also a great honor for John.

John was not told to deliver the message to many people but about many people. This is what John does in the rest of the chapters of Revelation. During the Tribulation, many peoples, nations, languages, and kings will open these last chapters and read what John has to say about them. If they are smart they'll listen and change while there is time.

CHAPTER CHECKUP

1. Describe how the mighty angel at the beginning of chapter 10 looks.
2. Who has the voice of seven thunders?
3. Give an explanation of the sweet scroll that turns sour once it is eaten.
4. What was the great commission that John was given by God?

CRASH COURSE

▶ Another mighty angel will come down from heaven wearing strange clothes and holding a little scroll. He will claim the land and sea for God. (Revelation 10:1–2)
▶ The angel standing on the sea and land will raise his right hand and declare that there will be no more delay for the judgment of earth. (Revelation 10:5–8)
▶ When John eats the scroll it will taste sweet at first but will turn his stomach sour. Learning God's Word can be exciting, but understanding the realities of its judgments is sickening. (Revelation 10:9)
▶ John was given the task of prophesying about many peoples, nations, languages, and kings. (Revelation 10:11)

Two Witnesses and an Ark

103

 LET'S DIVE IN

John gets going on his big job—extreme measuring. On earth a fight breaks out over who controls Jerusalem. A couple of dead guys cause the world's biggest party. Then God crashes the party by bringing the dead to life and shaking up the earth—literally.

As you read remember the big picture. God's anger against the world is bursting out. It's significant that God's anger will be first focused on Israel and the Temple. The conflict over Jerusalem will trigger the Second Coming and the Battle of Armageddon. Here's the background scoop:

- Israel and Jerusalem will be the storm center of the world. Israel has Jerusalem as its capital, but the Palestinian Liberation Organization wants Jerusalem to be its capital. In Zechariah 12 and 14 we read that God will make Jerusalem a place that sends the nations into confusion. The nations <u>will gather</u> against Jerusalem, the city will be captured, and half of the Jews living there will run away.
- The Jews want to rebuild the Temple on the site of the Old Testament Temple. They call this area the Temple Mount. But a building called the Dome of the Rock has

GO!
Zechariah 12:1–3;
14:1–3 (will gather)

GO!

Jeremiah 51:19–23
(shatter)

 HAPPENINGS

Israeli: *people who live in Israel, many of Jewish descent*

GO!

2 Chronicles 4:19
(golden)
1 Kings 8:64 (bronze)
John 3:36; Acts 4:12
(only sacrifice)
Hebrews 9:12; 10:12
(permanent solution)

Holy Place: *large room inside the door of the Temple*

Holy of Holies: *inner sanctuary of the Temple, held the Ark of the Covenant*

been built on this site. **Muslims** consider the site holy because they believe Muhammad ascended to heaven there. The continuing Middle East struggle is a battle of religions and whose God is the true God. God will use Israel to <u>shatter</u> the nations and show everyone who's boss.

*In December 2000, Muslim worshipers at Al-Aqsa mosque in Jerusalem pelted **Israeli** police with rocks on the second "day of rage" to mark the thirteenth anniversary of an earlier uprising in Israel. The Israelis responded with rubber-coated steel bullets and tear gas, killing four Palestinians.* [1]

> **Revelation 11:1–2**
>
> I was given a reed like a measuring rod and was told, "Go and measure the temple of God and the altar, and count the worshipers there." But exclude the outer court; do not measure it, because it has been given to the Gentiles. They will trample on the holy city for 42 months."

GET THE TAPE MEASURE

John was given a reed or long plant and told to use it like a tape measure. He measured the altar, and then he counted the worshipers. The fact that an altar and worshipers exist is important, because in the last days of the Temple (see illustration, page 105), one of its two original altars will be rebuilt. The altar that will be rebuilt was originally called the <u>golden</u> altar (see illustration, page 81) or the altar of incense. The altar that isn't going to be rebuilt was originally called the <u>bronze</u> altar. This altar was located in the outer court where the Gentiles will rule.

The Jews at this time will have returned to their old way of worship—sacrificing animals as an offering to God (see LWBI, pages 29–30). These Jews don't realize that Jesus, the Messiah, died and became their one and <u>only sacrifice</u>. Jesus is the <u>permanent solution</u> to sin.

John is told not to measure the outer court of the Temple. This may mean that only the **Holy Place** and the **Holy of**

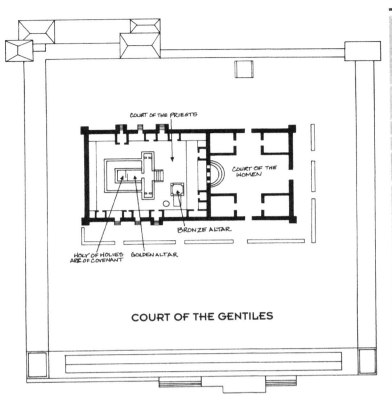

COURT OF THE PRIESTS

COURT OF THE WOMEN

BRONZE ALTAR

HOLY OF HOLIES
ARK OF COVENANT

GOLDEN ALTAR

COURT OF THE GENTILES

Layout of the Temple

When the Temple is rebuilt, Jews will use only the interior part. The Court of the Gentiles will probably not be rebuilt.

Holies will be rebuilt. It is possible that at this time Jews and Muslims will share the Temple Mount and that the walls around the outer court will not exist. This place could only be shared if these altars were built without disturbing the Dome of the Rock (see illustration, page 106). The forty-two months mentioned coincide with what Jesus taught: <u>Gentiles</u> will control Jerusalem and the Temple during the last three-and-one-half years of the Tribulation.

Hal Lindsey: The importance of the Temple Mount Site in Jerusalem to two faiths (Judaism and Islam) makes it the most strategic and potentially explosive piece of real estate on the face of the earth.[2]

GO!
Luke 21:24 (Gentiles)

OUTSIDE CONNECTION

sackcloth: *a tough cloth worn as a sign of sadness*

Revelation 11:3–4
"And I will give power to my two witnesses, and they will prophesy for 1,260 days, clothed in **sackcloth**." These are the two olive trees and the two lampstands that stand before the Lord of the earth.

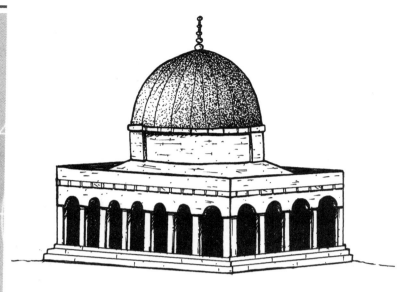

GO!
Deuteronomy 17:6;
19:15 (witnesses)
2 Kings 2:1 (Elijah)

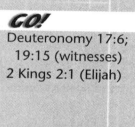

KEY SYMBOLS

Two Witnesses
Elijah and ? (no one knows)

devours: *destroys, ruins, kills*

Dynamic Duo

In the Old Testament, the law required two <u>witnesses</u> to agree before any testimony was accepted as true. So God sends two people to show that his message is true.

Who these witnesses are isn't known, but most experts agree that one of them will be Elijah. Experts think this because the Old Testament says, *"I will send you the prophet Elijah before that great and dreadful day of the Lord comes"* (Malachi 4:5–6). (You can read more about Elijah in GWBI pages 67–68.) Currently <u>Elijah</u> is in heaven, but if he is one of the witnesses spoken about here he will return to earth before the Tribulation. Imagine how Elijah might feel to be transported from heaven to this terrible time.

Both witnesses will stay and prophesy for 1,260 days or three-and-one-half years (the first half of the Tribulation).

Revelation 11:5–6

If anyone tries to harm them, fire comes from their mouths and **devours** their enemies. This is how anyone who wants to harm them must die. These men have power to shut up the sky so that it will not rain during the time they are prophesying; and they have power to turn the waters into blood and to strike the earth with every kind of plague as often as they want.

FLAME THROWERS AND RERUNS

Ever watch the old movie *The Ten Commandments*? God used Moses to send **plagues** on Egypt because Pharaoh would not let the Israelites go to worship God. The water of the Nile turned into blood. Frogs and locusts overran Egypt. Hail and darkness covered the land.

plagues: terrible events in nature that are sometimes viewed as acts of God

This is the rerun. Only this time things are worse. These two witnesses are tough dudes. They have the Word of God in their mouths and will be spitting fire. All they have to do is speak and their enemies are destroyed! Imagine what it would be like to have such power.

Without rain for three-and-one-half years almost every plant will die. The air will be dusty, and many people will starve to death because crops won't grow. As the water turns to blood, the fish and other sea life will die. We aren't told what the other plagues will be, but from what we've seen so far, it won't be pretty.

Tens of thousands of migrating birds have taken over water storage areas of a central Iran industrial sector because their normal resting places have disappeared following months of drought. Storks, ducks, and flamingos have recently arrived in large numbers from Siberia and northern Europe, but lakes, wetlands, and a river in the Iranian region of Isfahan on the birds' migratory path have disappeared.[3] Already water sources are drying up and animals and humans are suffering the consequences.

HAPPENINGS

Revelation 11:7
Now when they have finished their testimony, the beast that comes up from the Abyss will attack them, and overpower and kill them.

 ## BEATEN BY THE BEAST

The two witnesses are protected by God until their jobs are done. They tell people about their sin and God's judgment. This news makes people so angry they kill the witnesses—but only when God allows.

GO!

Revelation 13:1
(Antichrist)
Revelation 13:11
(False Prophet)

KEY SYMBOLS

First Beast
Antichrist

Second Beast
False Prophet

GO!

Isaiah 1:1–10
(Isaiah compared)
Ezekiel 16:1–62
(like Egypt)

Revelation mentions two beasts: the <u>Antichrist</u> and the <u>False Prophet</u>. The Antichrist will hate the two witnesses and will become furious when he hears them talking about Jesus. He will be jealous at the number of people who become Christians, so he will throw all of the power of the satanic government into an attack against them. The witnesses will be overpowered and killed. The Antichrist will think he is all that when he silences these witnesses.

> **Revelation 11:8**
> Their bodies will lie in the street of the great city, which is figuratively called Sodom and Egypt, where also their Lord was crucified.

Lying Dead in Jerusalem

When the witnesses are killed, they won't even be buried. Their bodies will be left to rot in the streets. It will be a gross sight but people will be happy because the witnesses won't be saying bad things against them.

The great city mentioned here must be Jerusalem. But why is Jerusalem called Sodom and Egypt? In the Old Testament, the prophet <u>Isaiah compared</u> Jerusalem to the cities of Sodom and Gomorrah because it was so sinful. Ezekiel, another Old Testament prophet, said Jerusalem was <u>like Egypt</u> because it was full of idols. In other words, Jerusalem is once again a place where sin is everywhere.

OUTSIDE CONNECTION

William T. James: A significant body of prophetic text predicts a generation just before the end of the age that will ultimately go into a materialistically mad frenzy where human love will be extinguished. At the same time, the appetite for money will become insatiable, and seducers and evildoers will grow worse and worse. . . . a judgment-deserving generation will plunge into what God's Word describes as earth's darkest hour—the Great Tribulation.[4]

> **Revelation 11:9–10**
>
> For three and a half days men from every people, tribe, language and nation will gaze on their bodies and refuse them burial. The inhabitants of the earth will gloat over them and will celebrate by sending each other gifts, because these two prophets had tormented those who live on the earth.

Gift-Giving Bonanza

People are going to party over the deaths of these witnesses. Can you imagine anyone giving gifts to celebrate a "deathday" rather than a birthday? It's a morbid thought, but it shows the state of the earth at this time. People from every tribe and nation will stare at the dead bodies of the witnesses.

OUTSIDE CONNECTION

John Hagee: Prophecy states that the whole world will, at the same time, be able to see the two witnesses in the streets of Jerusalem. My father's generation could not explain that. . . . Then came television, followed by international satellites, the Internet, and wireless communication.[5]

> **Revelation 11:11–13**
>
> But after three and a half days a breath of life from God entered them, and they stood on their feet, and terror struck those who saw them. Then they heard a loud voice from heaven saying to them, "Come up here." And they went up to heaven in a cloud, while their enemies looked on. At that very hour there was a severe earthquake and a tenth of the city collapsed. Seven thousand people were killed in the earthquake, and the survivors were terrified and gave glory to the God of heaven.

》》 DEAD MEN RISING

As internet cams and TV cameras focus on the corpses, they mysteriously begin to move. Life flows back into the bodies. The two witnesses stand up—alive.

People gasp. Parties stop. All are afraid. Everyone's eyes are glued to the scene.

A great voice calls the two witnesses to heaven. Before any of their enemies are able to harm them, the two figures disappear into heaven in a cloud.

As people stare at the sky, the earth will start to shake vio-

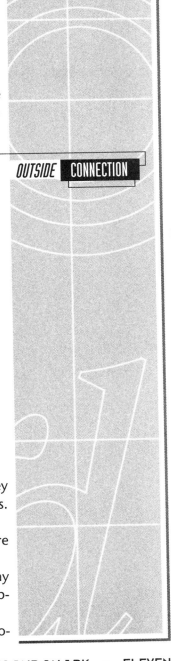

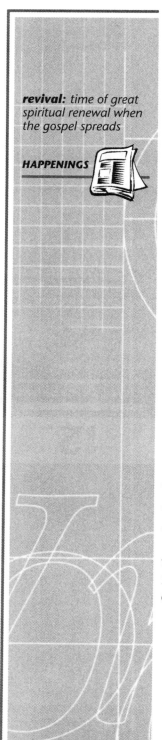

revival: time of great spiritual renewal when the gospel spreads

HAPPENINGS

lently. Ten percent of the buildings in Jerusalem will collapse, killing seven thousand people. The fear of God will enter the hearts of the survivors, and many will change their minds about the two witnesses, praise the God of heaven, and begin a Jewish **revival**. Oy vey! Praise the Lord!

Over ninety major earthquakes have taken place in Israel in the last two thousand years, with an average of twenty-seven years between each. In the twentieth century alone, over one thousand earthquakes of all measurable intensities have been recorded. Scientists predict another major earthquake in Israel, but they cannot say whether it will be next week or next century. Complete buildings, including the Dome of the Rock in 1546, and even whole cities (Safed in 1837) were totally destroyed in past centuries.[6]

> **Revelation 11:14–15**
> The second woe has passed; the third woe is coming soon. The seventh angel sounded his trumpet, and there were loud voices in heaven, which said: "The kingdom of the world has become the kingdom of our Lord and of his Christ, and he will reign for ever and ever."

It's God and Jesus' Kingdom Now!

The earthquake in Jerusalem marks the end of the second woe or the sixth trumpet. The seventh trumpet will sound soon and bring the third woe.

When the seventh trumpet sounds a heavenly voice says that God and his Son, Jesus, will soon be taking over. Although Satan and his powerful demons have had control of the earth, God and his Son will do away with them and reign forever.

> **Revelation 11:16–17**
> And the twenty-four elders, who were seated on their thrones before God, fell on their faces and worshiped God, saying: "We give thanks to you, Lord God Almighty, the One who is and who was, because you have taken your great power and have begun to reign."

Facedown and Praising

The announcement that God and Jesus will be taking over will cause a praise fest in heaven. The elders, or all the believers, will fall facedown and worship God. They will thank him because he is in charge.

From this point on, Satan's days of acting like he's king of the earth are almost over. There is about to be a hostile takeover! Jesus will begin to use his power over the nations and will go forth to conquer the forces of <u>evil</u> and bring in his reign, the Millennium.

> **Revelation 11:18**
> "The nations were angry; and your wrath has come. The time has come for judging the dead, and for rewarding your servants the prophets and your saints and those who reverence your name, both small and great—and for destroying those who destroy the earth."

They're Coming Down the Stretch

Satan knows his time will soon be up, so he will get people mad at God. When he does, God's wrath will become even more intense. It's as if God and Satan will be driving head-on toward each other on the Daytona Speedway. Satan will bring all of the nations crashing down against Jesus. The mother of all battles that will come as a result of their collision is called the **Battle of Armageddon**.

No one will escape God's judgment. Even the dead will be judged. The righteous will be rewarded for believing on the name of Jesus, and the wicked will be destroyed because they won't repent of their sin.

> **Revelation 11:19**
> Then God's temple in heaven was opened, and within his temple was seen the ark of his covenant. And there came flashes of lightning, rumblings, peals of thunder, an earthquake, and a great hailstorm.

KEY SYMBOLS

Seventh Trumpet
Believers give thanks

GO!
Psalm 37:9–17 (evil)

KEY POINT

The righteous will be rewarded for respecting the name of Jesus, and the wicked will be destroyed for their sin.

Battle of Armageddon: the last and greatest war before the Millennium

111

Since everyone is accountable to God, how do you feel about the sinful things in your life? _____

_____

What should you do about any sin in your life right now?_____

_____

_____

 What you do matters. God sees every action, knows every thought, and can even anticipate your emotions and intentions. He will one day judge everyone—even people who have died. The good news is that he also will reward those who choose to live for him. God is just, so you'll want to be sure you are on his good side! That can only be done by having faith in his Son, Jesus Christ!

 ALL HEAVEN BREAKS LOOSE

God's heavenly temple holds the ark of the covenant. The ark, with its mercy seat (see illustration below), is a reminder that God has always shown mercy to his people. The lightning, rumbling, thunder, earthquakes, and hailstorms will be signs of God's destruction to come, but God will show mercy by protecting Israel.

Ark of the Covenant

The ark of the covenant, shown here, was kept in the Temple inside the Holy of Holies and was a symbol of God's presence on earth. The mercy seat was between the outstretched wings of the two angels on the top of the ark. The heavenly temple also has an ark of the covenant with a mercy seat representing God's mercy for his people.

CHAPTER CHECKUP

1. Why was John told to measure the Temple but exclude the outer court?
2. Who were the two witnesses, and what was their purpose?
3. What will cause the world to rejoice and party during the Tribulation?
4. What happens to the two witnesses after three and one-half days of lying dead in the streets?
5. What is about to change on earth?

CRASH COURSE

▶ God will empower his two witnesses to prophesy for 1,260 days during which time they will be able to bring plagues to the earth and consume their enemies with fire. (Revelation 11:3–6)

▶ After prophesying for 1,260 days, the two witnesses will be killed by the Antichrist in Jerusalem. Their bodies will lie in the street while unbelievers celebrate. (Revelation 11:7–10)

▶ Three and one-half days after the witnesses are killed, God will raise the witnesses from the dead, call them home to heaven, and destroy a tenth of Jerusalem with an earthquake. (Revelation 11:11–13)

▶ A heavenly declaration proclaiming that Jesus will soon start his earthly reign will follow the seventh trumpet blast. (Revelation 11:15)

▶ God will open his heavenly temple revealing the ark of the covenant, which serves as a reminder that he has always shown Israel mercy. (Revelation 11:19)

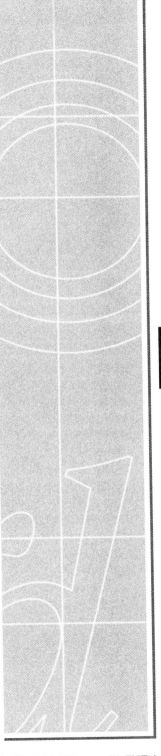

115

The Greatest Fall of All

 **LET'S DIVE IN**

A pregnant woman. A dragon. War between angels. An earthquake, and a great escape. This chapter has them all. John continues to prophesy about many peoples, nations, languages, and kings.

Revelation 12:1–2
A great and wondrous **sign** appeared in heaven: a woman clothed with the sun, with the moon under her feet and a crown of twelve stars on her head. She was pregnant and cried out in pain as she was about to give birth.

sign: symbol for something else

 WONDROUS SIGN

In the Book of Genesis a man named <u>Joseph</u> had a <u>dream</u>. Joseph's dreams usually got him in trouble, but that's another story! Joseph's father, Jacob (who was later named Israel), interpreted his son's dream. Joseph dreamed about the sun (representing Jacob), the moon (representing Jacob's wife Rachel), and a crown of twelve stars (representing Jacob's twelve children or the twelve tribes of Israel).

 GO!
Genesis 30:22–24; 37:3–4 (Joseph)
Genesis 37:9–11 (dream)

Notice that the three symbols in Joseph's dream (the sun, moon, and twelve stars) are all connected with this woman in Revelation 12. The first sign in heaven is this woman who represents the nation of Israel. The baby she is about to bear is Jesus. Her groans represent how the Israelites groaned before Jesus' birth when they had to obey Roman leaders and laws.

 RED DRAGON

The second sign in heaven is a huge red dragon (Satan) that is explained more in Revelation 12:9. He is large because of his great power, red because he has <u>killed</u> so many, and a dragon because of his fierce nature. And this is no fairy tale, believe me!

This red dragon will appear in heaven with seven <u>heads</u> (symbols of world governments), ten <u>horns</u> (symbols of powerful kings), and seven crowns (symbols of the seven regions controlled by the powerful kings).

Are you still with me? Don't zone out because it gets more complicated. The seven heads stand for the seven Gentile world governments that Satan has led since the world began. The ten horns stand for the ten kings that will rule with Satan during the entire Tribulation.

The Bible teaches that the nations will set up a world government, perhaps the United Nations. The world government will divide into ten regions with a king or leader over each region. One of those regions will be Europe. The Antichrist will rise to power in Europe and overthrow <u>three</u> of the ten kings or regions so that only seven will be left. At that point, the remaining seven will surrender to the Antichrist. Then he will control the world government.

 A one-world government controlled by Satan will be a terrible thing. Some say the Antichrist's government will make Adolf Hitler's reign look like a Sunday picnic. Satan is not to be taken lightly.

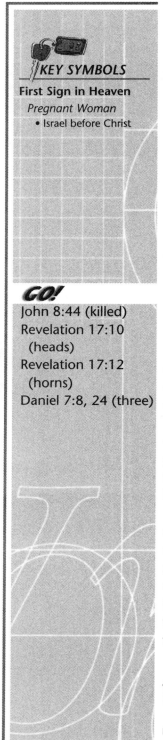

KEY SYMBOLS

First Sign in Heaven
Pregnant Woman
• Israel before Christ

GO!
John 8:44 (killed)
Revelation 17:10 (heads)
Revelation 17:12 (horns)
Daniel 7:8, 24 (three)

116

Ron Hutchcraft: Satanic themes, symbols, and darkness run all through much of their [teens'] music and many of their videos. One young man summed it up to me— "Kids in our school think Satan is a lot more interesting than God." [1]

> **Revelation 12:4**
> His tail swept a third of the stars out of the sky and flung them to the earth. The dragon stood in front of the woman who was about to give birth, so that he might devour her child the moment it was born.

FALLING ANGELS

The stars mentioned here represent angels. When Satan swept a third of the stars out of the sky, he caused one-third of the <u>angels</u> to fall from heaven. Millions of angels were forced to leave heaven when they rebelled and chose to follow Satan instead of God. A really bad move on their part.

Here are five ways Satan tried to destroy Jesus or Jesus' mission:

1. Satan waited for the birth of Jesus and then he stirred up King Herod to kill all the male babies in and around Bethlehem. God, however, stepped in by sending an angel to warn Joseph to run to Egypt and hide there until it was safe.
2. At the beginning of Jesus' ministry, Satan tempted Jesus with the <u>kingdoms</u> of the world if he would bow down and worship Satan, but Jesus refused.
3. When Jesus' disciple Peter tried to steer Jesus from the cross, Jesus said to him, *"Get behind me Satan"* (Matthew 16:23).
4. At the <u>Mount of Olives,</u> Satan tried to tempt Jesus to skip the cross. Jesus sweat drops of blood, but overcame. God sent an angel to strengthen Jesus from the agony that Satan caused.
5. Satan tried to keep Jesus from dying on the cross. When Jesus was hanging from the cross, people made fun of him and tried to tempt him to come down from the cross (Matthew 27:42–43). Satan even used the thieves who were crucified next to Jesus to insult him (Matthew

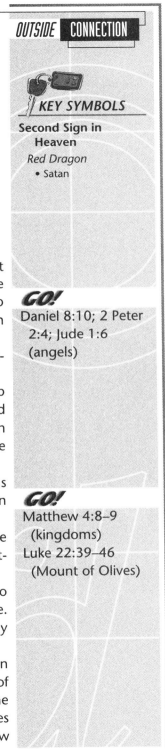

OUTSIDE CONNECTION

KEY SYMBOLS

Second Sign in Heaven
Red Dragon
• Satan

GO!
Daniel 8:10; 2 Peter 2:4; Jude 1:6 (angels)

GO!
Matthew 4:8–9 (kingdoms)
Luke 22:39–46 (Mount of Olives)

117

27:44). Nothing within Satan's power was successful in getting Jesus to change the plans that God had for him.

> ### Revelation 12:5–6
> She gave birth to a son, a male child, who will rule all the nations with an iron scepter. And her child was snatched up to God and to his throne. The woman fled into the desert to a place prepared for her by God, where she might be taken care of for 1,260 days.

Snatched Up

The woman gives birth to a son who will rule all the nations during the Millennium. Jesus will rule in a way that shows his authority—with an iron scepter. People will know for sure that Jesus is the all-powerful king. No one will dare stand up to his authority, similar to how first graders feel when they are approached by the school principal!

Israel's child being snatched up is a reference to when Jesus returned to heaven (the **ascension**) after his death and resurrection. Since Satan failed to keep Jesus from his saving mission, Satan now turns his attention to the woman—Israel. He wants to get her. But God has everything under control. The woman (Israel) runs to the desert and stays in a place prepared for her. Most prophecy experts believe this place is a mountainous area in the Jordan desert where a city called Petra (see illustration, page 119) was carved into the rocks centuries ago. Israel will hide there for the rest of the Tribulation (1,260 days).

Revelation 12:6 signals the middle of the Tribulation. Three and a half years (1,260 days) have passed.

> ### Revelation 12:7–8
> And there was war in heaven. Michael and his angels fought against the dragon, and the dragon and his angels fought back. But he was not strong enough, and they lost their place in heaven.

GO!

Acts 1:9 (ascension)
Luke 23:26–24:12 (resurrection)

ascension: *Jesus' return to heaven forty days after the resurrection*

Petra

The city of Petra is hidden at the end of a mile-long 1,000-foot-deep gorge. As you enter the city through this corridor, you can see columns of rose-red sandstone cut into the cliff.

▶▶ WAR BETWEEN GOOD AND EVIL

Once Israel is safely out of the picture, a great war will break out in heaven. God's angels will be led by the archangel Michael in the fight against Satan and his angels. This will be a spiritual, not earthly battle, because the last thing Satan wants is to be thrown literally out of heaven again! Satan and his angels will fight hard, but they won't win. They will lose their place in heaven forever.

Billy Graham: *Even as in the beginning of time angelic forces waged war in heaven, so in the very last days angels will wage still another war; Satan will make his last stand. As the time draws near he intensifies his activities. But it will be a victorious day for the universe, and especially planet earth, when the devil and his angels are thrown into the lake of fire, never again to tempt and destroy man.*[2]

OUTSIDE CONNECTION

Moviemakers love to depict good and evil, heroes and villains. (The movie character Indiana Jones is based on a real Indiana Jones who is an archaeologist in Israel. Some of the scenes where Indiana Jones is searching for the Holy Grail were shot at Petra.) Think of some recent movies where there was an obvious good and bad guy. How are these movie characters similar to the characters you have seen in Revelation 12?_____

_____

Why is Israel (Jesus' bloodline) so hard for Satan to destroy?_____

_____

_____

What can you do to strengthen your faith in Jesus, the winner of the battle?

_____

_____

There is no worse guy than Satan. He is sin, evil, and destruction all wrapped up in one. The good news is he's destined to lose. No matter what happens, Jesus has already won the battle. Satan is just killing time. It won't be long before his time is up.

Revelation 12:9
The great dragon was hurled down—that ancient serpent called the devil, or Satan, who leads the whole world astray. He was hurled to the earth, and his angels with him.

 HURLED TO EARTH

The good news is that Satan no longer will be bothering those in heaven, but the bad news is he has been hurled to earth where he can continue to do damage. And believe me when I say he is just getting going!

> **Revelation 12:10**
>
> Then I heard a loud voice in heaven say: "Now have come the salvation and the power and the kingdom of our God, and the authority of his Christ. For the accuser of our brothers, who accuses them before our God day and night, has been hurled down."

Party Hearty!

Heaven will party for several reasons: (1) Our salvation is complete and Satan no longer will be able to be in the presence of heaven; (2) all power will belong to Jesus; (3) God's kingdom will finally come to earth; and (4) Jesus will finally take control over what he won at the cross (the earth).

Satan today is constantly in God's face in heaven, accusing believers. We don't have to worry because Jesus is there to defend the believers before his Father. Once Satan is cast out of heaven for good, Jesus will no longer have to <u>defend</u> us; we will be **justified** once and for all!

Charles R. Swindoll: Whether young or old, those who pass into eternity have the same truth to claim . . . and so do those of us who remain. It is something you can cling to when it seems as though all hell has broken loose in your life. When the events of your days seem out of control, having neither rhyme nor reason. Deep within you are reminded that the end has yet to come. When He [Jesus] comes it will all make sense.[3]

> **Revelation 12:11–12**
>
> "They overcame him by the blood of the Lamb and by the word of their testimony; they did not love their lives so much as to shrink from death. Therefore rejoice, you heavens and you who dwell in them! But woe to the earth and the sea, because the devil has gone down to you! He is filled with fury, because he knows that his time is short."

By the Blood and the Word

Believers will be able to overcome Satan during the Tribulation by (1) trusting in the blood of the Lamb (Jesus' blood shed on the cross for sinners); (2) sharing their faith with others

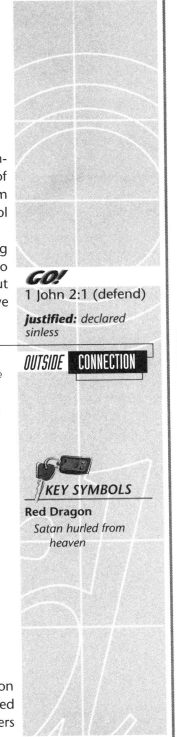

GO!
1 John 2:1 (defend)

justified: *declared sinless*

OUTSIDE CONNECTION

KEY SYMBOLS

Red Dragon
Satan hurled from heaven

121

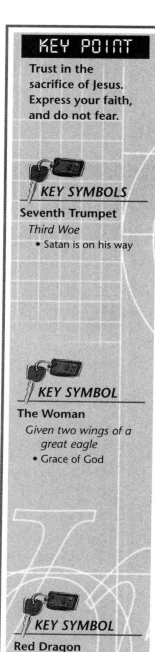

KEY POINT

Trust in the sacrifice of Jesus. Express your faith, and do not fear.

KEY SYMBOLS

Seventh Trumpet
Third Woe
• Satan is on his way

KEY SYMBOL

The Woman
Given two wings of a great eagle
• Grace of God

KEY SYMBOL

Red Dragon
Satan spewed water like a river

> ### Revelation 12:13–14
> When the dragon saw that he had been hurled to the earth, he pursued the woman who had given birth to the male child. The woman was given the two wings of a great eagle, so that she might fly to the place prepared for her in the desert, where she would be taken care of for a time, times and half a time, out of the serpent's reach.

Flying to Safety

Satan will have one major target when he returns to earth— the Jews. He will chase after them because the nation of Israel was responsible for bringing Jesus into the world. Jesus is Satan's biggest enemy.

God knew, even before Satan was kicked out of heaven, that Satan would go after Israel first thing. God is ahead of the game. He has already made an escape plan for Israel. God sweeps Israel away to a secret place much as an eagle swiftly comes and goes. God takes care of her by supernaturally providing food, water, clothing, protection, and anything else she needs. This will go on for three and a half years (*"a time, times and half a time"*). God will keep Israel safe for the second half of the Tribulation.

> ### Revelation 12:15
> Then from his mouth the serpent spewed water like a river, to overtake the woman and sweep her away with the torrent.

Attempted Drowning

When Satan sees Israel running away into the wilderness, he will probably speak through the Antichrist or his False Prophet, using their mouths to create an attack on the terrified Jewish people. He will try to pour many troops into the wilderness, and drown Israel (the woman) with an overwhelming force.

Gulp, Gulp

God isn't about to abandon his people. No, he moves on their behalf by allowing a natural disaster, likely a great earthquake, to destroy Satan's army. The earth literally will open up and swallow them. That is why the Jews should not go back for any stuff when they see the Antichrist setting up his image or idol at the Temple. And unlike **Jonah** who was swallowed by a whale, these armies won't be spit back out and given a second chance!

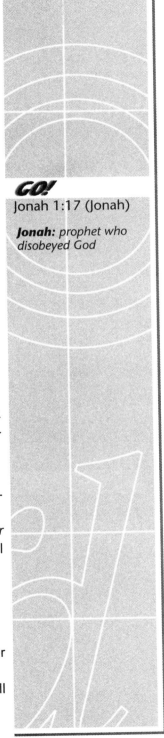

GO!
Jonah 1:17 (Jonah)

Jonah: *prophet who disobeyed God*

 WHO'S NEXT?

"Okay," Satan will say, "if I can't get her I'll get her relatives!" He will go after anyone who is a believer. He will actively seek out *"those who obey God's commandments and hold to the testimony of Jesus."*

Notice two things:

1. We have now started reading about things that will happen during the second half of the Tribulation.
2. There will be Gentile believers on earth at this time. *"Her offspring"* is a reference to Gentile believers. Satan will go on a rampage to destroy believers.

CHAPTER CHECKUP

1. Who is the woman we keep reading about? What is her significance?
2. What is the meaning of the number 1,260 and what will happen now?
3. Who is the angel that will cast Satan out of heaven?

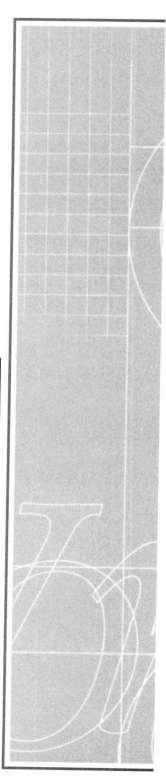

4. Why is Satan so angry? What will he do now?
5. What powers do believers have for overcoming Satan?

CRASH COURSE

▶ Israel represented as a woman clothed with the sun is the first sign in heaven. She is pregnant with a child. (Revelation 12:1–2)

▶ A great, red dragon, symbolic of Satan, is the second sign in heaven. He will cause a third of the angels to fall to earth due to rebellion. (Revelation 12:3–4)

▶ Satan will war against God in heaven, but God's angel will overpower him, expel him, and throw him to earth. (Revelation 12:7–9)

▶ After Satan's heavenly defeat he will try to attack God's people on earth, so he will send an army to drown them. (Revelation 12:15)

▶ The earth, however, will help God's people by swallowing these troops in an earthquake. (Revelation 12:16–17)

The Beasts Arrive

🔷🔷 LET'S DIVE IN

A lot has happened. Let's review. In chapter 10 John is told to eat the little book and prophesy about many peoples, nations, languages, and kings. In chapter 11 John writes about the Temple being rebuilt, the two witnesses who are killed but come back to life, and the impact these witnesses have on the world. In chapter 12 John writes about Satan getting the boot out of heaven and this will impact Israel and other believers.

Now in chapter 13 John tells us about two serious dudes of the Tribulation—the Antichrist (top political leader), and the False Prophet (top religious leader). These two end-time rulers will form a partnership and deceive many. They will be the deadly duo of destruction and death.

> **Revelation 13:1–2**
> And the dragon stood on the shore of the sea. And I saw a beast coming out of the sea. He had ten horns and seven heads, with ten crowns on his horns, and on each head a **blasphemous** name. The beast I saw resembled a leopard, but had feet like those of a bear and a mouth like that of a lion. The dragon gave the beast his power and his throne and great authority.

blasphemous: showing serious disrespect for God

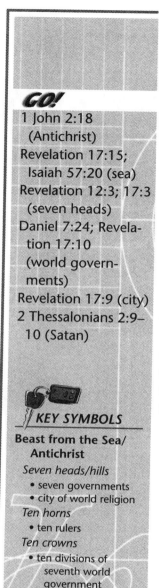

GO!

1 John 2:18
(Antichrist)
Revelation 17:15;
Isaiah 57:20 (sea)
Revelation 12:3; 17:3
(seven heads)
Daniel 7:24; Revelation 17:10
(world governments)
Revelation 17:9 (city)
2 Thessalonians 2:9–10 (Satan)

126

KEY SYMBOLS

Beast from the Sea/ Antichrist
Seven heads/hills
  • seven governments
  • city of world religion
Ten horns
  • ten rulers
Ten crowns
  • ten divisions of seventh world government

Although it gets complicated, this next part is the pregame hoopla for the end of the world. So hang in there.

The Antichrist, the beast, will come up out of a sea of wickedness that will control the earth when the church is no longer around. The Antichrist will rule with ten leaders (symbolized by the ten horns) during the Tribulation. The *"seven heads"* mean two things. First, they represent seven world governments (see chart, page 127). Six of these governments are past, but one is future. Second, the *"seven heads"* represent the city of seven hills where the one-world religion will have its headquarters during the Tribulation. The ten crowns mentioned will be ten branches of the seventh or last world government. This seventh or last world government will be split up into ten divisions, each with its own ruler. All ten divisions will be wicked and show disregard for God.

The seventh world government will be run by the Antichrist, who is controlled by Satan. This new government will begin in Europe and quickly grow to three groups of nations. Eventually, the Antichrist will gain total control of the world. This is the way it will happen:

• Phase 1: The world will form a world government, perhaps the United Nations.
• Phase 2: The world will divide itself into ten regions with a leader over each region.
• Phase 3: The Antichrist will rise to power in Europe and take control of that region (called lion).
• Phase 4: The Antichrist will take control of two more regions, possibly a group of Arab nations and Russia (called leopard and bear).
• Phase 5: The other seven regions will surrender control to the Antichrist.

OUTSIDE CONNECTION

Dr. William R. Goetz: *Events among the nations of earth—the Arab oil producers, the European Union, China, Russia—appear to be taking shape in the pattern that was foretold. The "pieces of the puzzle" adjacent to Israel seem to be falling into place.*[1]

Seven Heads/Hills (seven world governments)	**Ten Horns/Crowns** (ten divisions/rulers)	**Chart of Seven World Governments**

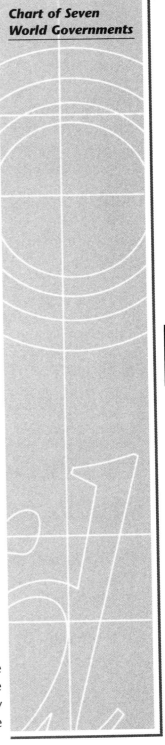

1 Assyrian

2 Egyptian

3 Babylonian

4 Medo-Persian

5 Greek

6 Roman (Old Roman Empire)

7 Revived Roman Empire
   (run by the Antichrist)

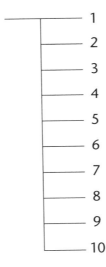

1
2
3
4
5
6
7
8
9
10

Revelation 13:3–4

One of the heads of the beast seemed to have had a fatal wound, but the fatal wound had been healed. The whole world was astonished and followed the beast. Men worshiped the dragon because he had given authority to the beast, and they also worshiped the beast and asked, "Who is like the beast? Who can make war against him?"

 FATAL ATTRACTION

What's up with this fatal wound? Well, the Antichrist will be mortally hurt with a sword (he is the *"wounded head"*). People will think he's dead, but then somehow he will be completely healed. It will be freaky, yet captivating. All who see this miracle will believe that the Antichrist has risen from the dead (a sad attempt at copying Jesus' resurrection) and these actions will convince people that the Antichrist can do anything. People will be willing to go to war for him, walk through fire with him, and do whatever he wants them to do.

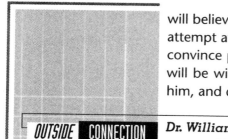

Dr. William R. Goetz: *The Antichrist will be awesome, empowered by Satan. He will blaspheme God. He will apparently rise from the dead, or at least from what would be considered a fatal wound. He will take control of the world through unprecedented political authority and will be worshiped by all except the saints of God. He will appear to be invincible.* [2]

 Don't blindly follow people or leaders. Jesus said, *"If a blind man leads a blind man, both will fall into a pit"* (Matthew 15:14).

> **Revelation 13:5–7**
> The beast was given a mouth to utter proud words and blasphemies and to exercise his authority for forty-two months. He opened his mouth to blaspheme God, and to slander his name and his dwelling place and those who live in heaven. He was given power to make war against the saints and to conquer them. And he was given authority over every tribe, people, language, and nation.

Ruler of All

The Antichrist will be *it*—top dog, head honcho, numero uno. The Antichrist will give great speeches that charm listeners into doing what he wants. (He'll be much more interesting than today's politicians!) The leaders of the world's regions will be so impressed they will say, "<u>Here</u>, run my country." The Antichrist will <u>call himself God</u> and will spout <u>blasphemies</u> about the true God. By the time the Antichrist is miraculously healed, the end of the Tribulation will be forty-two months away.

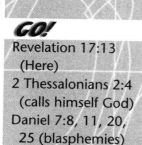

GO!
Revelation 17:13 (Here)
2 Thessalonians 2:4 (calls himself God)
Daniel 7:8, 11, 20, 25 (blasphemies)

128

BOOK OF LIFE

Imagine a world filled with Satan worshipers. However horrible you can picture that world being, that's how bad things will be—and worse.

But God doesn't want us to despair. John reminds us he's not talking about believers. The verse above refers to the people whose names have not been written in this book. Jesus not only knows those who belong to him but also those who do *not* belong to him. These people have chosen to worship the beast, Satan. There is <u>no hope</u> for them.

Jesus has already written the names of those who have trusted in him in his Book of Life. We don't have to sweat all this stuff we're learning about.

Doing Their Part

Review time! Do you recognize the first phrase above? It appeared in chapters 2 and 3 and was followed by the words, *"let him hear what the Spirit says to the churches."* The fact that these last words are left out here proves that the Rapture of the church occurs before the Tribulation.

During this time in the Tribulation, <u>revenge</u> will be normal. Those who kill will be killed. The tribulation saints, however, will have to face persecution patiently. God will avenge their suffering, but in his own time. They are not to take matters into their own hands.

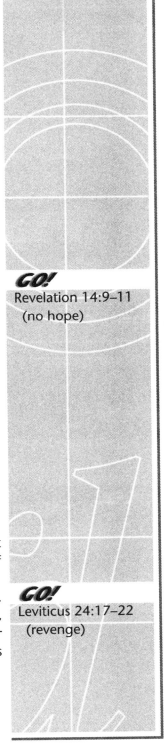

GO!
Revelation 14:9–11
(no hope)

GO!
Leviticus 24:17–22
(revenge)

129

KEY POINT

Believe in God, *trust* in Jesus, and *look* to the resurrection of the dead.

GO!

Revelation 17:15;
Isaiah 57:20 (sea)
Psalm 25:13 (earth)
John 1:29 (lamb)

KEY SYMBOLS

First Beast from Sea
Antichrist

Second Beast from Earth
False Prophet

Revelation 13:11–12

Then I saw another beast, coming out of the earth. He had two horns like a lamb, but he spoke like a dragon. He exercised all the authority of the first beast on his behalf, and made the earth and its inhabitants worship the first beast, whose fatal wound had been healed.

The Second Beast

The first beast came out of the <u>sea</u>, but this next beast comes out of the <u>earth</u> (a symbol of the land of Israel).

This second beast will have two horns and will look like a <u>lamb</u>. He will fool people into thinking he's gentle. He will talk about loving, accepting, showing tolerance, and so on. He will look down on racism, sexism, poverty, and all forms of discrimination. He'll sound good, but his actions will show that he's a terrible dragon.

This second beast (the False Prophet) will hold as much authority as the first beast (the Antichrist). He will not use his great authority to lift himself up. Instead, he'll use it to lift up the Antichrist. He will imitate the way the Holy Spirit works to draw attention to Christ. The False Prophet will pretend to be a miracle worker and healer, taking credit for healing the Antichrist's fatal wound. He'll fulfill the prophecy where Jesus said, *"For false Christs and false prophets will appear and perform great signs and miracles to deceive even the elect—if that were possible"* (Matthew 24:24).

Revelation 13:13–14

And he performed great and miraculous signs, even causing fire to come down from heaven to earth in full view of men. Because of the signs he was given power to do on behalf of the first beast, he deceived the inhabitants of the earth. He ordered them to set up an image in honor of the beast who was wounded by the sword and yet lived.

Right Where He Wants Them

The False Prophet will "wow" everyone by causing fire to come down from heaven in front of a huge crowd. The fire itself won't prove that he is from God, but many people will see this sign and believe that he is. It's not like everyone can do some-

Whom do you admire and why? _____

_____

What kinds of traits do you look for in a leader? _____

_____

_____

Name some of Jesus' qualities that make him a good leader._____

_____

_____

The Antichrist and the False Prophet are deceiving leaders. Learning about them can help you be aware of how easy it is to follow the wrong person. In the world right now there are good and bad leaders. It's important to evaluate the people who lead. The next time you find yourself following or copying someone, take a minute to see if he or she is someone Jesus would want you to imitate.

thing like that! People will follow him and gladly do what he commands—including making an idol to worship. Halfway through the Tribulation he will set up an image of the Antichrist in the Temple area.

Revelation 13:15–17

He was given power to give breath to the image of the first beast, so that it could speak and cause all who refused to worship the image to be killed. He also forced everyone, small and great, rich and poor, free and slave, to receive a mark on his right hand or on his forehead, so that no one could buy or sell unless he had the mark, which is the name of the beast or the number of his name.

🗝️ KEY SYMBOLS

False Prophet
Comes from earth
- possibly a Jew

Has two horns like a lamb
- imitates Christ

Speaks like a dragon
- deceitful

Makes others worship Antichrist
- imitates Holy Spirit's focus on another

 SATANIC TATTOO

The False Prophet will give breath to the idol, and it will appear to come to life—a real-life Pinocchio, only this creature

mark of the beast:
mark on right hand or forehead needed for buying or selling products

GO!
Revelation 14:1
(forehead)
Leviticus 19:28
(marks)

won't be cute. This idol will be able to speak, perhaps by demonic power or some technological feat, and will condemn to death those who refuse to worship it.

Not only will the False Prophet create this idol, but he will also require every person alive to get something like a tattoo known as the **mark of the beast**. People will be able to choose to get this mark on their right hand or their forehead. These marks will be vital because without them people will not be allowed to buy or sell anything. By doing this the False Prophet will succeed in merging government and religion. People will no longer be able to worship anyone other than the Antichrist, and those who refuse will likely starve.

OUTSIDE CONNECTION *William T. James: Revelation 13:16–17 approaches ever closer. . . . Technology is swamping humanity in a gigantic wave of liberty-crushing power to control.*[3]

OUTSIDE CONNECTION *Tim LaHaye: Physically speaking, it will be necessary for men to have the Mark of the Beast. Spiritually speaking, it will be fatal. For we have repeatedly seen that those who are redeemed by the Lamb, those who have the seal of God, do not have the Mark of the Beast. But those who receive the Antichrist's mark will have made the final decisions for eternity to reject Christ and worship his archenemy.*[4]

GO!
Revelation 14:9–11
(fatal)

HAPPENINGS

ATMs. Debit and credit cards. Online banking. The world is moving toward a cashless society. The countries that make up Europe are already using one currency, the euro, making it easier to buy and sell things across country lines. One day no money will be used, only a mark like the one mentioned in Revelation 13.

> **Revelation 13:18**
> This calls for wisdom. If anyone has insight, let him calculate the number of the beast, for it is man's number. His number is 666.

132

666—NUMBER OF TERROR

God tells us to use **wisdom** in figuring out who the Antichrist will be. People will eventually be able to recognize the Antichrist, but wisdom will be necessary.

- The Antichrist can't appear until after Israel becomes a nation because he will sign a <u>covenant</u> with them, so Hitler was not the Antichrist.
- The Antichrist will rise to power in Europe, I think, because the prophet Daniel told of the destruction of the Temple by the <u>Romans</u> and that the Antichrist would come out of that people group.
- The Antichrist will not be revealed until <u>after the Rapture</u>.

Many theories have been suggested to explain the meaning of the number 666. Some people have even assigned numbers to letters and by various calculations have thought the Antichrist was Nero, Hitler, or Henry Kissinger.

Others think the number 666 should be viewed symbolically. For instance, the Bible associates the <u>number 7</u> with God and perfection. Since man falls short of perfection, his symbolic number is 6. The number 666 may be a way of emphasizing how far the Antichrist is from God's standards.

CHAPTER CHECKUP

1. How will people be saved during the Tribulation?
2. What part will miracles play in the Tribulation?
3. What two spiritual things will the saints need to endure the Tribulation? Why?
4. Is the mark your social security number, credit card number, or driver's license number?

CRASH COURSE

▶ The dragon will give his power and authority to the Antichrist, so the world will be deceived and worship the dragon. (Revelation 13:1–4)
▶ The Antichrist will receive what appears to be a fatal wound that will be healed. The world will marvel at this "miracle" and follow him. (Revelation 13:3–4)

wisdom: *right use of knowledge*

 GO!

Daniel 9:27
(covenant)
Daniel 9:26 (Romans)
2 Thessalonians 2:1–8
(after the Rapture)
Revelation 3:1; 5:6
(number 7)

KEY POINT

The mark of the beast is the "bright" idea of the False Prophet who helps the Antichrist gain control of people's hearts, minds, and wallets.

133

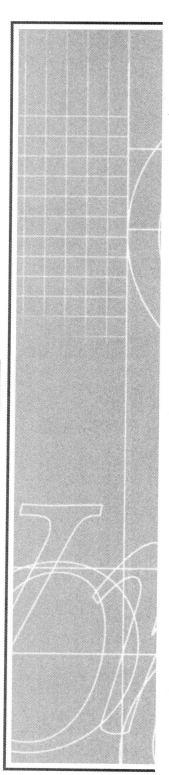

- The False Prophet will perform miracles to deceive people and force them to worship the Antichrist. (Revelation 13:11–13)
- The False Prophet will get people to make an image of the Antichrist and worship it. Anyone who doesn't will be killed. (Revelation 13:14–15)
- Everyone who wishes to buy or sell will be forced to take the mark of the beast. This mark is man's number, 666. (Revelation 13:16–18)

134

Armageddon and Babylon

 **LET'S DIVE IN**

In John's writing Armageddon isn't the name of a movie. It's a giant war! We'll learn about Armageddon as well as hear more about tribulation saints, Jerusalem, and the mark of the beast. Those 144,000 Jewish witnesses are still around and a holy (not grim!) reaper makes an appearance too.

> **Revelation 14:1–2**
> Then I looked, and there before me was the Lamb, standing on Mount Zion, and with him 144,000 who had his name and his Father's name written on their foreheads. And I heard a sound from heaven like the roar of rushing waters and like a loud peal of thunder. The sound I heard was like that of harpists playing their harps.

 STORM BEFORE THE CALM

John looks around Mount Zion in <u>Jerusalem</u>, and he is not alone. Around him are 144,000 Jewish witnesses unharmed by the <u>Antichrist</u>, False Prophet, and disasters that have happened on earth. God has <u>preserved</u> them. John notices that

GO!
1 Chronicles 11:4–8 (Jerusalem)
Revelation 13:16–17 (Antichrist)
Proverbs 2:8 (preserved)

KEY POINT

Jesus knows how to protect his own.

136

celibate: abstaining from all sexual activity

each one has the name of Jesus and his Father written on his <u>forehead</u>.

Then John hears a loud sound coming from heaven; *wham-kaboom*—it is like the roar of rushing waters and a loud crash of thunder all at the same time. Then he hears a soothing sound like a musician playing a <u>harp</u>.

Revelation 14:3

And they sang a new song before the throne and before the four living creatures and the elders. No one could learn the song except the 144,000 who had been redeemed from the earth.

 EXCLUSIVE SONG

If you can't carry a tune, don't worry. If you aren't one of the 144,000 you won't have to sing this song. Only the 144,000 can sing this song because they have had all the experiences that give them the passion to sing it.

The next two verses give us an idea of why this group was able to understand and learn this heavenly song. It shows us what this group of people endured for Jesus.

Revelation 14:4–5

There are those who did not defile themselves with women, for they kept themselves pure. They follow the Lamb wherever he goes. They were purchased from among men and offered as firstfruits to God and the Lamb. No lie was found in their mouths; they are blameless.

Pure Followers

There is some buzz around this verse's meaning. Some say *"did not defile"* means that the 144,000 were **celibate**. Others believe they did not commit adultery or get divorced or get married. Still others believe *"did not defile"* means they refused to worship idols and did not teach false things. It's hard to say who is right, but we can be sure of some things: (1) During the Tribulation, it will be difficult for these men to be married and to be good husbands and fathers, and (2) they will remain pure in spite of living in a world filled with immoral things and idol worship.

Tim LaHaye: *The Bible does not teach celibacy; in fact, no hint of it is found in Scripture. The Bible everywhere advocates that Christians be holy and virtuous, undefiled by the world. Misuse of sex has always been one of man's greatest problems; infidelity and immorality one of man's greatest temptations.*[1]

> **Revelation 14:6–7**
> Then I saw another angel flying in midair, and he had the eternal gospel to proclaim to those who live on the earth—to every nation, tribe, language, and people. He said in a loud voice, "Fear God and give him glory, because the hour of his judgment has come. Worship him who made the heavens, the earth, the sea, and the springs of water."

 ANGEL IN MIDAIR!

Right now on earth it's the duty of Christians to spread the gospel. If you aren't doing this every day, it's time to get to it, pronto! At the time of the events John is writing about, however, the church will be in heaven, so it will be up to these 144,000 Jews, two witnesses, and this angel to preach the message of Jesus Christ. This angel will go to great lengths to give the world one last chance to hear the gospel—the same gospel Christians today preach.

People who hear this gospel will have two choices: (1) believe the Antichrist and his lie and worship him, or (2) **fear God** alone and give him the glory. One of these beliefs will lead to eternal death, and one will lead to eternal life. Life's choices don't get much more clear than this!

> **Revelation 14:8**
> A second angel followed and said, "Fallen! Fallen is Babylon the Great, which made all the nations drink the maddening wine of her adulteries."

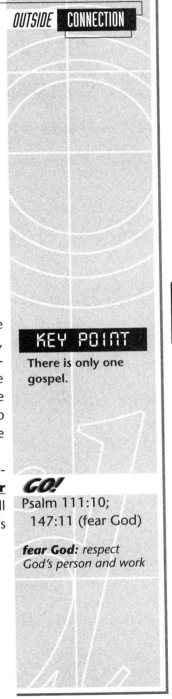

OUTSIDE CONNECTION

137

KEY POINT

There is only one gospel.

GO!
Psalm 111:10; 147:11 (fear God)

fear God: respect God's person and work

Babylon's Fall

The first angel in this chapter brings a message of hope or judgment—depending on people's choices. This angel mentions Babylon as an object lesson of what happens to a city when God judges it. Babylon (see illustration below) was once a great city, but was overthrown and destroyed. In the 1980s and 1990s, Saddam Hussein spent millions of dollars trying to rebuild this city.[2] During the Tribulation, it will again become a modern center of religion. (Instead of being a place where the <u>tower</u> of Babel was built, it will be a place where people exchange a whole lot of babble against the true God!)

Babylon is known as the city of Satan because of its long history of idol worship, **astrology**, witchcraft, and other things of the **occult**. Its influence will again lead people away from the truth of God.

The word *fallen* is repeated two times because there will be two separate falls or judgments. The false religious system will fall first when the Antichrist destroys it just after the middle of the Tribulation. The rebuilt city of Babylon will fall next when it is burned to the ground in one hour near the end of the Tribulation (more to come on this in chapter 17).

GO!
Genesis 11:1–9
(tower)

astrology: *use of the sky and stars to predict future events*

occult: *false religion that honors satanic things*

138

Map of Babylon

This map shows the location of the ancient city of Babylon between the Tigris and Euphrates Rivers. Babylon is in present-day Iraq.

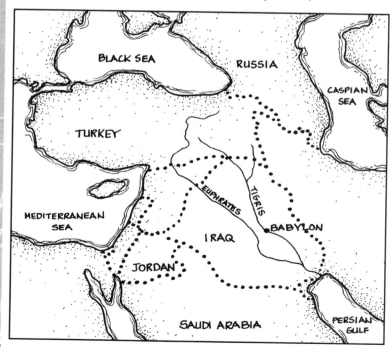

> **Revelation 14:9–10**
>
> A third angel followed them and said in a loud voice: "If any-one worships the beast and his image and receives his mark on the forehead or on the hand, he, too, will drink of the wine of God's fury, which has been poured full strength into the cup of his wrath. He will be tormented with burning sulfur in the presence of the holy angels and of the Lamb."

REFUSE THE MARK!

This is a chapter of angel sightings! The first angel preaches the gospel. The second angel announces the fall of Babylon, and the third angel warns people not to worship the Antichrist or take the mark of the beast.

No matter what hardships people living in this time face, it will be better for them to die than to worship the Antichrist and take his mark. Those who do so will face God's anger and be tormented with burning sulfur!

> **Revelation 14:11–12**
>
> "And the smoke of their torment rises for ever and ever. There is no rest day or night for those who worship the beast and his image, or for anyone who receives the mark of his name." This calls for patient endurance on the part of the saints who obey God's commandments and remain faithful to Jesus.

No Rest for Beast Worshipers

Those who worship the beast and take his mark will be tormented forever. They will run, but will never, ever, be able to hide from God.

When the Antichrist takes over and causes destruction, people will be helpless against him. People who believe in Jesus will have to be patient and wait for God's perfect time of judgment. They will have to <u>remain faithful</u>, and let God take charge.

> **Revelation 14:13**
>
> Then I heard a voice from heaven say, "Write: Blessed are the dead who die in the Lord from now on."
>
> "Yes," says the Spirit, "they will rest from their labor, for their deeds will follow them."

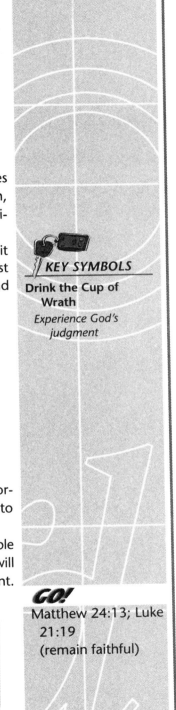

KEY SYMBOLS

Drink the Cup of Wrath
Experience God's judgment

GO!
Matthew 24:13; Luke 21:19
(remain faithful)

Rest for the Righteous

God doesn't want his followers to be afraid of death. If people die knowing Jesus, then they are blessed! A time will come during the Tribulation when it will be better for the saved to <u>die</u> than to live. What's cool is that when these believers get to heaven, they will be able to relax and hang out because their hard work of dying for Christ will bring them <u>heavenly rewards</u>. They will be way better off than those still on earth who took the mark and are destined for hell.

GO!
2 Timothy 2:11–12
(die)
Matthew 6:20
(heavenly rewards)

OUTSIDE CONNECTION

Billy Graham: You may be filled with dread at the thought of death. Just remember that at one moment you may be suffering, but in another moment, you will be instantly transformed into the glorious likeness of our Savior. The wonders, beauties, splendor and grandeur of heaven will be yours. You will be surrounded by these heavenly messengers sent by God to bring you home where you may rest from your labors, though the honor of your works will follow you.[3]

> **Revelation 14:14**
> I looked, and there before me was a white cloud, and seated on the cloud was one "like a son of man" with a crown of gold on his head and a sharp sickle in his hand.

HOLY REAPER

The grim reaper is often portrayed in movies or on TV as a ghost wearing black, carrying a large sickle, and taking people from the earth to death when their time to live is up. Did you know there is a holy reaper? The *"son of man"* described here, Jesus, will take a seat in the <u>clouds</u> and will come back to claim his harvest.

GO!
Daniel 7:13 (clouds)
Matthew 13:39–42
(weeds)

harvest: here the gathering of the wicked nations for judgment

This harvest will be grim, way bleak, for those who have chosen not to believe in Jesus Christ for their salvation. When Jesus returns wearing a gold crown on his head he will **harvest** the earth and will pull up the <u>weeds</u>—those who have turned their backs on him. And trust me when I say you really don't want to be a weed when it comes time for Jesus' gardening!

140

How do you feel when you think about your own death?_____

_____

What are you most afraid of?_____

_____

_____

How can placing your faith in Jesus Christ and having the assurance that you'll
go to heaven help ease your fears?_____

_____

_____

 When Jesus Christ rose from the dead, he defeated death once and for all. We can trust in what he did and know that he has prepared a place for us in heaven. Believers don't need to fear death, but it's natural to be nervous about it. Focusing on the great things waiting for us in heaven can help us get through this life's ups and downs.

Wim Malgo: *The sharp sickle is raised in preparation for the harvest. This term is never used for the gathering of good grain, and therefore it means something terrible: He is coming here as the Judge of the world.*[4]

OUTSIDE CONNECTION

> **Revelation 14:15–16**
> Then another angel came out of the temple and called in a loud voice to him who was sitting on the cloud, "Take your sickle and reap, because the time to reap has come, for the harvest of the earth is ripe." So he who was seated on the cloud swung his sickle over the earth, and the earth was harvested.

KEY SYMBOLS

Crown of Gold
Jesus as king

Sharp Sickle
Coming judgment

Time to Reap What's Been Sown

It's go time. The chance for unbelievers to turn to Jesus has come and gone. The angel will tell Jesus, *"The time to reap has come."* The people of the earth have had more than enough time on the vine, so to speak; they are now so ripe they are rotting. It's time for Jesus to judge the earth.

Another angel came out of the temple in heaven, and he too had a sharp sickle. Still another angel, who had charge of the fire, came from the altar and called in a loud voice to him who had the sharp sickle, "Take your sharp sickle and gather the clusters of grapes from the earth's vine, because its grapes are ripe."

KEY SYMBOLS

Clusters of Grapes
Followers of Antichrist

Earth's Vine
Antichrist

True Vine
Christ

GO!
John 15:1
(True Vine)

GO!
Isaiah 34:1–8 (wrath)

horses' bridles: *about four feet high*

1,600 stadia: *about 180 miles*

 ANGELS OF DOOM

If you think action movies have lots of violence, this next scene makes those films seem tame. One angel will come directly from the presence of God with a sharp sickle just like the one Jesus will have. The next angel will come from the altar in the heavenly temple, where the tribulation saints are calling on God to avenge their blood. The clusters of grapes from the earth's vine are those who follow the Antichrist, instead of Jesus, the <u>True Vine</u>.

Verse 18 indicates two things: (1) God will eventually answer the prayers of the tribulation saints who cry out for revenge, and (2) the wickedness on the earth will be at its peak.

The angel swung his sickle on the earth, gathered its grapes and threw them into the great winepress of God's <u>wrath</u>. They were trampled into the winepress outside the city, and blood flowed out of the press, rising as high as the **horses' bridles** for a distance of **1,600 stadia**.

 A BLOODY MESS

The fourth angel will use his sickle to gather all of the wicked nations of the earth. They will be squeezed like grapes being turned into wine. They will not come out alive from God's winepress of wrath. As these ripe "grapes" are pressed, blood will rise as high as the horses' bridles for approximately 180 miles, and millions will die.

You may be thinking, "This is terrible! How can a loving God do this?" Keep in mind that God is righteous and just. These people have had many chances to repent and turn to him before he takes his wrath out on them.

KEY POINT

God will give the world many chances to repent before he destroys it.

CHAPTER CHECKUP

1. What virtue did the 144,000 who were redeemed from the earth possess?
2. Why shouldn't people have the Antichrist's mark put on their forehead or hand?
3. Who will do the harvesting on earth during the Tribulation, and what will they harvest?
4. How will the sinful nations finally be judged?

CRASH COURSE

▶ The 144,000 will stand with Jesus on Mount Zion and sing a new song since they will be redeemed from the earth and offered as firstfruits. These are also the ones who kept themselves pure during the Tribulation. (Revelation 14:1–5)

▶ An angel will fly through the air proclaiming the gospel to all the earth's inhabitants and warning them that the hour of God's judgment is near. (Revelation 14:6–7)

▶ A second angel will proclaim the fall of Babylon because she caused the nations of the earth to sin. (Revelation 14:8)

▶ A third angel will warn the people of earth to not worship the Antichrist or receive his mark. Those who follow the Antichrist will suffer God's wrath forever.

▶ Two harvests of the earth will occur. The first one will be by Christ, and the second by an angel who will throw his harvest into the winepress of God's wrath. (Revelation 14:14–20)

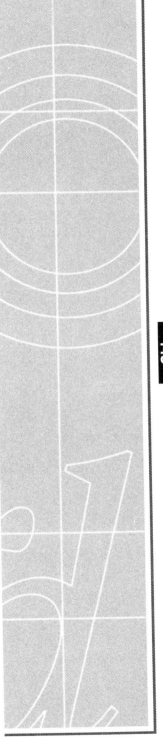

Short, Not Sweet

 **LET'S DIVE IN**

This is the shortest chapter of Revelation, but it is packed with gloom and doom for those who refuse to believe in Jesus for their salvation. There are predictions of what will happen in heaven right before the final judgments begin. Most Bible scholars believe this chapter should be combined with the next chapter because it is the introduction to the seven bowl judgments of chapter 16 (see chart, page 64).

> **Revelation 15:1–2**
> I saw in heaven another great and marvelous sign: seven angels with the seven last plagues—last, because with them God's wrath is completed. And I saw what looked like a sea of glass mixed with fire and, standing beside the sea, those who had been victorious over the beast and his image and over the number of his name. They held harps given them by God . . .

 **END OF IT ALL**

You might say John knew sign language. Altogether John saw three great signs in heaven. The sun-clothed woman who represented Israel (Revelation 12:1), the great red dragon who was Satan (Revelation 12:3), and the seven angels with seven final plagues (Revelation 15:1–3). What's unusual about this last sign is that it proclaims doom for Satan and is promised by God to be the end of it all. This means that when these plagues are through, God's anger at the sin of the world will be through.

John had seen a sea in heaven prior to this vision—one that was clear as <u>crystal</u>. The <u>sea</u> described here sounds like a polluted beach resort. The fire symbolizes God's judgment on humankind.

The tribulation saints will come up out of this sea because they have been through fiery hardships. (Remember these saints are people who became believers during the Tribulation and who were persecuted for their faith.) The pain and difficulties they faced on earth will melt away as they joyfully play songs to God. It will have been worth it all in the end!

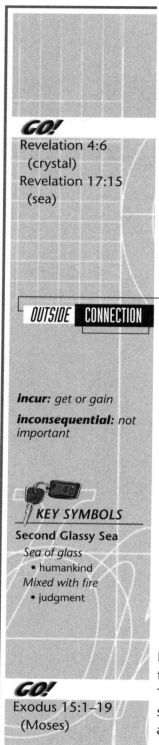

GO!
Revelation 4:6
(crystal)
Revelation 17:15
(sea)

OUTSIDE CONNECTION

incur: get or gain

inconsequential: not important

Tim LaHaye: *Death at the hands of a murderous dictator or anti-Christian persecutor is only defeat as man looks upon the situation. People living during the Tribulation will think the Antichrist is overcoming the saints, but in reality he is sending them out into eternity to be with the Lord. . . . If man does not* **incur** *blessings in this life, he considers that defeat, not realizing that what man gains in this life is* **inconsequential** *in comparison to what he gains in the life to come.*[1]

Revelation 15:3–4

. . . and sang the song of Moses the servant of God and the song of the Lamb: "Great and marvelous are your deeds, Lord God Almighty. Just and true are your ways, King of the ages. Who will not fear you, O Lord, and bring glory to your name? For you alone are holy. All nations will come and worship before you, for your righteous acts have been revealed."

KEY SYMBOLS

Second Glassy Sea
Sea of glass
• humankind
Mixed with fire
• judgment

▶▶ YOU ALONE ARE HOLY

It will be party time as these tribulation saints happily sing two tunes: (1) the song of Moses, and (2) the song of the Lamb. The song of <u>Moses</u> is in the Old Testament and was a praise song sung when Israel was brought out of slavery in Egypt and crossed the Red Sea.

GO!
Exodus 15:1–19
(Moses)

146

LEARN THE WORD • REVELATION FOR TEENS

The song of the Lamb celebrates God's victory over all nations, and the words are right here in verses 3 and 4. It's a universal anthem, so to speak, that represents Jesus' marvelous deeds. Jesus should be feared because he alone is holy. All nations will worship and bow down to him. No one will worship idols; everyone will worship Jesus, the true God. In the last days Jesus' righteous acts will be revealed. It's only proper that holy Jesus will deal with the ungodly in a righteous and just way.

KEY SYMBOLS

Seven Angels
Seven plagues
  • the wrath of God
Clean, shining clothes
  • righteousness
Golden sashes
  • royal priesthood

> **Revelation 15:5–6**
>
> After this I looked and in heaven the temple, that is, the tabernacle of the Testimony, was opened. Out of the temple came the seven angels with the seven plagues. They were dressed in clean, shining linen and wore golden sashes around their chests.

▶▶ HERE COMES TROUBLE

John looked up and saw that the temple in heaven was opened up. In addition, the Holy of Holies and the ark of the covenant that holds the <u>Ten Commandments</u> will also be open. (Finally that ark that Indiana Jones searched for in the movies will, in real life, be revealed!) In Old Testament times Israelites were <u>forbidden</u> to enter these holy places. If an ordinary Israelite man, for instance, wanted to approach God, he had to have a priest sacrifice an animal in his place. There were even <u>strict rules</u> for the priest to follow.

John's vision here symbolizes that believers will be able to approach God's most holy place. They won't need a human priest or an animal sacrifice; Jesus is their high priest. The angels' clothing shows that they belong to Christ and are part of his royal priesthood. Unbelievers will be judged according to the Ten Commandments.

GO!
Exodus 20:2–17
(Ten Commandments)
Leviticus 16:17;
17:32–34
(forbidden)
Leviticus 16:24
(strict rules)

> **Revelation 15:7**
>
> Then one of the four living creatures gave to the seven angels seven golden bowls filled with the wrath of God, who lives for ever and ever.

How can Christians approach God?_____

_____

Do you think it's fair for God to punish unbelievers? Why or why not?_____

_____

_____

No one is able to approach God on his or her own merit. But those who have put their faith in what Jesus Christ did on the cross can approach God through Jesus. They no longer need to be afraid of God. Jesus will represent them before God because he is their high priest. Unbelievers, however, will be judged by God's righteous law, and they won't measure up.

GO!
Revelation 6:1–8 (creatures)
Leviticus 16:14 (Day of Atonement)

mercy seat: *lid covering the ark of the covenant*

⟫⟫ A GIFT YOU DON'T WANT

The four living <u>creatures</u> will give the seven angels seven bowls filled with seven plagues of the wrath of God. Pretty powerful stuff!

In the Old Testament, once a year on the <u>Day of Atonement</u> the high priest would take a bowl of blood from one of the animals sacrificed and go into the Holy of Holies and dump it on the **mercy seat** of the ark of the covenant (see illustration, page 112). God commanded that this be done so the people could be forgiven of their sins. Since the Antichrist and his followers will not accept the blood of Jesus to cover their sins, these priest-like angels will dump God's anger on them instead.

Charles R. Swindoll: Since we are living in a day when animal sacrifices are not performed, it is necessary that we familiarize ourselves with what that meant. . . . Even though the idea of offering sacrifices seems strange to us, it was as common to people in the early days as the courtroom scene is to us.[2]

And the temple was filled with smoke from the glory of God and from his power, and no one could enter the temple until the seven plagues of the seven angels were completed.

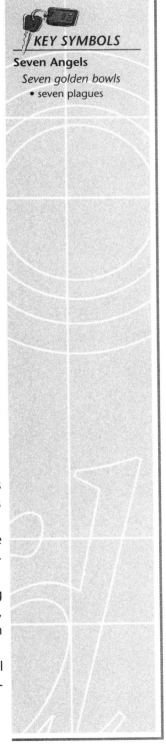

 SMOKIN'

Once this temple area is covered with smoke, those who have forsaken Jesus will no longer have the opportunity to accept him as Savior. God won't show mercy to these people any more. He'll instead give the go-ahead to the angels to pour out his wrath in the form of these last seven plagues. The earth is about to become a very terrible place! Look out below!

CHApTeR cHeCkUp

1. What are the three signs from heaven?
2. What will the tribulation saints be doing as they stand next to the sea of glass mixed with fire?
3. What does the Bible mean when it says, "You alone are holy"?
4. What will the golden bowls have in them?
5. Why will smoke fill the Temple?

CRASH COURSE

▶ The third great sign John will see will be seven angels carrying the seven last plagues, which will complete God's wrath. (Revelation 15:1)

▶ Standing beside the sea of glass mixed with fire will be those who will be victorious over the Antichrist. (Revelation 15:2–4)

▶ Those who overcome the Antichrist will sing the song of the Lamb. They will sing about his marvelous actions, his just and true ways, and his holiness. (Revelation 15:3–4)

▶ Anyone who rejects Christ and his gift of eternal life will be judged according to the Law of Moses (the Ten Commandments). (Revelation 15:5)

149

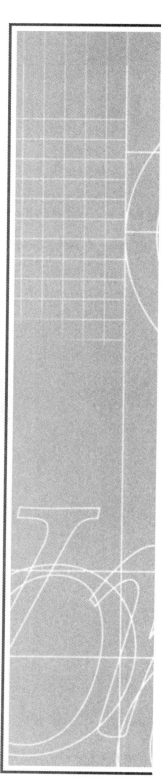

▶ When the heavenly temple opens, the seven angels with the seven last plagues will come out of it. Once the angels leave the temple, smoke from God's glory will fill it preventing anyone from seeking mercy and obtaining one last chance. (Revelation 15:5–8)

CHAPTER CAPTURE

● Gross Sores

● Blood Angel

● Battle Tactics

● Armed Robbery!

● Major Shake-Up

Goodness, Gracious, Great Bowls of Wrath

151

 LET'S DIVE IN

Check out what happens when the seven bowls of God's wrath are poured out on a sinful world. Refer to the chart in chapter 6, page 64 for help in understanding the events in this chapter. Although God is extremely angry with the wicked people on earth, he wants them to realize that he is the all-powerful God. Will they finally listen?

KEY SYMBOLS

Seven Bowls
Seven portions of God's wrath

KEY POINT

The first bowl judgment will bring ugly, painful sores.

Revelation 16:1–2
Then I heard a loud voice from the temple saying to the seven angels, "Go, pour out the seven bowls of God's wrath on the earth." The first angel went and poured out his bowl on the land, and ugly and painful sores broke out on the people who had the mark of the beast and worshiped his image.

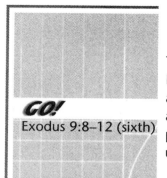

GO!
Exodus 9:8–12 (sixth)

GO!
Revelation 8:8–9 (sea)

KEY POINT

The second bowl judgment will turn the sea to blood, and everything in it will die.

GO!
Revelation 8:10–11 (freshwater)

 **GROSS SORES**

The first bowl judgment will cause ugly, painful, stinky sores. It will be like the <u>sixth</u> plague God sent on Egypt when Moses asked Pharaoh to free the Israelites. When the Antichrist isn't able to heal his own sores, much less the sores of his followers, people will realize that he isn't the powerful leader he's cracked up to be.

> **Revelation 16:3**
> The second angel poured out his bowl on the sea, and it turned into blood like that of a dead man, and every living thing in the <u>sea</u> died.

Belly-Up

The second bowl judgment will be worse than the second trumpet judgment when one-third of the sea was polluted. Now *everything* in the water will die! The ocean will be completely ruined. The water will be bloody from all the dead and decaying creatures. As fish and other creatures go belly-up, it won't be a pretty sight or smell!

> **Revelation 16:4–6**
> The third angel poured out his bowl on the rivers and springs of water, and they became blood. Then I heard the angel in charge of the waters say: "You are just in these judgments, you who are and who were, the Holy One, because you have so judged; for they have shed the blood of your saints and prophets, and you have given them blood to drink as they deserve."

BLOOD ANGEL

The third bowl judgment will be worse than the third trumpet in which one-third of <u>freshwater</u> is polluted. Now *all* of the water, sea and freshwater, will turn gross. The water that people depend on for drinking and cooking is suddenly blood! Can you imagine blood coming out of faucets? How terrifying that will be!

After this bowl judgment has fallen on the rivers and springs, the angel in charge of the waters will praise God. Most people

152

don't realize that God has designated certain angels to take charge of various tasks related to his creation. In this case, there is an angel who has the job of caring for the earth's water supplies. Instead of getting upset or angry, this angel gives God glory because he realizes that God's judgment against the waters is just and well deserved. The tribulation saints and the Old Testament prophets were killed by unbelievers. It's time for their deaths to be avenged. It's like God says, "You want blood? Okay, I'll give you blood!"

KEY POINT

The third bowl judgment will cause all rivers and springs to turn to blood.

Wim Malgo: We can only grasp the full extent of this judgment when we consider the reason for it. If the voice of the blood of one single person who was murdered (Abel) cries to the Lord, how much louder must the blood of all the innumerable murdered people cry to heaven?[1]

OUTSIDE **CONNECTION**

GO!
Genesis 4:10 (Abel)

> **Revelation 16:7**
> And I heard the altar respond: "Yes, Lord God Almighty, true and just are your judgments."

True and Just Judgments

When the fifth seal was opened, the martyred tribulation saints under the altar asked God how long it would be until he judged the people of the earth and avenged their blood. God told them to wait until more Christians were killed. Now, with the third bowl judgment, God responds to the bloodshed of the Antichrist and his followers by turning the water into blood. When he does this, the martyred tribulation saints cheer. The bad guys are finally getting their due!

GO!
Revelation 6:9–11 (saints)

> **Revelation 16:8–9**
> The fourth angel poured out his bowl on the sun, and the sun was given power to scorch people with fire. They were seared by the intense heat and they cursed the name of God, who had control over these plagues, but they refused to repent and glorify him.

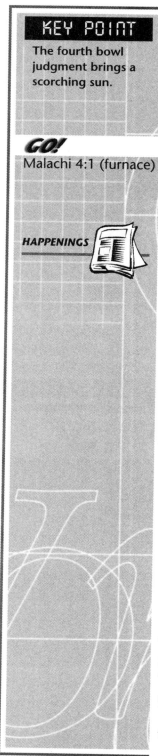

Global Warming

The fourth bowl judgment will cause the sun to burn people with fire. Ouch! Major sizzle is an understatement. No air conditioning unit or SPF lotion will be able to counteract this kind of heat. It will be global warming times ten. The Old Testament prophet Malachi predicted a day when the earth would burn like a <u>furnace</u>. Those who remain in sin will suffer a real hell on earth. But instead of turning for help to the God who controls nature, these people will curse him.

The past five years have produced evidence that human activities are influencing climate and that the earth is likely to get hotter than previously predicted, a U.N. panel of climate scientists said. "Global warming is a real problem and it is with us and we are going to have to take this into account in our future planning," said Kevin Trenberth, head of climate analysis section at the National Center for Atmospheric Research in Boulder, Colorado.[2]

Animals are also big contributors to global warming, and various countries have begun tracking the amount of methane gas they produce in the form of waste and—believe it or not—burps! Researchers are even developing a vaccine to reduce the burps of cows and sheep.[3]

> **Revelation 16:10–11**
> The fifth angel poured out his bowl on the throne of the beast, and his kingdom was plunged into darkness. Men gnawed their tongues in agony and cursed the God of heaven because of their pains and their sores, but they refused to repent of what they had done.

Dark Days

The fifth bowl judgment will mark a turning point. God will begin to focus on his biggest enemy on earth—the Antichrist. Total darkness will cover the planet, and even the sun, moon, and stars will be hidden from view.

As people sit in darkness they will also be in great pain from their sores and sunburn. They will be nervous and afraid. Some will chew on their tongues as if insane. They will curse the God of heaven but still won't be sorry for what they've done. They'll continue to follow the Antichrist and the False Prophet.

🗡🗡 BATTLE TACTICS

The Euphrates River (see illustration, page 138) is mentioned more than twenty-five times in the Bible, sometimes called the *"great river."* This great river has kept people of the East from coming over to the West. When the sixth angel pours out his bowl, this river will dry up, and the barrier will be gone. The kings of the East with their army of 200 <u>million</u> will attack Israel in what is called the Battle of Armageddon. The attackers will likely be an alliance of several Eastern nations.

Dr. William R. Goetz: It is significant that the Red Chinese leaders on several occasions in recent years, have boasted that they can field a "people's army" of 200 million militia.[4]

Don't Croak

John tells us that three evil spirits will come burping out of Satan's, the Antichrist's, and the False Prophet's mouths. We can't know for sure what these demons will look like, but a frog-like appearance is likely. The idea of frogs and demonic forces is not new. In ancient Egypt there was a frog-headed goddess named Heka, who was said to have demonic powers. Frogs are also associated with witches, spells, and the occult.

Demons aren't goofing off today, but they will be mega-busy during the Tribulation. The apostle Paul said, *"In later times some will abandon the faith and follow deceiving spirits*

KEY POINT
The fifth bowl judgment means darkness over all the earth.

GO!
Revelation 9:14–16 (million)

155

OUTSIDE **CONNECTION**

KEY SYMBOLS
Sixth Bowl Judgment
Euphrates River will dry up

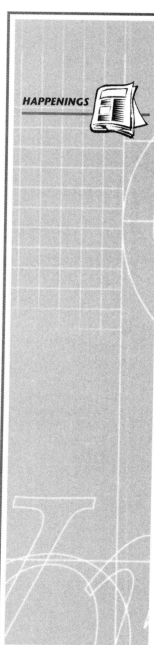

and things taught by demons" (1 Timothy 4:1). Be aware that Satan's demons are alive and well.

Hawaii's Big Island is being overrun by a dramatic population explosion of tree frogs, reaching a density in some places of as many as 8,000 per acre. The numbers of two types of non-native Caribbean frogs in Hawaii County have soared more than tenfold in less than two years. Earl Campbell, a biologist with the U.S. Agriculture Department, said the noisy frogs are moving to more areas of the Big Island, posing a threat to the economy and native wildlife, as well as preventing residents from sleeping. A single male frog's whistle-like call can reach up to 90 decibels. The jump in the number of amphibians could threaten native ecosystems. Every night, the frogs consume tens of thousands of insects, which normally would be eaten by native birds.[5]

> **Revelation 16:14**
> They are spirits of demons performing miraculous signs, and they go out to the kings of the whole world, to gather them for the battle on the great day of God Almighty.

Death Trap

When the sixth bowl is poured out, spirits of demons will use miracles to trick the leaders of the world. These leaders will be deceived and will follow the Antichrist and his demons right into the death trap called the great day of God Almighty or the Battle of Armageddon. Satan plans to gather a great army to go against God—an army, however, destined to fail!

Don't be deceived by sensational miracles. We often forget demons have limited power to do miracles. Jesus was talking about the end times when he said, *"False Christs and false prophets will appear and perform great signs and miracles to deceive even the elect—if that were possible. See, I have told you ahead of time"* (Matthew 24:24–25). We've been forewarned! Jesus, himself, wants us to be on the lookout for fakes.

Have you ever encountered a person who deceived you? Describe
what happened. _____

_____

How can you be on the lookout for fakes?_____

_____

_____

How can you know if a person is a false religious teacher or leader?_____

_____

_____

GET REAL Jesus warned us that fake teachers and prophets would come. These people will be convincing, and they will lead many away from the truth. Reading the Bible and understanding what it says is a great way to protect yourself from fakes. (Check out 2 Peter and LWBI, pages 225–227.) Also, if you're unsure about what people claim as truth, call them on it. Ask questions and search the Bible for answers. Watch how they live. It's important to be on guard and not believe *everything* you hear or see.

> **Revelation 16:15**
> "Behold, I come like a thief! Blessed is he who stays awake and keeps his clothes with him, so that he may not go naked and be shamefully exposed."

 ## ARMED ROBBERY!

Action movies often depict stakeouts where the cops sit outside the criminals' house, eating junk food and waiting endless hours for the bad guys to come home so they can arrest them. That is sort of the picture of this verse. Those who wait patiently and watch for Jesus will be rewarded.

This verse is a reference to the coming of Jesus at the end of the Tribulation. The demons will gather the armies of the world

at Armageddon, and only then will Jesus return and catch them all by surprise! Jesus will come like a thief in the night.

Some people may think this verse refers to the Rapture, but that has already happened.

> **Revelation 16:16**
> Then they gathered the kings together to the place that in Hebrew is called Armageddon.

Judgment Day

Armageddon is where it will all go down—the world as we know it, full of sin and ruin. Only one more bowl of judgment will take place before Jesus returns to rule as king. This is almost it, guys—the end of the age. After this comes the Millennium.

This is the only time the word *Armageddon* is found in the Bible. It has a ring to it, doesn't it? Armageddon is Hebrew and is the name of a place in northern Israel that is a large hill just west of the Jordan River in the plain of Esdralon (look for Megiddo on the map on page 159). When translated, the word means "Mount of Megiddo." Demons will gather the world's armies in Armageddon. The Euphrates River will dry up to allow this army of 200 million to approach from the East.

OUTSIDE CONNECTION

Dr. William R. Goetz: This seven-year period culminates with the war of Armageddon, when the armies of the world ruler (called the Antichrist), the Arab confederacy, a 200-million man force from the Far East and the remnant of the Russian power bloc, will converge on Palestine.[6]

KEY SYMBOLS

Seventh Bowl Judgment
"It is done!"

> **Revelation 16:17**
> The seventh angel poured out his bowl into the air, and out of the temple came a loud voice from the throne, saying, "It is done!"

The Grand Finale

The seventh bowl judgment will be it—the final blow. The phrase *"It is done!"* is similar to Jesus' last words on the cross, *"It is finished"* (John 19:30). The remaining events will bring an end to Satan's reign on earth. As we say in sports arenas, "Na na na na, na na na na, hey-eh-eh, good-bye."

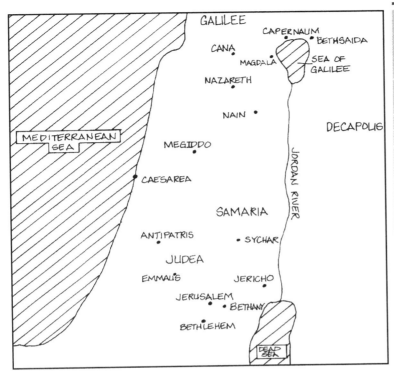

Map of Megiddo

This map of Israel shows the location of the city of Megiddo. It has become a symbol for the final battle of good and evil because Armageddon translated is "Mount of Megiddo."

159

> **Revelation 16:18**
> Then there came flashes of lightning, rumblings, peals of thunder and a severe earthquake. No earthquake like it has ever occurred since man has been on earth, so tremendous was the quake.

 ## MAJOR SHAKE-UP

When the ground starts rumbling, there will be no forgetting it. This will be the earthquake of all earthquakes! It will be a wake-up call for the world. When the seventh bowl pours into the air, the world will go absolutely nuts! Exploding flashes of light, loud rumblings, and clashes of thunder. The earth will act like a giant yo-yo, spinning out of control as the ground crumbles in all directions and fires break out.

 **HAPPENINGS**

Recent Deadly Quakes

Date of Earthquake	Place	Strength	How Deadly
January 26, 2000	India	Magnitude 7.9	Over 50,000 killed
January 13, 2000	El Salvador	Magnitude 7.6	Over 700 killed
September 21, 1999	Taiwan	Magnitude 7.6	2,400 killed
August 17, 1999	Western Turkey	Magnitude 7.4	17,000 killed
January 25, 1999	Western Columbia	Magnitude 6.1	171 killed
February 4, 1998	Northeast Afghanistan	Magnitude 6.1	5,000 killed

 GO!

Zechariah 12; 14
(Jerusalem)
Isaiah 13:4–6, 19–20;
Jeremiah 51:7, 25–
26 (prophets)

Split in Three

Babylon, the great city, will be divided into three parts as a result of this earthquake, but it won't be totally destroyed. All other cities, except <u>Jerusalem</u>, will be piles of rubble. In Revelation 14:8, one of the three angels predicted that Babylon would fall. A second angel then followed and declared Babylon *"Fallen."* Old Testament <u>prophets</u> also foretold the destruction of Babylon long before the angel did. The time for those prophecies to be fulfilled has come.

Heavy Stuff

The whole earth will be changed. Islands will slide into the ocean and mountains will be no more. Hail weighing a hundred pounds will fall from the sky! Imagine it! It will be raining ice stones the size of big sheep or Saint Bernard dogs. People will be crushed to death by these hailstones, and those who survive will curse God. People are still too stubborn to repent of their sins. They will cry out at God in anger rather than submission.

CHAPTER CHECKUP

1. What is the first bowl judgment?
2. What is the second bowl judgment?
3. What is the third bowl judgment?
4. What is the fourth bowl judgment?
5. What is the fifth bowl judgment?
6. What is the sixth bowl judgment?
7. What is the seventh, and last, bowl judgment?

CRASH COURSE

▶ When the seven bowls of God's wrath are poured out his judgments will come to an end.
▶ After the third bowl is emptied, the angel in charge of the waters and the tribulation saints will proclaim these judgments to be just and true. (Revelation 16:5–7)
▶ The Euphrates River will dry up to make way for the coming of the kings from the East. (Revelation 16:12)
▶ Three spirits will come out of the mouths of Satan, the Antichrist, and the False Prophet to call the kings of the earth together for the Battle of Armageddon. (Revelation 16:13–16)
▶ After the seventh bowl is poured out a great earthquake will rock the planet, destroying all cities except Jerusalem and Babylon, which will split into three parts. (Revelation 16:18–19)

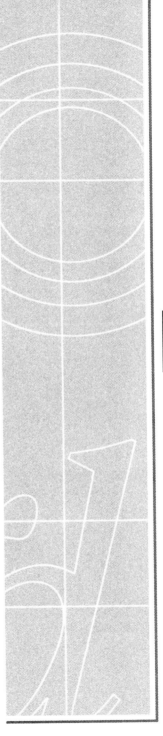

Babylon, Mother of False Religions

 LET'S DIVE IN

Hang on for some tough stuff! Chapter 17 tells us about a Babylonian woman who is both a mother and a city. This might not make any sense, so think "big picture" instead of little details.

As a mother, Babylon is a failure. Babylon turned against God. She messed up by giving birth to her "daughters," who are false religions: New Age, Satan worship, Mother Earth worship, globalism, humanism, Hinduism, and Islam. The followers of Babylon's daughters are religious people who will be left behind when the true church is raptured.

As a city, Babylon messed up by allowing false religions and leaders to meet within her city limits. During the Tribulation, Babylon the city will be filled with **adulterous** kings. This is a place where one-world religion and one-world trading will be

adulterous: here, people who believe false religions

Babylon
Daughters
• false religions
City of sin
• center of one-world government

intoxicated: drunk

Exodus 34:15–16;
2 Chronicles 21:
11–13 (often uses)
Revelation 4:6 (sea)
Revelation 17:15
(waters)
Revelation 17:1
(masses)

164

encouraged. Eventually, Jesus will return and completely destroy Babylon the mother *and* Babylon the city. Some day that will be!

Revelation 17:1–2
One of the seven angels who had the seven bowls came and said to me, "Come, I will show you the punishment of the great prostitute, who sits on many waters. With her the kings of the earth committed adultery and the inhabitants of the earth were **intoxicated** with the wine of her adulteries."

 SNEAK PEAK

John is invited to look at the punishment of Babylon the mother. She is called a religious prostitute because she is the one behind false religions. The Bible <u>often uses</u> the words *adultery* and *prostitute* to refer to the actions and people who do not follow God. John is getting a sneak peak at Babylon's not-so-pretty fate.

In the Bible, <u>sea</u> and <u>waters</u> stand for great numbers of people. They represent people, nations, and languages. The fact that this woman is pictured sitting upon these great <u>masses</u> shows that she will influence and be supported by large numbers of people.

The false religious system will commit adultery (cheat) with the political system or the leaders of the earth. Babylon will try to produce an accepted mix of religion and government.

OUTSIDE CONNECTION

Ed Hindson: *This will be the final phase of the New World Order. The idea of a new world religion of peace and cooperation is already being proposed. Religious unity has been endorsed by Pope John Paul II, the Dali Lama, and leaders of the World Council of Churches.*[1]

Revelation 17:3
Then the angel carried me away in the Spirit into a desert. There I saw a woman sitting on a scarlet beast that was covered with blasphemous names and had seven heads and ten horns.

Along for the Ride

John was under the control of the Holy Spirit when he was carried away into a desert and saw a woman sitting on a red beast. We already know the beast with seven heads and ten horns is the Antichrist. Since the woman will be sitting on the beast (beware of this duo), we can assume that her prostitute religion and the Antichrist will be on the earth at the same time.

At first the Antichrist will support her one-world religion and be under her authority, but things will eventually get unfriendly. Their relationship will be hurt by the woman's double identity. (Remember she is both the mother, the false religious system, and the <u>great city</u> Babylon, the economic center.) We see from this verse that all three—the false religious system, the city of Babylon, and the Antichrist—will exist during the first half of the Tribulation.

> ### Revelation 17:4
> The woman was dressed in purple and scarlet, and was glittering with gold, precious stones, and pearls. She held a golden cup in her hand, filled with **abominable** things and the filth of her adulteries.

All Dressed Up with Nowhere to Go

God hates when people worship anything or anyone but him. He calls that adultery. Through the power of demons, this wealthy-looking woman succeeds in encouraging people to worship anything and everything but God. The gold cup she holds is full of terrible things and false religions. The people who are enchanted with this woman will be spiritually blind. They will drink the wine of adultery—symbolic of **<u>deceiving spirits</u>**.

Hal Lindsey: I have found this about religion. The more false a religion is, usually the more wealth it has. And the more true a religion is, usually the less material things it has. And it doesn't seem to care about it. And I've seen the Christian church become poverty stricken spiritually as they have become wealthy materially.[2]

KEY POINT

The saved, regardless of their denomination, will be raptured, and the lost, regardless of their religious beliefs, will be left behind.

GO!
Revelation 17:18
(great city)

abominable: hateful

GO!
1 Timothy 4:1
(deceiving spirits)

OUTSIDE CONNECTION

deceiving spirits: demons

Do you believe in demons? Why or why not?_____

_____

In what ways do you think demons work today?_____

_____

_____

What might Satan want to do through his demons at your school or in your community?_____

_____

_____

 Your Move

 GET REAL

Many unbelievers today think they are too well educated to believe in the existence of demons. If you believe the Bible is true, you can't disregard the reality of demons. Satan is real. He's sly. He's slick. It's hard to fight against an enemy if you don't believe it's there! People who have trusted in Jesus Christ as Savior are much more powerful than Satan and his army. Satan's time is limited and his earthly rule will soon come to an end.

mystery: *a hidden truth*

abominations: *terrible sins*

> Revelation 17:5
>
> This title was written on her forehead: **MYSTERY** BABYLON THE GREAT THE MOTHER OF PROSTITUTES AND OF THE **ABOMINATIONS** OF THE EARTH.

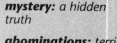 **GO!**
Genesis 11:1–9 (tower)

 **FULL CIRCLE**

The prostitute's title reveals where she will come from and what she will do. She will try to fake Christianity and promote a world religion. The one-world religious movement began at the <u>tower</u> of Babel, which was located at Old Testament Babylon (see illustration, page 138). That Babylon was destroyed, but it is being rebuilt along with the tower of Babel in Iraq. The prostitute is going full circle. She was born in Babylon and will be associated with that city again during the Tribulation. She will be known as the Mother of Prostitutes and the Mother of Abominations (sins) because many evil practices will flow from her.

> I saw that the woman was drunk with the blood of the saints, the blood of those who bore testimony to Jesus. When I saw her, I was greatly astonished. Then the angel said to me: "Why are you astonished? I will explain to you the mystery of the woman and of the beasts she rides, which has the seven heads and ten horns."

Mystery Woman

This prostitute will not only make other people drunk, she, herself, will be drunk as a skunk! She will be drunk, not on alcohol, but on the blood of the tribulation saints. She will be so determined to create her one-world religion that she will actually be responsible for killing many believers.

John was pretty confused and amazed when he saw this woman, so God used an angel to help clear up his astonishment. This angel explains two things to John: (1) the mystery of the woman, and (2) the mystery of the beast with the seven heads and ten horns. Stay tuned for the explanation in the rest of chapter 17.

Revelation 17:8

> "The beast, which you saw, once was, now is not, and will come up out of the **Abyss** and go to his destruction. The **inhabitants** of the earth whose names have not been written in the book of life from the creation of the world will be astonished when they see the beast, because he once was, now is not, and yet will come."

Abyss: place where God is holding the worst of the demonic spirits

inhabitants: people who live in an area

A RIDDLE

The explanation the angel gives might make you want to roll your eyes. The angel seems to be speaking in riddles—a beast *"who once was, now is not, and yet will come."* Say what?

Well, the beast existed before John was born—*"once was."* This beast did not exist when John received this revelation—*"now is not."* However, this beast will reappear at some unspecified time in the future—*"will come."* The beast will have ties to Satan and the demonic spirits imprisoned beneath the earth's surface. He will come out of the Abyss and will eventu-

GO!
Revelation 19:20
(Lake of Fire)

KEY SYMBOLS

Seven Heads/Hills
Seven kings
• kingdoms or world governments

GO!
Jeremiah 51:24–25;
Daniel 2:35–45
(mountains)

Gentile: non-Jewish people

ally go to his destruction when God throws him in the <u>Lake of Fire</u>. When this happens, the beast will take his followers, *"the inhabitants of the earth whose names have not been written in the book of life from the creation of the world,"* with him.

> **Revelation 17:9**
> "This calls for a mind with wisdom. The seven heads are seven hills on which the woman sits."

Wise Up

Figuring out this verse requires an understanding of Scripture (not geography). The seven heads on the beast are seven hills on which the woman sits. This seems pretty basic, but it isn't as easy as it seems. Revelation 17:10 says that these seven hills are not really seven hills, but instead are seven world governments. The problem is figuring out if the hills are (1) a religious system or a city that sits on seven hills, (2) seven kings or kingdoms, or (3) both.

The Bible tells us that hills or <u>mountains</u> are symbolic of kingdoms. So it is possible that these seven hills are seven kings or kingdoms. However, some experts say the seven hills are a reference to Rome (the city on seven hills). If that view is right, this is saying the prostitute will control and be supported by Rome. The bottom line is we don't know for sure!

> **Revelation 17:10–11**
> "There are also seven kings. Five have fallen, one is, the other has not yet come; but when he does come, he must remain for a little while. The beast who once was, and now is not, is an eighth king. He belongs to the seven and is going to his destruction."

 **MORE RIDDLES**

Just when you thought you had it all figured out, we come to some even more confusing stuff! The seven heads are seven hills, and they are also seven kings. The word kings can also be translated *kingdoms*. It makes more sense to say the seven heads are seven kingdoms because history and Scripture show that there have been seven **Gentile** world kingdoms.

"*Five have fallen*" refers to the five Gentile world kingdoms (Assyrian, Medo-Persian, Greek, Egyptian, and Babylonian) that existed before John's lifetime. "*One is*" refers to the sixth kingdom (Roman) that existed *during* John's lifetime, and "*the other has not yet come*" refers to a seventh future kingdom (the revived Roman Empire) which will exist after John's lifetime. Bring on the gladiators! This seventh kingdom will remain ("*he must remain for a little while*") for the time of the seven-year Tribulation.

"*The beast who once was, and now is not*" is the Antichrist. He is an eighth king (or kingdom). "*He belongs to the seven*" means he will be one of the seven already mentioned. Since he is yet to come, he must come out of the seventh Gentile world kingdom, which will be the revived Roman Empire.

As "*an eighth king*" the Antichrist will take over the seventh Gentile world kingdom and establish his own brand of world government—a New World Order or one-world government. The Antichrist will become a powerful leader in that government, take it over, and turn it into a satanic state. You got all that, right?

> ### Revelation 17:12
> "The ten horns you saw are ten kings who have not yet received a kingdom, but who for one hour will receive authority as kings along with the beast."

▶▶ MEN OF THE HOUR

The ten horns mentioned are ten kings that will rule with the Antichrist. A world government will be established and divided into ten regions with a ruler over each region. The Antichrist will rise to power in the European region and take it over. He will forcefully take over two more regions, and then the leaders or kings of the remaining seven regions will surrender their authority to him.

These ten kings will receive authority for one hour. It doesn't mean they'll get to sit on their throne for sixty minutes before being booted out! In this case, "*one hour*" is a Bible term that means a short time—the Tribulation. This is important because Jesus promised to keep his faithful believers from the "***hour of***

169

KEY POINT
God will keep the faithful from the hour of trial.

hour of trial:
Tribulation

trial" that is coming upon the world. This helps support the idea of a pre-Tribulation Rapture (Revelation 3:10). The church will not be on earth during the short rule of the ten kings with the Antichrist.

> **Revelation 17:13–14**
> "They have one purpose and will give their power and authority to the beast. They will make war against the Lamb, but the Lamb will overcome them because he is Lord of lords and King of kings—and with him will be his called, chosen, and faithful followers."

Kings with No Backbone

These kings won't have minds of their own. They will follow the orders of the Antichrist. They will do everything he says and will be powerless without his influence.

At the end of the Tribulation, the Antichrist and his ten kings will make war against the Lamb and his <u>called</u>, <u>chosen</u>, and <u>faithful</u> followers. The outcome of this war was decided long ago. No surprise here! The Lamb will win the Battle of Armageddon because he is the Lord of lords and King of kings. These kings and the Antichrist don't stand a chance!

Dictators usually come to power by using one or more of these tactics: violence, force, or political tricks. After coming to power, they usually have to continue to use force to stay in power. Because of this they usually make laws that take away basic freedoms such as freedom to gather in groups, freedom of speech, and freedom of worship. Adolf Hitler, who ruled Germany during World War 2, was one such dictator.

> **Revelation 17:15**
> Then the angel said to me, "The waters you saw, where the prostitute sits, are peoples, multitudes, nations, and languages."

Wrapped around Her Finger

Behind the prostitute's popularity and power are the people groups that she's tricked into following her. She has fooled people on a worldwide scale. They are totally hooked by her wicked religion.

> **Revelation 17:16**
> "The beast and the ten horns you saw will hate the prostitute. They will bring her to ruin and leave her naked; they will eat her flesh and burn her with fire."

🔺🔺 A VIOLENT END

During the first half of the Tribulation, the Antichrist will put up with religious Babylon (the mother and her false religious system). Now John tells us that the Antichrist and the ten kingdoms (or kings) have had enough of her. About time! They will rise up against Babylon at the midpoint of the Tribulation and will *"bring her to ruin."*

The Antichrist will enter the Jewish Temple in Jerusalem and will declare that he <u>is God</u>! Since the Antichrist is claiming to be God, he will no longer want another religion competing with him. The Antichrist and his allies will destroy the prostitute's religious system. They'll take her wealth and torture and kill her unsuspecting followers. The fact that they will *"eat her flesh and burn her with fire"* indicates the lengths to which they will go to have religious Babylon destroyed.

GO!
2 Thessalonians 2:4
(is God)

OUTSIDE CONNECTION

Dr. William R. Goetz: *Thus, at the midpoint of the seven-year treaty the Antichrist decides he no longer needs the false church. He and the False Prophet, energized by Satan, have become wonder workers in their own right. Thus, he proclaims himself to be god, and the prostitute is destroyed by him. How ironic!*[3]

> **Revelation 17:17**
> "For God has put it into their hearts to accomplish his purpose by agreeing to give the beast their power to rule, until God's words are fulfilled."

Okaying a Mini-Rule

The Antichrist doesn't know it, but God is toying with him. God is allowing him to rule and be powerful, but only for a short time. We sometimes wonder why God would allow the Antichrist and these ten kings to get so much <u>power</u>. God does this so they will be strong enough to destroy all the false religions. Without so much power they could not do that. The uproar would be too great. If the church was doing its job, these false religions would not exist and the Antichrist and his ten puppet kings would not be needed. But after the true church is raptured, the false church will be a part of the false religious system. So God will put it in the heart of the Antichrist and his ten kings to destroy this false religious system.

> **Revelation 17:18**
> "The woman you saw is the great city that rules over the kings of the earth."

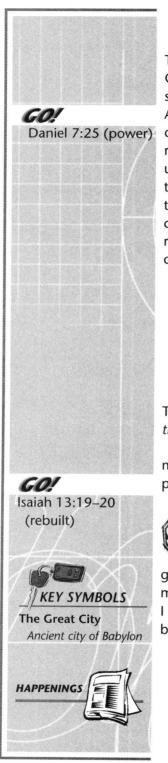

Side panel:

GO!
Daniel 7:25 (power)

GO!
Isaiah 13:19–20 (rebuilt)

KEY SYMBOLS
The Great City
Ancient city of Babylon

HAPPENINGS

BABYLON REBUILT

This verse says that the woman is *"the great city that rules over the kings of the earth."*

There are several prophecies about the city of Babylon that must be fulfilled. Chapter 18 covers the fulfillment of these prophecies. Although Babylon had fallen, she is now <u>rebuilt</u>.

STOP Some people are afraid to take this verse literally and speculate that the city mentioned is Rome, Jerusalem, New York, the United States, part of the European group of nations, or a nation in control of those nations. We must not attempt to read into Scripture things that aren't there. I believe these verses teach that Babylon will be literally rebuilt.

Sometime during the 1980s Iraq started rebuilding the ancient city of Babylon with the hope of turning it into a major tourist attraction. About $6 million a year was being spent on archaeological work and construction. At the same time the nation was involved in a war with

Iran and Saddam Hussein was looking for a way to stir Iraqi anger against the Iranians. He remembered that Persia (Iran) helped destroy ancient Babylon. He reminded his people of this as he poured millions of dollars into the city. Many of the ancient buildings, including the famous tower of Babel, have now been rebuilt.[4]

CHAPTER cHECKUP

1. Describe Babylon the mother and Babylon the city.
2. What influence was John under when he saw the vision of a woman sitting on a scarlet beast?
3. What do the ten horns represent?
4. Who will overcome the Antichrist and the kings (or king-doms)?
5. Who will give the beast and the ten kings power and why?

CRASH COURSE

▶ An angel will show John the punishment of the prostitute who sits on the scarlet beast. She is the one with whom the people of the earth will commit adultery. (Revelation 17:1–5)

▶ The woman who sits on the beast is Babylon the Great. She, the Mother of Prostitutes, will kill so many of the saints who follow Jesus that she will be drunk on their blood. (Revelation 17:5–6)

▶ The beast who will come out of the Abyss and go to his destruction will astonish many because he was, wasn't, and yet will come. His seven heads represent seven king-doms—the beast is the eighth kingdom that will come out of the seventh. (Revelation 17:8–11)

▶ The ten horns are ten kings who will rule with the Anti-christ during the Tribulation. Their only purpose is to give their power to the eighth king (the beast). (Revelation 17:11–14)

▶ God will accomplish his purpose by planting the idea of destroying Babylon, the mother, into the minds of the beast and his ten kings. (Revelation 17:16–17)

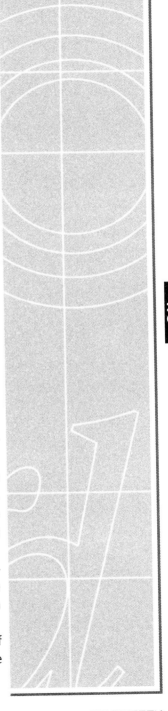

173

Babylon, City of Sin

175

 LET'S DIVE IN

The world is already working toward a one-world government, a one-world religion, and a one-world currency. All that is left to be developed is one-stop shopping. This will come, and it will be called Babylon.

Certain scholars suggest the great city described in this chapter cannot be the literal Babylon. They seem to think the current city of Babylon is too small, too remote, and more of a tourist attraction. They underestimate what the Antichrist could do if several dozen nations flew in work crews and materials from around the world. (Look at how fast Las Vegas has grown as a world attraction.) A hundred nations with unlimited financing, hundreds of engineers, modern equipment, and thousands of workers could turn Babylon into a great city virtually overnight.

> **Revelation 18:1–2**
> After this I saw another angel coming down from heaven. He had great authority, and the earth was **illuminated** by his splendor. With a mighty voice he shouted: "Fallen! Fallen is Babylon the Great! She has become a home for demons and a haunt for every evil spirit, a haunt for every unclean and **detestable** bird."

illuminated: shined brightly

detestable: undesirable

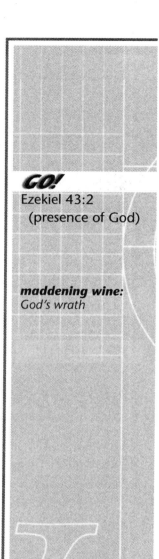

BABYLON—A HAUNTED HOUSE

John gets to see it all. First, in chapter 17, he witnesses the coming destruction of the one-world religious system. Now John sees another angel of doom proclaiming that Babylon, the one-world political and economic center, will also fall. This angel will be bright like the sun because he will come directly from the <u>presence of God</u>. He will prophesy about the future of Babylon the Great. Babylon is destined to become the home of demons, evil spirits, and unclean birds. Good-bye Babylon. Hello destruction.

GO!
Ezekiel 43:2
(presence of God)

> **Revelation 18:3**
> "For all the nations have drunk the **maddening wine** of her adulteries. The kings of the earth committed adultery with her, and the merchants of the earth grew rich from her excessive luxuries."

maddening wine:
God's wrath

All the Rage

Babylon will become the hub of cool. Governments and businesses will be totally caught up in this concept of Babylon the Great. The excitement over this city will be like getting drunk! Just as the internet and websites took off in the early 1990s, this city will be hailed as the next big thing. No one will want to be left out of the idea of one-world government and one-world trade. Those who invest in Babylon will become filthy rich!

HAPPENINGS

In 1994 over two hundred religious leaders met in Sudan to discuss beginning a world council of religions. Representing all faiths, this council would foster cooperation among the world's religions. The conference members weren't content to call for peace and religious harmony. They called for a new political order too![1]

OUTSIDE CONNECTION

Ed Hindson: The fall of communism has paved the way for a world economy and a world government. The global web is tightening around us every day.[2]

SINS PILED MILES HIGH

God still cares about what happens to his people. He doesn't want them to suffer when he takes out his wrath on Babylon. He is warning his people to get out, and get out quick. Babylon's sins are piled up to heaven, and God is ready to unleash terrible plagues on her. Look out!

In the Old Testament, God didn't overlook what Babylon did when she tried to build a <u>tower</u> to heaven. God confused the people's language, so they couldn't understand each other. Building stopped, and people scattered throughout the world. Now, in order to stop Babylon's sins from piling up any higher, God has chosen to burn her to the ground.

Double Payback

It will seem for a time that Babylon is getting away with the murder of God's people. Time is ticking, however, on Babylon's lifeline. She's about to become toast. God will deal with her the way she dealt with others—with no <u>mercy</u>.

It is predicted that in less than thirty years there will be no Christians in the Palestinian-controlled areas of Israel. Palestinian persecution is driving them out of the land where Christ was born.

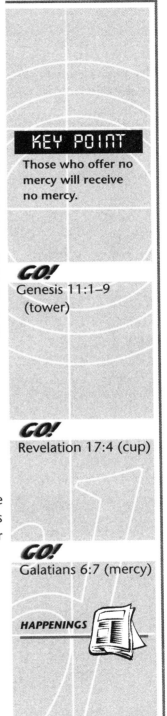

KEY POINT

Those who offer no mercy will receive no mercy.

GO!
Genesis 11:1–9 (tower)

177

GO!
Revelation 17:4 (cup)

GO!
Galatians 6:7 (mercy)

HAPPENINGS

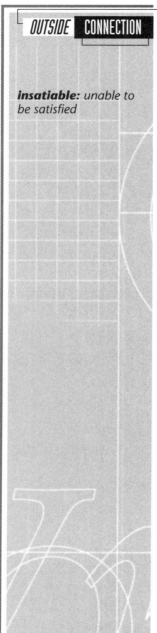

insatiable: *unable to be satisfied*

*William T. James: A significant body of prophetic text predicts a generation just before the end of the age that will ultimately go into a materialistically mad frenzy where human love will be extinguished. At the same time, the appetite for money will become **insatiable**, and seducers and evildoers will grow worse and worse.*[3]

> **Revelation 18:7**
> "Give her as much torture and grief as the glory and luxury she gave herself. In her heart she boasts, 'I sit as queen; I am not a widow, and I will never mourn.'"

Big Time Bragger

The people who live and work in Babylon will be blind to the possibility of destruction. They will brag about how great they are and how wonderful their city is. Babylon will think she has no reason to deny herself every comfort. Babylon will become conceited and forget that the God who brought her down before can bring her down again. In the end, the great sadness of the godly will be turned into glory, and the glory of the godless will be turned into great sadness.

> **Revelation 18:8**
> "Therefore in one day her plagues will overtake her: death, mourning, and famine. She will be consumed by fire, for mighty is the Lord God who judges her."

Gone, Just Like That

Babylon will go from being all that to being nothing. As the home of one-world government and global trade, Babylon will think of herself as unstoppable. Unfortunately for her, God is able to stop her easily. What no earthly army can do, God will accomplish in one day! First, the angel of death will pass over Babylon. Second, this city, which just finished saying, *"I will never mourn,"* will cry out loud. Third, this rich city will suddenly run out of food, and finally, it will be burned to the ground. Sizzle!

Babylon will go from being the richest place to the poorest in a matter of minutes. Why do you think Babylon will fall that way?_____

_____

_____

How important do you think money and power are today?_____

_____

_____

What role do you think money should play in a Christian's life?_____

_____

_____

GET REAL Money isn't wrong. Planning for the future isn't bad either. What's important is to keep God in the center of your life and trust him to take care of you. The city of Babylon will fall not because it is prosperous, but because it refuses to acknowledge God.

Revelation 18:9–10

"When the kings of the earth who committed adultery with her and shared her luxury see the smoke of her burning, they will weep and mourn over her. Terrified at her torment, they will stand far off and cry: 'Woe! Woe, O great city, O Babylon, city of power! In one hour your doom has come!'"

COLOSSAL COLLAPSE

When Babylon falls, world leaders and those who supported her will see the smoke and will cry. The nations that thrived financially from Babylon will be poor. The value of businesses and property will tumble. People will panic. They won't care about the city; they will care about themselves.

A few experts suggest that *"one hour"* could mean a short space of time or an event spread over a few days. But most think it means sudden or instant destruction. That would add to the panic and terror the people feel.

cargoes: *merchandise, stuff*

> ### Revelation 18:11–13
> "The merchants of the earth will weep and mourn over her because no one buys their **cargoes** anymore—cargoes of gold, silver, precious stones, and pearls; fine linen, purple, silk and scarlet cloth; every sort of citron wood, and articles of every kind made of ivory, costly wood, bronze, iron, and marble; cargoes of cinnamon and spice, of incense, myrrh and frankincense, of wine and olive oil, of fine flour and wheat; cattle and sheep; horses and carriages; and bodies and souls of men."

Clearance Sale

Purple and scarlet clothing were worn only by the rich and famous in John's day. Silk was so scarce it was outlawed. Citron wood was so valuable that people didn't build with it, but used it only for decoration. During the Tribulation, Babylon will be rich enough to import these valuable materials for frequent use. Babylon will be the world's biggest market for luxury items. It will be a place where millionaires and billionaires hang out. The companies that deal in Babylon will do anything to get rich, even sell human beings into slavery. Then, all of a sudden, as God doles out his judgment, stores and salespeople won't find any buyers.

OUTSIDE CONNECTION

David Hocking: One is astonished to find among the items that will be lost to these merchants, the bodies and souls of men (Revelation 18:13). Human life will be cheap, and people will be sold as merchandise. One cannot help but wonder if the prostitution and pornography enterprises of our world are not indicated by these words.[4]

HAPPENINGS

Slavery is a tragic reality in some parts of the world. In Sudan slavery is conducted regularly, and there is no outcry from the world's public leaders or human rights activists. The holy war being fought against Christians and non-Muslims in Sudan has caused the death of about three million people. Christian and non-Muslim villages are being burned, men are being killed, and women and children are being sold in open slave markets for sometimes as little as $10–15 apiece.

> **Revelation 18:14–16**
>
> "They will say, 'The fruit you longed for is gone from you. All your riches and splendor have vanished, never to be recovered.' The merchants who sold these things and gained their wealth from her will stand far off, terrified at her torment. They will weep and mourn and cry out: 'Woe! Woe, O great city, dressed in fine linen, purple and scarlet, and glittering with gold, precious stones, and pearls!'"

POOF, VANISHED!

Even though the business world has lost a bundle, these investors will be too chicken to approach Babylon's destruction and see it for themselves. Instead, they will likely watch the city's destruction on TV from the comfort of their majestic homes—like cowards. Their distance from the situation, however, won't ease their losses. When people make <u>money</u> a god and forget to worship the real God, all that is left when their riches fail them is sadness and shock.

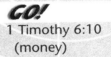

GO!
1 Timothy 6:10
(money)

> **Revelation 18:17–19**
>
> "'In one hour such great wealth has been brought to ruin!' Every sea captain, and all who travel by ship, the sailors, and all who earn their living from the sea, will stand far off. When they see the smoke of her burning, they will exclaim, 'Was there ever a city like this great city?' They will throw dust on their heads, and with weeping and mourning cry out: 'Woe! Woe, O great city, where all who had ships on the sea became rich through her wealth! In one hour she has been brought to ruin!'"

Sail Away

The sudden destruction of such great <u>treasure</u> in such a short time will be terrible. First, we read that the kings, dictators, and politicians who supported Babylon will cry. Then, we read that the businesspeople who traded with her will weep. Now we learn the workers on the sea who transported her goods will be upset.

Hauling the merchandise of Babylon will be big business, but in one short hour everything will be gone. All the people

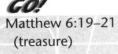

GO!
Matthew 6:19–21
(treasure)

GO!
Revelation 18:10, 17
(one hour)

GO!
Isaiah 13:19–22;
Jeremiah 50:38–40
(prophets)
James 5:1–6
(apostles)

millstone: *large doughnut-shaped stone used for grinding grain*

KEY POINT
In the end, Babylon will have brought this judgment on herself for mistreating God's people.

who earned a good living transporting goods by sea will mourn the loss of their jobs and businesses.

Three times we're told that Babylon will fall in <u>one hour</u>. Some think this one hour could mean an atomic or nuclear explosion. The fact that people will not go near the city is another indication of this.

> **Revelation 18:20**
>
> "'Rejoice over her, O heaven! Rejoice, saints and apostles and prophets! God has judged her for the way she treated you.'"

Heaven Rejoices

"God has judged her for the way she treated you." In other words, it's payback time. God is just. Babylon's destruction is something the Old Testament <u>prophets</u> and New Testament <u>apostles</u> predicted, and the tribulation saints continuously pray for. We should join the angels in heaven in rejoicing when God's Word is fulfilled and the prayers of God's people are answered. See how differently God's people react (with happiness) from how the godless react (with horror).

> **Revelation 18:21–22**
>
> Then a mighty angel picked up a boulder the size of a large **millstone** and threw it into the sea, and said: "With such violence the great city of Babylon will be thrown down, never to be found again. The music of harpists and musicians, flute players and trumpeters, will never be heard in you again. No workman of any trade will ever be found in you again. The sound of a millstone will never be heard in you again."

CHUCKED INTO THE SEA

This is the third time we've read about the mighty angel. We don't know whether these are three different angels or the same angel. So let's tackle this boulder being thrown violently into the sea. This symbolizes the sudden, violent, and eternal destruction of future Babylon. *Kerplunk!* She's gone. The music that came out of a festive Babylon will disappear. The hustle and bustle of the happening city will be heard no more.

> ### Revelation 18:23–24
> "The light of a lamp will never shine in you again. The voice of bridegroom and bride will never be heard in you again. Your merchants were the world's greatest men. By your magic spell all the nations were led astray. In her was found the blood of prophets and of the saints, and of all who have been killed on the earth."

 **LIGHTS OUT**

Can you imagine what would happen if every light in New York City went out at the same time? Not only would it be eerie, but it would be dangerous, frightening, and the financial loss would be huge.

Babylon was a city that glowed 24/7. She was booming, thriving, and brightly lit. The owners and builders of Babylon were great men on earth. They used black magic, sorcery, and demonic practices to get what they wanted—until God turned off their lights and shut them down.

Don't pity them. Babylon has a long history as the city of Satan. The False Prophet will make his headquarters there during the last half of the Tribulation. He will worship the Antichrist and have no tolerance for the people of God. He will kill all those who don't have the mark of the beast. Babylon's destruction will be well deserved.

Jesus warned that false prophets will deceive many in the last days (Matthew 24:11). Be careful of any religious teacher who says bad things about Jesus and is against the Bible. Any message that says Jesus is not the Son of God and that he didn't die on the cross or rise again is not from God.

OUTSIDE CONNECTION

Larry Richards: These two chapters [Revelation 17 and 18] are among the most difficult to interpret in Revelation. However, it is clear that the dominant figure—Mystery Babylon—represents the unification of the western world under the Antichrist. But the apparent success of this agent of Satan is to be short-lived. All that the Antichrist builds—a

one-world religion and a totally materialistic society—soon comes tumbling down.[5]

CHAPTER CHECKUP

1. Who lives in Babylon?
2. What will call God's people out of Babylon?
3. How high are Babylon's sins piled up?
4. What will happen to Babylon in the end?
5. Why will merchants, businesses, wealthy investors, and sea captains be sad?
6. Why will heaven, the saints, and the apostles rejoice?

CRASH COURSE

▶ An angel will come from the presence of God and declare the destruction of the great city, Babylon. (Revelation 18:1–3)
▶ A heavenly voice will call God's people out of Babylon so that they will not share in her crimes and judgment. (Revelation 18:4–7)
▶ Babylon will be destroyed by God in one hour. Her sudden destruction will leave the world crying over the loss of money. (Revelation 18:8–19)
▶ Those in heaven, who suffered at Babylon's hands, will rejoice over God's judgment of her. (Revelation 18:20)
▶ A mighty angel will throw a boulder into the sea. This represents Babylon's total destruction; she will never rise again. (Revelation 18:21–24)

The Beginning of the End

 LET'S DIVE IN

It's time—time for Jesus to take over the world. The terrible judgments of the Tribulation are about over. Humankind's effort to bring peace on earth *without* God is done. Jesus will finally return to earth and bring joy and blessing to all believers.

> **Revelation 19:1**
> After this I heard what sounded like the roar of a great multitude in heaven shouting: **"Hallelujah!** Salvation and glory and power belong to our God, . . ."

Hallelujah: Hebrew word meaning "praise the Lord"

 THE REAL HALLELUJAH CHORUS

After Babylon is destroyed and people around the world are crying, the roar of a great multitude will be heard in heaven. Those doing the shouting will most likely be the tribulation saints, but will include others such as the Old Testament saints, the church, and the angels. The cheering and hoopla will be directed at God because he is able to save, judge, and overcome his enemies! Plan to be there to participate in this chorale!

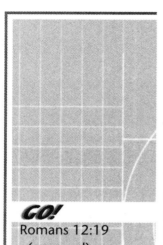

> ### Revelation 19:2–3
> ". . . for true and just are his judgments. He has condemned the great prostitute who corrupted the earth by her adulteries. He has avenged on her the blood of his servants." And again they shouted: "Hallelujah! The smoke from her goes up for ever and ever."

Justice Is Served

Those in heaven will praise God and declare that his judgments are *"true and just."* God has destroyed the one-world religious system and has <u>avenged</u> the death of his people. Keep in mind that the wicked never get away with their sins forever. God will repay, or judge, everyone who has ever harmed his people. His judgments are fair because he gives people what they deserve. This verse refers to more than just the destruction of Babylon. It celebrates the eternal destruction of those who hurt God's people.

GO!
Romans 12:19
(avenged)

> ### Revelation 19:4–5
> The twenty-four elders and the four living creatures fell down and worshiped God, who was seated on the throne. And they cried: "Amen, Hallelujah!" Then a voice came from the throne, saying: "Praise our God, all you his servants, you who fear him, both small and great!"

Wonderful Worship

The <u>elders</u> and the four living creatures will fall down as they did before and <u>worship God</u> who sits on the heavenly throne. It is impossible to say whose voice comes from the throne because both God the Father and God the Son will be on the throne. We do know, however, that the voice will invite everyone who serves the Lord to join in!

GO!
Revelation 4:4
(elders)
Psalm 106:47–48;
 Revelation 5:8, 14,
 7:11; 11:16
(worship God)

> ### Revelation 19:6–7
> Then I heard what sounded like a great multitude, like the roar of rushing waters and like loud peals of thunder, shouting: "Hallelujah! For our Lord God Almighty reigns. Let us rejoice and be glad and give him glory! For the wedding of the Lamb has come, and his bride has made herself ready."

186

HERE COMES THE BRIDE

A popular praise song chorus repeats the words "our God reigns." That's pretty much the gist of this verse. In response to the invitation in Revelation 19:5, the church and all God's servants will shout praises to God because he is so great and mighty.

It's time for the Lamb's (Christ's) marriage to the church. The church, sometimes called the bride of Christ, is ready just like a bride waiting to walk down the aisle. (Guys will be part of this bride too; it's not just a wedding for girls.) God's servants will rejoice and be glad because this wedding will be the greatest wedding celebration of all. It will be the party of all parties!

A special union will exist between Jesus and the church, similar to the union that a husband and wife share. In both instances the two <u>become one</u>. <u>Jesus</u> is coming back to earth where he and his <u>bride</u> will be together as one. Before they can rule together, though, they have to be married. Jesus will not come back to earth without his people, and his people will not rule the earth without him.

> **Revelation 19:8**
> "Fine linen, bright and clean, was given her to wear." (Fine linen stands for the righteous acts of the saints.)

 ## WHITE WEDDING

A bride wouldn't think of appearing at her wedding without a special dress. She spends hours preparing for the day. In the same way Christians have the opportunity to prepare for their marriage to Christ. We will wear fine linen, which stands for our righteous acts. But Christians are only able to do good things because they have Christ's power in them. <u>Faith</u> in God makes our righteous acts possible. When the marriage takes place, we will lay our own righteousness to the side and put on the holiness and righteousness of Jesus Christ.

KEY POINT

The church is the bride of Christ.

 **GO!**

Ephesians 5:22–25 (become one)
Matthew 22:1–14 (Jesus)
2 Corinthians 11:2 (bride)

KEY SYMBOLS

Wedding of the Lamb
Equipping saints to rule with Christ

 **GO!**

Philippians 3:9 (faith)

KEY SYMBOLS

Fine Linen
Our righteous acts on earth

187

Our need for the right kind of clothes should not be taken lightly. We cannot go to this wedding without Christ's gift of clothing—his righteousness. We must be properly dressed, or we will be thrown into outer darkness where there will be weeping and **gnashing** of teeth (Matthew 8:12).

gnashing: *grinding together*

> **Revelation 19:9**
>
> Then the angel said to me, "Write: 'Blessed are those who are invited to the wedding supper of the Lamb!'" And he added, "These are the true words of God."

Supper Bell's a Ringing

Every wedding has a reception. Our marriage to Christ will be followed by a big wedding banquet too. Again John heard an angel tell him to write. This time he is told to write about the invitations to the wedding supper of the Lamb. It's hotter than the hottest celebrity after-Grammy-party guest list. The guests must be saved people who are not part of the church.

Three passages from the New Testament can help us better understand this idea of a marriage between Jesus and the church:

GO!
Matthew 25:1–13 (ten virgins)

parable: *story with a heavenly meaning used to illustrate unfamiliar things*

1. *The **parable** of the ten virgins*—Just as the ten virgins (people) heard that the bridegroom (Jesus) and his bride (the church) were coming back for their wedding banquet, so too will Jesus come back to earth with his church at the end of the Tribulation for the marriage supper of the Lamb. Only those who have received Jesus as their Savior (those with oil) will be allowed to attend this banquet on earth.

GO!
Matthew 22:1–14 (wedding banquet)
Matthew 26:29 (fruit)

2. *The parable of the wedding banquet*—This parable tells us about a king (God) who prepared a wedding banquet for his son (Jesus). He sent out invitations, but many of those invited (unbelievers) made excuses for not attending, so he invited others (believers). One man (an unbeliever) was not wearing the right kind of clothes (fine linens) so he was escorted out. The wedding clothes signify the kind of righteousness needed to attend the banquet. God provides the right clothes to those who accept Jesus as their Savior. Those who do not have the

188

A testimony is a true account of how a person came to a certain place in his or her life and often involves a religious conversion experience. Have you ever heard a person give a testimony, and what did you think about it?_____

_____

What would you say if you gave a testimony about Jesus?_____

_____

What testimony does Jesus give about himself?_____

_____

The testimony of Jesus has to do with his predictions about himself and the fulfillment of those predictions. Jesus said he would <u>die, be buried, and be raised</u> from the dead. Jesus also said he would <u>come again</u> to earth. These things all came true and are a part of his testimony. As a Christian, you can share your testimony with others. You may think you don't have anything to say, but if you tell others what Jesus means to you, that testimony may have eternal results.

189

right clothes are not prepared to spend eternity with God.

3. *The **Last Supper***—This occasion in Scripture provides insight as well. Jesus said he will not drink of the <u>fruit</u> of the vine again until he drinks it in his Father's kingdom. His Father's kingdom is his **Millennial Kingdom** on earth.

GO!
1 Corinthians 15:3–4 (die, be buried, and be raised)
Matthew 24:27; John 14:3 (come again)

Last Supper: *last meal Jesus ate before he was crucified*

Millennial Kingdom: *one-thousand-year reign of Jesus on earth*

Revelation 19:10
At this I fell at his feet to worship him. But he said to me, "Do not do it! I am a fellow servant with you and with your brothers who hold to the testimony of Jesus. Worship God! For the testimony of Jesus is the spirit of prophecy."

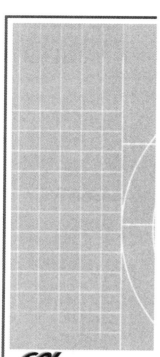

Stop Worshiping Me!

When John fell at the angel's feet and started worshiping the ground the angel walked on, the angel was not pleased. He called John on it. John was bowing to the wrong guy! The angel wanted him to *"worship God!"*

The *"testimony of Jesus"* means Jesus' finished work on the cross and the fulfillment of prophecies when he died and rose again.

> **Revelation 19:11**
> I saw heaven standing open and there before me was a white horse, whose rider is called Faithful and True. With justice he judges and makes war.

 SPECTACULAR RETURN

This verse just might be the most exciting verse in the entire Bible! The Old Testament prophets predicted this event, <u>Jesus</u> said it would come to pass, and the New Testament writers wrote about it. Everything we've studied so far in Revelation has been building up to this great event—Jesus' return to earth! Jesus' return will be a wonderful sight for the saints who are still alive on earth, but a scary sight for the Antichrist and his followers.

Heaven will open. It opened the first time when <u>John went up</u> to heaven identifying the Rapture of the church. It will open a second time when Jesus comes back with his church.

A second rider on a white horse will appear. (The <u>first rider</u> on a white horse was the Antichrist.) The second rider (Jesus) will be called *"Faithful and True"*—faithful because he has done and will do everything God asks him to do, and true because Jesus will do everything he said he would. Jesus said he would return, and, bravo, he will appear from heaven, fulfilling his own prophecy.

"With justice he judges and makes war" is the reason why he will <u>come back</u>. He will return to settle a big score. He'll be a warrior who will <u>judge</u> all the people of the earth. He will deal with their sin, settle their eternal destiny, and take over as King. What he does will be just and right.

190

GO!
Matthew 24:30
(Jesus)

GO!
Revelation 4:1–2
(John went up)
Revelation 6:2
(first rider)
Matthew 16:27
(come back)
Revelation 14:14–20
(judge)

KEY SYMBOLS

Second Rider on White Horse
Jesus

> **Revelation 19:12**
> His eyes are like blazing fire, and on his head are many crowns. He has a name written on him that no one knows but he himself.

A Secret Name

When Jesus comes back to earth as judge, he will be unstoppable. Christ's <u>fiery eyes</u> will reveal his insight, knowledge, and anger. He knows everything and will use those eyes to see right through each and every human's heart and soul.

Jesus' many crowns reveal his royalty, authority, and majesty. He will have complete power in heaven and on the earth.

We know Jesus by many names: Christ, Lord, Son of God, Son of man, Wonderful, Almighty God, Prince of Peace. When Jesus returns to earth, he will wear a special, secret name that only he and God will know. Christians know his name is great, but our human minds aren't big enough to understand that greatness.

> **Revelation 19:13**
> He is dressed in a robe dipped in blood, and his name is the Word of God.

 ## ROBE DIPPED IN BLOOD

The *"robe dipped in blood"* is symbolic of what is about to take place. The prophet Isaiah tells us that this blood-soaked robe represents the <u>blood</u> of Jesus' enemies. When Jesus comes back, he will deal harshly with hundreds of millions of unbelievers at the Battle of Armageddon. This battle will be the bloodiest on record. No one who is against God will be left standing. The score: God—100; Man—0.

Jesus' name is the *"Word of God."* Here's the scoop:

1. There is the written Word of God (John 5:39).
2. There is the spoken Word of God (John 3:34; 6:63).
3. There is the living Word of God (John 1:1, 14; Hebrews 4:12).

GO!
Revelation 1:14; 2:18 (fiery eyes)

KEY SYMBOLS

Jesus
Eyes like blazing fire
  • insight, knowledge, and anger
Many crowns
  • royalty, authority, and majesty

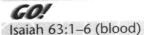

GO!
Isaiah 63:1–6 (blood)

KEY SYMBOLS

Jesus
White robe dipped in blood
  • blood of his enemies
Word of God
  • expression of God in the flesh

KEY SYMBOLS

Sharp Sword
Word of God

Iron Scepter
God's standards

Winepress of His Wrath
Judgment of the nations

Ephesians 6:17
(Word of God)
Romans 8:37 (loved)
Psalm 2:9; Revelation
2:27 (iron scepter)

The Bible is the written Word of God. The message of the Holy Spirit that filled preachers, evangelists, and others is the spoken Word of God. Jesus is the living Word of God. He is the one who fulfills both the *written* and the *spoken* Word of God.

> **Revelation 19:14–15**
> The armies of heaven were following him, riding on white horses and dressed in fine linen, white and clean. Out of his mouth comes a sharp sword with which to strike down the nations. "He will rule them with an iron scepter." He treads the winepress of the fury of the wrath of God Almighty.

Word Power

The armies of heaven, made up of Christ's followers, will follow Jesus out of heaven. They will be dressed in fine linens, and will be white and clean.

Jesus is the only one in the great heavenly army who needs any sort of weapon. The only weapon he needs is a sharp sword that he will use to strike down the nations. This weapon is the <u>Word of God</u>. Jesus will be the one who conquers. The victory doesn't belong to Christians. If it weren't for Jesus who <u>loved</u> us, we would be in the wrong army and would be defeated.

Once Jesus comes, the Millennium will begin. During this time, Jesus will rule with an *"iron scepter."* In other words, he'll establish his standard for living. There will no longer be any tolerance for lies, war, murder, theft. He'll stomp them out like grapes are stomped when wine is made. For a thousand years, Jesus will rule in righteousness. All people will follow the Lord and worship him.

OUTSIDE CONNECTION *J. Vernon McGee: Christ is going to be a dictator. A chicken won't peep, a rooster won't crow, and a man will not move without his permission.*[1]

> **Revelation 19:16**
> On his robe and on his thigh he has this name written: KING OF KINGS AND LORD OF LORDS.

Name of Names

Jesus' name will forever be known upon his return. He won't just be called Jesus, but he will be known as the King of kings and Lord of lords. Jesus will be so much greater than any king, emperor, or president the world has ever known. There will never be another ruler.

> **Revelation 19:17–18**
> And I saw an angel standing in the sun, who cried in a loud voice to all the birds flying in midair, "Come, gather together for the great supper of God, so that you may eat the flesh of kings, generals, and mighty men, of horses and their riders, and the flesh of all people, free and slave, small and great."

Calling All Vultures

The supper mentioned here is meal number two for this chapter. The first supper was the big wedding feast mentioned in Revelation 19:9. That meal was beautiful; this meal is gruesome.

Have you ever seen what a vulture does to its prey? Well, the angel and the birds circling here will do similar damage. They are getting ready to eat and destroy those who are at Armageddon. The mighty men, horses, and riders will become bird feed. It will be a tragic end for those who turn their backs on Jesus and follow the Antichrist.

> **Revelation 19:19**
> Then I saw the beast and the kings of the earth and their armies gathered together to make war against the rider on the horse and his army.

Waging War

These followers of Satan won't know when they've been whipped. Instead of surrendering and begging for mercy, these troops will take on the Almighty God.

The Antichrist is named first because he will lead these armies. The ten kings who follow him will gather up all of their

GO!

Revelation 9:16
(200 million)

deluded: *fooled, tricked*

Lake of Fire: *final place for Satan and followers*

194

troops to take on Jesus and the armies that follow him out of heaven. The kings of the east alone will have <u>200 million</u> troops. This will be the war to end all wars. Every weapon known to humankind will be used. Never before and never again will so many troops line up to fight.

> **Revelation 19:20–21**
> But the beast was captured, and with him the false prophet who had performed the miraculous signs on his behalf. With these signs he had **deluded** those who had received the mark of the beast and worshiped his image. The two of them were thrown alive into the fiery lake of burning sulfur. The rest of them were killed with the sword that came out of the mouth of the rider on the horse, and all the birds gorged themselves on their flesh.

>> FEEDING FRENZY

Of all of the millions of people at the Battle of Armageddon, only two will be captured—the Antichrist and the False Prophet. They will pay immediately for their sins by being thrown alive into the **Lake of Fire**! Ouch!

Everyone who followed the Antichrist will be killed by the powerful Word of God. The birds will swoop down and will stuff themselves on the flesh of those who rejected Jesus. And after this, Jesus will set up his rule on earth.

 **David Jeremiah with C. C. Carlson:** *I believe the Bible. It tells us that heaven and hell are real. It also tells us that Jesus is coming again.*[2]

 **J. R. Church:** *Christ, the victor, will judge the nations, set up his glorious kingdom and rule over the earth for a thousand years!*[3]

CHAPTER CHECKUP

1. What shout of praise will be heard in heaven?
2. Who is the Lamb, and who is his bride?

3. What will the saints be wearing, and what do these garments represent?
4. Who did John bow down before? Why was he scolded?
5. What will the rider on the white horse be called?
6. What will happen to the Antichrist and the False Prophet and their followers?

CRASH COURSE

▶ Those in heaven will rejoice and praise God because he has destroyed Babylon and because the wedding of the Lamb has come. (Revelation 19:1–8)
▶ All those who are invited to the marriage supper of the Lamb will be blessed. (Revelation 19:9)
▶ The Second Coming of Jesus will be marked by his return on a white horse with the armies of heaven behind him. He will destroy the nations of the earth with the Word of God. (Revelation 19:11–16)
▶ At the Battle of Armageddon Christ will destroy the armies of the earth. He will capture the Antichrist and False Prophet and throw them into the Lake of Fire. (Revelation 19:19–21)
▶ An angel standing in the sun will invite all the birds of the air to God's supper where they will feast on the dead bodies of those who opposed Christ at Armageddon. (Revelation 19:17–19, 21).

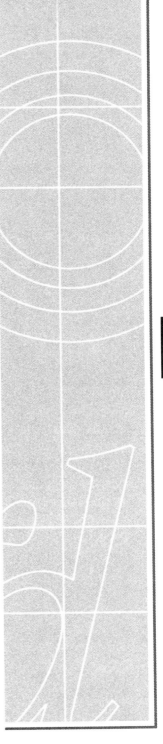

195

PART 3
THE MILLENNIUM AND BEYOND

"I CAN'T GO TO THE MOVIES WITH YOU, ELENORE.
I'M STILL GROUNDED FOR SOMETHING I DID IN 1937!"

A Thousand-Year Reign

 **LET'S DIVE IN**

So much happened in chapter 19 and you may find it hard to believe that anything more can take place. Don't forget, though, Satan is still out in the world. The Antichrist and False Prophet no longer can harm, but Jesus can't begin his rule on earth until all of his unfinished business is taken care of.

Chapter 20 reveals something that is mentioned nowhere else in the Bible—a thousand-year reign of Jesus on earth, or the Millennium. Before this peaceful rule can take place, two things have to happen: Jesus *must* return, and Satan's rule *must* come to an end. Chapter 19 covered Jesus' return, so now let's see what happens to Satan!

Most Christians take one of three views about the Millennium:

1. *Amillennialism*—This view says the thousand-year reign is a symbolic length of time, not a literal one thousand years. They believe Christ already reigns in believers' hearts. People who believe this view think Satan's power will be restrained and the church will do the work of the kingdom during this time period.
2. *Premillennialism*—This view takes the thousand-year reign literally. People who believe this view think Christ will

take believers out of the world (Rapture) and then return to rule the world from Jerusalem (Millennium). During this one-thousand-year rule, Satan will be a prisoner. At the end of this period, Satan will be released for a final struggle with God, who will win the battle between good and evil. I have written this book using the premillennial view.

3. *Postmillennialism*—This view also takes the thousand-year reign literally. People who hold this view believe the church will have a great impact in bringing about the reign of Christ. They believe Christ will return to earth *after* the Millennium.

> **Revelation 20:1**
> And I saw an angel coming down out of heaven, having the key to the Abyss and holding in his hand a great chain.

UNLOCKING THE ABYSS

An angel will come down out of heaven holding an important key—the key to the Abyss (or the bottomless pit). This angel obtained this key when Satan was thrown out of heaven in Revelation 12:7–9. This angel also has a great chain in his hand. This isn't a key chain, but rather is a strong link-chain that could be used to tie up someone.

> **Revelation 20:2**
> He seized the dragon, the ancient serpent, who is the devil, or Satan, and bound him for a thousand years.

QUICK CAPTURE

Not much is said here about Satan resisting arrest, so it's likely a quick deal. Remember, God is so much more powerful than Satan. At God's command an angel is sent to grab Satan, and presto, just like that, Satan is under lock and key. No sneaking out!

Since God is all-powerful and all-knowing, he could have grabbed Satan at any time. But the Bible says that Satan will be allowed to rule the earth until the end of the Tribulation. God doesn't rush things, but waits for the perfect time.

> **Revelation 20:3**
> He threw him into the Abyss, and locked and sealed it over him, to keep him from deceiving the nations anymore until the thousand years were ended. After that, he must be set free for a short time.

A New Generation

The angel will throw Satan, all tied up, into the Abyss. Satan won't be able to tempt the nations and people during this thousand-year period. Survivors from the Tribulation (the tribulation saints and the surviving Jews) will repopulate the earth, and people from all nations will go to Jerusalem once a year to worship Jesus.

Multitudes of people will be born during the Millennium. The children of the tribulation saints and Jews won't have a clue what it's like to fall into <u>temptation</u>. Their faith will never be tested. That is why Satan is released one last time—to try their faith. Unfortunately, during this test, many will be deceived by Satan and fail.

> **Revelation 20:4**
> I saw thrones on which were seated those who had been given authority to judge. And I saw the souls of those who had been beheaded because of their testimony for Jesus and because of the word of God. They had not worshiped the beast or his image and had not received his mark on their foreheads or their hands. They came to life and reigned with Christ for a thousand years.

Up from the Dead

The church and the tribulation saints who were killed because of their faith will sit on thrones and rule with Jesus during the Millennium. They will be given the authority to <u>judge</u> the entire world.

KEY POINT

God is holy, and he has to do right even in the eyes of Satan and his demons.

GO!
Zechariah 14:16 (worship Jesus)
Isaiah 2:4; 11:9 (temptation)

201

KEY SYMBOLS

Thrones
Judgment seats for Christians

GO!
1 Corinthians 6:2–3 (judge)

GO!
Matthew 27:52–53;
Daniel 12:1–3
(Old Testament
saints)
1 Thessalonians 4:13–
18 (church)
Revelation 11:11–12
(two witnesses)

> **Revelation 20:5**
> (The rest of the dead did not come to life until the thousand years were ended.) This is the first resurrection.

 ## TWO RESURRECTIONS

The first resurrection is called the resurrection of life or resurrection of believers. The second resurrection is called the resurrection of damnation or resurrection of unbelievers. This verse tells us that there will be one thousand years between these two resurrections.

Confused? Take a look at the following sequence of events:

1. *First Resurrection*—Believers raised in four phases that began over 1,900 years ago.
   - Phase 1—The resurrection of Jesus Christ and some Old Testament saints. (When Jesus rose from the dead, some saints who had been dead also arose and appeared to many people.)
   - Phase 2—The resurrection of the church at the Rapture when Christians are taken to heaven.
   - Phase 3—The resurrection of the two witnesses who were killed by the beast.
   - Phase 4—The resurrection of the tribulation saints and the remainder of the Old Testament saints at the end of the Tribulation. God will raise and avenge all who have been killed by the Antichrist and the False Prophet.
2. *Second Resurrection*—Unbelievers raised at the end of one-thousand-year Millennium.

The 144,000 and those believers who survive the Tribulation will not be resurrected since they will still be alive at the start of the Millennium.

> **Revelation 20:6**
> Blessed and holy are those who have part in the first resurrection. The second death has no power over them, but they will be priests of God and of Christ and will reign with him for a thousand years.

⟫⟫ WAY-COOL BOSS

If you've ever wanted to rule the world, this is your chance! Believers will work for Jesus and rule for a thousand years. Talk about teamwork. This will be the best! All who do will spend eternity being happy. Thanks to what Jesus has done for them on the cross, these people will no longer have to be afraid of death or suffer the consequences of their sins and be thrown into the Lake of Fire.

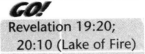

GO!
Revelation 19:20;
20:10 (Lake of Fire)

> **Revelation 20:7–8**
> When the thousand years are over, Satan will be released from his prison and will go out to deceive the nations in the four corners of the earth—Gog and Magog—to gather them for battle. In number they are like the sand on the seashore.

Look Who's Baaack

An enormous amount of people will be born during the Millennium. Those people won't have experienced temptation. They will be vulnerable to sin when Satan is let go from prison. They will need to have their faith tested just like people born before the Millennium. Some of these people will have appeared to obey and worship God, but their hearts will be ripe for revolt against him.

When the Millennium is over, the Abyss will be opened one more time, and Satan will go back to his old tricks. Once Satan's free, he'll roam the earth and deceive the nations. One of the things that the Millennium will prove is that a perfect environment does not change our sinful <u>nature</u>. Being rebellious comes naturally for people, and unless we are born again, we will never be perfectly good.

At the battle of Gog and Magog Satan will try one last time to become <u>greater than God</u>. He will gather a huge number of people from all over the world, including **Gog** and **Magog**.

203

KEY POINT

Those born during the Millennium will be tested.

GO!
Jeremiah 17:9;
Romans 8:7–8
(nature)
Isaiah 14:12–13;
Revelation 12:9
(greater than God)
Genesis 10:1–2;
Ezekiel 38:2–3
(Magog)

Gog: *title meaning leader, dictator, or prince*

Magog: *area ruled by Gog, possibly Russia*

> **Revelation 20:9**
> They marched across the breadth of the earth and surrounded the camp of God's people, the city he loves. But fire came down from heaven and devoured them.

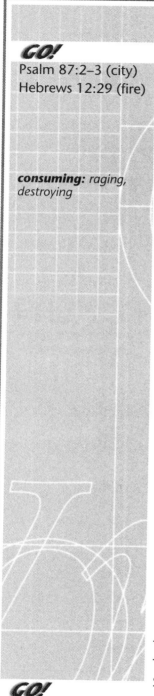

 SHORT-LIVED REBELLION

GO!
Psalm 87:2–3 (city)
Hebrews 12:29 (fire)

Jesus will set up his kingdom on earth in Jerusalem, the <u>city</u> of God (*"the camp of God's people"*) during his millennial reign. The multitude of people who haven't known temptation will try to fight Jesus and the people in Jerusalem. Satan's army will march across the entire earth and surround Jerusalem. The battle, however, will be short-lived because God will use fire from heaven to destroy them.

consuming: *raging, destroying*

God is a loving God, but he is also called a **consuming fire**. Although a large army of believers lives in Jerusalem, it isn't needed for this battle. God takes care of these rebels on his own and protects the people he loves.

> Revelation 20:10
> And the devil, who deceived them, was thrown into the lake of burning sulfur, where the beast and the false prophet had been thrown. They will be tormented day and night for ever and ever.

That's All Folks

Satan will finally be gone from the earth, forever. He will no longer be able to tempt, torment, and control people. His time will be up. Satan will wind up in the same place as the Antichrist and False Prophet who were thrown into the Lake of Fire before him. Unfortunately for them, their suffering will have no end. The fire won't destroy them. It will torture them for eternity.

> Revelation 20:11
> Then I saw a great white throne and him who was seated on it. Earth and sky fled from his presence, and there was no place for them.

Judgment Day

The great white throne is the judgment seat of Almighty God. This judgment is *only* for those who haven't accepted Jesus as Savior (unbelievers).

GO!
John 5:22
(committed)

This verse doesn't say who is on that throne, but all judgment has been <u>committed</u> to Jesus, so most likely Jesus will be on that throne.

"Earth and sky fled from his presence." This isn't something we know much about. Most Bible experts believe earth and sky will be removed to make room for a <u>new earth</u> and new heaven. *"There was no place for them"* appears to say that the <u>old</u> earth and old heaven will be destroyed.

GO!
Isaiah 66:22
(new earth)
Matthew 24:35 (old)

> **Revelation 20:12**
> And I saw the dead, great and small, standing before the throne, and books were opened. Another book was opened, which is the book of life. The dead were judged according to what they had done as recorded in the books.

KEY SYMBOLS
Great White Throne
God's judgment seat for unbelievers

Bummer of a Book

Imagine standing before a great king in a huge room full of people. Imagine the king reading aloud all your thoughts and a list of all the things you ever did—including the stuff you did when you thought no one was looking. "Let me outta here!" you'd say.

All the non-Christians who have ever lived or died will experience just such humiliation when they stand before Jesus as he sits on this Great White Throne. Nobodies and famous people, poor and rich, workers and managers, country folks and kings—every one will have his or her turn before the throne. Several books will be opened. These books will hold the thoughts, words, and actions of each person, and by these things they will be judged.

When the judgment begins, the dead will be judged by what they have done. They are in for an unpleasant surprise because none of these people <u>will reach heaven</u>. All that is awaiting these unbelievers is punishment. Believers, however, won't have to fear this judgment. Their names are written in the <u>Lamb's Book of Life</u>. All whose names are recorded in the Lamb's Book of Life have eternal life to look forward to.

KEY POINT
Unbelievers will be judged by their thoughts, words, and actions.

GO!
Galatians 3:10
(will reach heaven)
Revelation 21:27
(Lamb's Book of Life)

Zach Arrington, college freshman: There is no higher moral power watching over me, except God. In a lot of ways, that's scary. God doesn't ground you. He just lets you do your own thing until you destroy yourself. That, ultimately, is a lot worse that getting grounded.[1]

OUTSIDE **CONNECTION**

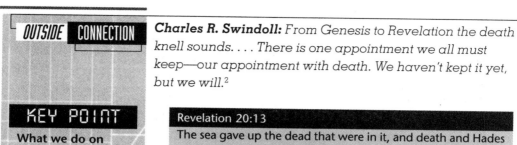

Charles R. Swindoll: *From Genesis to Revelation the death knell sounds. . . . There is one appointment we all must keep—our appointment with death. We haven't kept it yet, but we will.*[2]

> **Revelation 20:13**
> The sea gave up the dead that were in it, and death and Hades gave up the dead that were in them, and each person was judged according to what he had done.

No Escape

Even those who have drowned and sunk to the bottom of the ocean floor won't be able to escape judgment. All unbelievers who have died and gone to **Hades** will be brought before this great throne. No one will escape the judgment of God because he will raise them all from the dead. All will be judged as individuals according to the things they have done or not done.

Hades: *temporary hell for unbelievers*

Remember the Bible teaches that all humans are destined to die once and then face judgment. This death refers to the end of life on earth. Believers and unbelievers will be raised separately and judged separately. Believers will go before the Judgment Seat of Christ where the things they have done will be judged. These believers have already received salvation through Jesus' finished work on the cross. The purpose of this judgment for believers is for them to be rewarded for the good things they've done on earth. Christians will receive crowns as rewards.

Hebrews 9:27
 (die once)
Romans 14:10;
 2 Corinthians 5:10
 (Judgment Seat)
2 Timothy 2:8;
 1 Peter 5:4
 (receive crowns)

Unbelievers, on the other hand, will go before the Great White Throne mentioned in verse 11. Instead of rewards, they will get varied degrees of punishment for their sins.

David Hocking: *The word Hades is used eleven times in the New Testament and is to be distinguished from the word Gehenna, which refers to the final hell, the Lake of Fire. Hades is certainly like hell, a place of terrible torment, but it is the temporary **abode** of the wicked dead who await the Great White Throne Judgment and their final sentencing.*[3]

abode: *home*

> **Revelation 20:14**
> Then death and Hades were thrown into the lake of fire. The lake of fire is the second death.

Second Death

This is the end of the first death—physical death. This is good news for believers, but really bad news for unbelievers. Those who don't know Jesus as their Savior will want to die physically to end their pain, but they won't be able to. Instead, they will have new bodies that cannot be destroyed in the Lake of Fire. These new bodies will allow them to suffer forever. Hades will also be no more. Instead of Hades, these people will be <u>cast into hell</u>. When the earth is destroyed, people will be in one of two places: the **Heavenly City** or hell.

GO!
Matthew 25:41, 46
(cast into hell)

Heavenly City: the new Jerusalem (future home of believers)

> **Revelation 20:15**
> If anyone's name was not found written in the book of life, he was thrown into the lake of fire.

Name some ways people think they will get into heaven. _____

Your Move

What could you do to help these people realize the awful fate that awaits them unless they believe in Jesus Christ?_____

_____

If you fail to witness to someone, what can you do about it?_____

_____

_____

GET REAL

Two teenage sisters from Montreal, Suzy and Christi McVeigh, started a magazine called *Flame Resistant* to spread their Christian faith to lovers of punk rock music.[4] While we all don't have the time or talents to do what Suzy and Christi do, we all know people in our schools and neighborhoods who need to hear the good news of Christ.

Some people think everyone will go to heaven. Others think they are good enough to get there on their own. A few people know they need a savior and welcome news about Jesus. The Holy Spirit is the one who convicts each person of sin, but we can play a vital part as we live for Jesus and share his love with others.

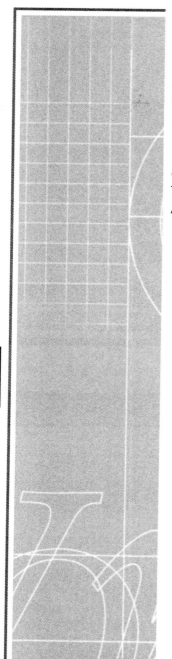

 DROPPING NAMES

When all is said and done, a person's eternal destiny won't be decided by the things he or she does on earth. No, the deciding factor will be whether or not a person's name is in the Book of Life. God will make a careful search of the heavenly list to determine who will be allowed into heaven.

The names of those who did not accept Jesus before they died will have been erased or crossed out of the Book of Life. Their names will not be found, and they will join Satan, the Antichrist, and the False Prophet in the Lake of Fire forever.

CHAPTER CHECKUP

1. What will the angel coming down out of heaven have?
2. How long will Satan be tied up?
3. Who was given authority to judge?
4. What will Satan do when he is released after a thousand years?
5. What will happen to Satan and his army?
6. What will take place at the Great White Throne judgment?

CRASH COURSE

▶ An angel will tie up Satan and throw him in the Abyss for a thousand years to keep him from deceiving the nations. (Revelation 20:1–3)

▶ Those believers who died during the Tribulation will be raised in the last phase of the first resurrection and will rule with Christ for the Millennium. Those who take part in the first resurrection will be blessed because they will not face the second death. (Revelation 20:4–6)

▶ After a thousand years, Satan will be released briefly to test the faith of the nations. Unfortunately, many will fall and make war against God. God will destroy them with fire and cast Satan into the Lake of Fire where he will suffer never-ending torture. (Revelation 20:7–10)

▶ Christ will sit on the Great White Throne and judge the dead. Those whose names are not found in the Book of Life will be thrown into the Lake of Fire to suffer the second death. (Revelation 20:11–15)

Out with Old, In with New

 LET'S DIVE IN

Have you ever wondered what heaven will be like? Well, stay tuned because this chapter gives you a glimpse. Heaven is a greater place than any human can imagine, and those who trust in Jesus Christ for salvation will have a chance to experience it. How cool is that!

> **Revelation 21:1**
> Then I saw a new heaven and a new earth, for the first heaven and the first earth had passed away, and there was no longer any sea.

 BRAND NEW START

John must have been totally amazed by what he saw—a new heaven and a <u>new earth</u>! These will replace the present heaven and earth with one major difference—the oceans or other large bodies of water will no longer exist.

GO!
Isaiah 65:17; 2 Peter 3:13
(new earth)

Bible experts believe there will no longer be large bodies of water to allow (1) more room for people; (2) the climate to change, reducing storms; and (3) the social distance between countries to end.

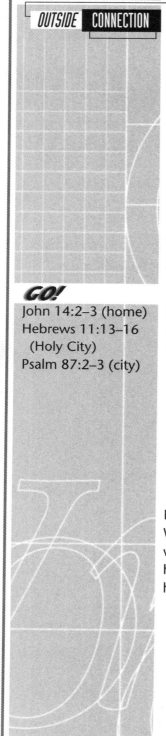

Jim Petersen: God is making everything new. He is creating a new heaven and earth where even our familiar laws of physics will be useless.[1]

> **Revelation 21:2**
> I saw the Holy City, the new Jerusalem, coming down out of heaven from God, prepared as a bride beautifully dressed for her husband.

Here Comes the Bride

Do you ever wonder who you'll marry, what he or she will look like on your wedding day, and what your home together will look like? The Holy City, the new Jerusalem, will come down from heaven looking like a bride on her wedding day.

The church will spend eternity with Jesus the bridegroom. The bride's new <u>home</u> will be a <u>Holy City</u>. Jerusalem has always been a <u>city</u> of God, but now it is a perfect place with no sin, a new Jerusalem. God is the power source of this city, and it will glow, *"as a bride beautifully dressed for her husband."*

GO!
John 14:2–3 (home)
Hebrews 11:13–16
  (Holy City)
Psalm 87:2–3 (city)

> **Revelation 21:3**
> And I heard a loud voice from the throne saying, "Now the dwelling of God is with men, and he will live with them. They will be his people, and God himself will be with them and be their God."

Home at Last

Right now, the Holy Spirit lives in the hearts of all believers. When the new Jerusalem comes down from heaven, things will change. Instead of living *in* his people, God will live *with* his people and will physically live in the new Jerusalem where he will walk and talk with his very own people, the church.

> **Revelation 21:4**
> "He will wipe every tear from their eyes. There will be no more death or mourning or crying or pain, for the old order of things has passed away."

When was the last time you cried?_____

_____

What made you cry?_____

_____

_____

How did you feel after you cried?_____

_____

_____

 Crying is a strange thing. Usually we cry because we feel sadness or hurt. Sometimes people cry because they are happy. Crying is something God created as a means for human beings to release pent-up emotions. Jesus cried about the death of his good friend Lazarus. John even cried in heaven. Crying is an earthly thing. We won't have any need to do it in this new world.

⏵⏵ NO REASON TO CRY

When Jesus reigns on the new earth, there no longer will be any reason for humans to cry. All the things that make us sad—broken friendships, loneliness, sickness, depression, anger, diseases, suffering, even death—will not exist. Jesus will completely do away with all sad things. Everything on earth now that makes people heave a deep sigh or cry will be gone. Jesus will wipe away all tears. Never, ever, will tears fall to the ground!

GO!
John 11:35
(Jesus cried)
Revelation 5:3–5
(in heaven)

Revelation 21:5
He who was seated on the throne said, "I am making everything new!" Then he said, "Write this down, for these words are trustworthy and true."

Trustworthy and True

The world as we've known it will no longer exist; however, that won't be a bad thing. The new world Jesus will make will

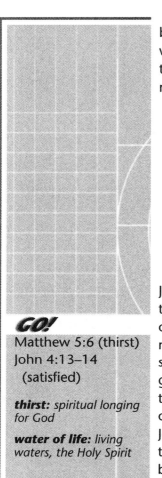

be wonderful. It's a promise you can take to the bank. Jesus' words are always true. Maybe John was so overwhelmed by the new world that he forgot to keep writing and had to be reminded.

> **Revelation 21:6–7**
> He said to me: "It is done. I am the Alpha and the Omega, the Beginning and the End. To him who is thirsty I will give to drink without cost from the spring of the water of life. He who overcomes will inherit all this, and I will be his God and he will be my son."

 ## ULTIMATE THIRST QUENCHER

Jesus was with God in the beginning of the world, and now, at the end of the world, he still is here. Jesus wants to give everyone who is thirsty the ultimate **thirst** quencher—himself. Here near the end of Revelation, Jesus still is calling people to himself to drink of the **water of life**. He is the only one who can get rid of the empty feeling that all human beings possess in their souls. Jesus died on the cross and rose again so that anyone who believes in him will be <u>satisfied</u>. If you have trusted in Jesus Christ as your Savior, then you have a wonderful inheritance to look forward to—better than anything money can buy—an eternally secure family tie with God.

> **Revelation 21:8**
> "But the cowardly, the unbelieving, the vile, the murderers, the sexually immoral, those who practice magic arts, the idolaters and all liars—their place will be in the fiery lake of burning sulfur. This is the second death."

Sin God Won't Tolerate

People who live a lifestyle of continual sin—not commit the sins listed in this verse once or twice—will not enter the heavenly city. Their physical death is the first death. Their eternal spiritual punishment is the second death.

GO!
Matthew 5:6 (thirst)
John 4:13–14 (satisfied)

thirst: *spiritual longing for God*

water of life: *living waters, the Holy Spirit*

212

Kevin Johnson: We're rebels. God's foes. Mercenaries in the wrong army. We do bad. We neglect to do good. The Bible's lists of sins and sinners nail all of us. . . . But we don't have to stay far from God. God's penalty for rebellion is death, yet God's Good News is that Jesus paid the penalty for us.[2]

> **Revelation 21:9**
> One of the seven angels who had the seven bowls full of the seven last plagues came and said to me, "Come, I will show you the bride, the wife of the Lamb."

Jesus' Bride

A unique <u>union</u> will exist between Jesus and the church, similar to the special bond a bridegroom and bride share. The bride mentioned here is the church, but here the angel refers to the city as the bride of the Lamb. As far as God's concerned, the Holy City and his holy people are one and the same. The Holy City will look like a city with rivers, trees, streets, and mansions, but the real identity of the city will be the Lamb (Jesus) and his bride (the church).

GO!
Revelation 19:7
(union)

KEY SYMBOLS

The Holy City
God's holy people
  • Lamb and his bride

213

> **Revelation 21:10–12**
> And he carried me away in the Spirit to a mountain great and high, and showed me the Holy City, Jerusalem, coming down out of heaven from God. It shone with the glory of God, and its brilliance was like that of a very precious jewel, like a jasper, clear as crystal. It had a great, high wall with twelve gates, and with twelve angels at the gates. On the gates were written the names of the twelve tribes of Israel.

Carried Away

While John was *"in the Spirit,"* the angel carried him away to a great mountain where he could see for miles. John had a unique spiritual experience where he was in close touch with God and saw a vision. John was able to witness this awesome city coming down out of heaven with his own eyes.

Bible scholars disagree about the descent of the city. Maybe it will come to rest on the new earth, or maybe it will hover above.

This great city will shine from the presence of God—no

GO!
Revelation 1:10; 17:3
(in the Spirit)

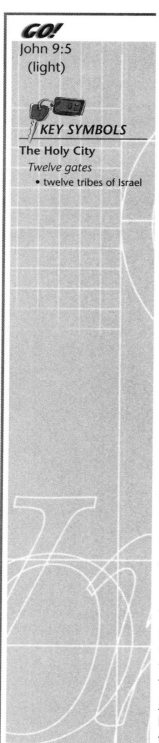

GO!
John 9:5
(light)

KEY SYMBOLS

The Holy City
Twelve gates
• twelve tribes of Israel

power source needed! God's pure <u>light</u> will sparkle like expensive jewelry. The Holy City will be surrounded by thick, high walls and will have twelve gates surrounding it. Each of the twelve tribes of Israel will have its name above a gate to remind everyone that Jesus, the words of the Bible, and ultimately salvation, came through the Jewish people. Without them the Holy City would not be needed, and all non-Jewish people would be without hope.

Why does the Holy City need a security wall and guarding angels? No one knows for sure, but some suggest it is a symbol that not everyone has access to God.

> **Revelation 21:13–14**
> There were three gates on the east, three on the north, three on the south and three on the west. The wall of the city had twelve foundations, and on them were the names of the twelve apostles of the Lamb.

 A GATED COMMUNITY

How can a wall have twelve foundations? We don't really know. Some experts say these foundations will be stacked on top of each other and will make up the basic "cement" of the city's structure. Others say these foundations will be large columns extending down to the new earth like legs or posts.

Whatever form these foundations take, they will have the name of one of the twelve apostles of Jesus on it. This is important because it fulfills Scripture. Ephesians 2:20 says, the church is being *"built on the foundation of the apostles and prophets, with Christ Jesus himself as the chief cornerstone."* Acts 1:1–2 says that Jesus gave *"instructions through the Holy Spirit to the apostles he had chosen."* These twelve followers of Jesus, with the Holy Spirit's help, gave the church its start. They preached the gospel, helped people get saved, started churches, wrote down things that later became the New Testament, selected church deacons, and taught their followers. Their life was tough. They gave up money and comfort for Jesus and were threatened, beaten up, put in prison, and even killed. They earned the right to have their names carved on the foundations of the Holy City.

> **Revelation 21:15–16**
>
> The angel who talked with me had a measuring rod of gold to measure the city, its gates, and its walls. The city was laid out like a square, as long as it was wide. He measured the city with the rod and found it to be 12,000 stadia in length, and as wide and high as it is long.

GIGANTIC GOLDEN CUBE

The angel took a gold measuring stick and measured the city. The place is huge! Some experts suggest the city will be a pyramid, but others think it will be a cube. Its length will be the same as its width, and it will be as tall as it is long. Twelve thousand stadia is about 1,500 miles (approximately the distance from New York City to Dallas, Texas). A city 1,500 miles long and 1,500 miles wide will be gigantic!

> **Revelation 21:17–18**
>
> He measured its wall and it was 144 cubits thick, by man's measurement, which the angel was using. The wall was made of jasper, and the city of pure gold, as pure as glass.

In the Thick of Jasper and Gold

Can you imagine the price tag on this great city? Even Donald Trump or Bill Gates couldn't afford it. There will be so much jasper and gold even former Las Vegas residents will be dazzled. The wall around the Holy City will be 144 cubits (216 feet) thick. This thick wall will make the city ultrasafe. People will be able to look through it into the Holy City, and the <u>light</u> of God will shine out of the city.

GO!
Isaiah 60:19
(light)

> **Revelation 21:19–21**
>
> The foundations of the city walls were decorated with every kind of precious stone. The first foundation was jasper, the second sapphire, the third chalcedony, the fourth emerald, the fifth sardonyx, the sixth carnelian, the seventh chrysolite, the eighth beryl, the ninth topaz, the tenth chrysoprase, the eleventh jacinth, and the twelfth amethyst. The twelve gates were twelve pearls, each gate made of a single pearl. The great street of the city was of pure gold, like transparent glass.

GO!
1 John 1:5 (light)

GO!
1 Thessalonians 4:17 (with the Lord)

KEY POINT

The glorious presence of the Father and the Son will shine through the entire city.

KEY SYMBOLS

The Holy City
No temple
• Free access to God

Birthstone Bonanza

Each one of the twelve foundations of the city walls will be different. You'll recognize the names of some of these stones as birthstones. God's <u>light</u> shining through the different stones and gems will make the place look like a stained-glass window. Add humongous pearls and gold streets, and the city is too incredible for words!

> **Revelation 21:22**
> I did not see a temple in the city, because the Lord God Almighty and the Lamb are its temple.

A Living Place of Worship

In Bible times the center of a city was usually its temple, so John looked for the center of this city. He found no temple. Then it dawned on him. Sin will not exist in the Holy City. Believers will be <u>with the Lord</u> and will no longer be separated from his presence because of sin. God the Father and Jesus the Son (called the Lamb in the verse above) will fill this city with glory and light. The whole city will be a living place of worship, a temple.

The Bible is full of things that are tough to understand, but fun to think about at the same time. One of them is mentioned in 1 John 3:2: *"When he appears, we [believers] shall be like him."* We don't fully understand what that means, but we will be changed for the better. We won't have a sin nature. We'll be full of wisdom, love, and everything else that Jesus has. We will be able to come before God and Jesus without fear or shame.

> **Revelation 21:23**
> The city does not need the sun or the moon to shine on it, for the glory of God gives it light, and the Lamb is its lamp.

A BRIGHT FUTURE

What if New York City, Los Angeles, Denver, and Dallas no longer needed any power grids for electricity? The people in the city in the verse above can be 100 miles away from God

216

and still won't need a light. The light of God will cover an area almost as large as the eastern half of the United States and be so bright it will be visible in outer space!

The Father and Son are the source of physical light for this Holy City. They <u>created</u> the sun and the moon and the stars to <u>light</u> up the earth, but those lights won't be necessary.

GO!
Genesis 1 (created)
Isaiah 60:19–20; John 1:3–5; 8:12 (light)

> **Revelation 21:24**
> The nations will walk by its light, and the kings of the earth will bring their **splendor** into it.

splendor: *display of praise, thanksgiving, worship, and honor*

Righteous Residents

Bible experts don't agree on what *"nations"* means in this verse. I believe the people living on the new earth (the Jewish people) will travel to the Holy City—not to live there—to worship God. The Holy City will be the future home of the church. The new earth will be the future home of Israel and all others who are saved after the Rapture.

> **Revelation 21:25–27**
> On no day will its gates ever be shut, for there will be no night there. The glory and honor of the nations will be brought into it. Nothing impure will ever enter it, nor will anyone who does what is shameful or deceitful, but only those whose names are written in the Lamb's Book of Life.

An Open, Not Shut, Case

The people of ancient cities opened their gates during the day and closed them at night. God's city gates will always be open. They will never need to be shut and locked like we shut the doors of our homes at night to keep out burglars. There will be no night because God's light will continuously shine. No impure thing or person will ever enter the Holy City. Only those who have their names in the Lamb's Book of Life will be allowed in.

Larry Richards: *We cannot know how wonderful eternity will be for those who have trusted God until we are welcomed into the new heaven and earth God will create.*[3]

OUTSIDE CONNECTION

CHAPTER CHECKUP

1. Why was John told to write the phrase, *"these words are trustworthy and true"*?
2. Why can Jesus give the *"water of life"*?
3. Describe the Holy City that will come down from heaven.
4. What is the significance of having the names of the twelve tribes of Israel on the twelve gates of the Holy City?
5. Who will enter this Holy City?

CRASH COURSE

▶ God will create a new heaven and new earth because the old ones will pass away. (Revelation 21:1)
▶ God will send the Holy City, the new Jerusalem, to the new earth. He will live among his people and will wipe away every tear from their eyes. (Revelation 21:2–4)
▶ Everyone who rejected God during their lifetime will be thrown into the Lake of Fire, which is the second death. (Revelation 21:8)
▶ The new Jerusalem will be built on twelve foundations and have twelve gates. It will be laid out like a square and be made of pure gold and precious stones. (Revelation 21:9–21)
▶ The new Jerusalem will not have a temple because God and Christ will be the temple. The city also will not need a sun or moon because the Father and Son will be the light. (Revelation 21:22–25)

22

Jesus Is Coming

 LET'S DIVE IN

Well, here we are at the last chapter of Revelation. Your mind is probably spinning with all of the information you've absorbed. At the same time you probably still have bunches of unanswered questions. God doesn't tell us everything, but he definitely has told us everything he wants us to know about the end times. <u>In his time</u> he'll make everything clear to us, even if we have to wait until Jesus' return to earth. For now, John explains further about the believer's final home, Christ's final promise, a final invitation, and a final warning.

GO!
Daniel 12:8–10
(in his time)

> **Revelation 22:1–2a**
> Then the angel showed me the river of the water of life, as clear as crystal, flowing from the throne of God and of the Lamb down the middle of the great street of the city.

 LIFE-GIVING RIVER

Up until now, the angel has been showing John the city's basic layout: foundations, walls, gates, and a street. The Holy City isn't just made up of beautiful structures, it also contains water, trees, and fruit. Here we see that it will have a river called

GO!
John 4:13–14
  (living water)
John 7:37–39
  (Holy Spirit)
John 3:1–8
  (life-giving)

KEY SYMBOLS

River of the Water of Life
The Holy Spirit

GO!
Revelation 2:17
  (manna)
Revelation 2:7
  (tree of life)
Genesis 3:22–24
  (Eden)

GO!
Genesis 3:14–19
  (curse)

"the river of the water of life." In other places in the Bible, this water of life is called <u>living water</u> and is symbolic of the <u>Holy Spirit</u>.

God uses something we know and recognize (water) to help explain a spiritual truth. Living water flows pure, clear, and fresh. This river is not like a green, mossy, swamp full of gnats and mosquitoes. This water possesses <u>life-giving</u> qualities that no one can live without. The source of this river is the *"throne of God and of the Lamb."* This river will provide life-giving water and the Holy Spirit to the Holy City. The Trinity (the Father, Son, and Holy Spirit) will be present to meet all our needs.

> **Revelation 22:2b**
> On each side of the river stood the tree of life, bearing twelve crops of fruit, yielding its fruit every month. And the leaves of the tree are for the healing of the nations.

 HEAVENLY FOOD

If you have ever wondered if there is food in heaven, here's your answer. Yes! Believers will diet on <u>manna</u> and fruit from the <u>tree of life</u>. The tree of life mentioned here was originally mentioned in the Garden of <u>Eden</u>. Before Adam and Eve sinned, they could have eaten from it and lived forever.

Believers won't eat the leaves of the tree because those will be for the health of those who live on the new earth. It's likely the healing mentioned here is in reference to healed relationships between nations. These leaves will provide healthiness.

> **Revelation 22:3**
> No longer will there be any curse. The throne of God and of the Lamb will be in the city, and his servants will serve him.

BROKEN CURSE!

All of the bad things that exist on the earth today will be gone in the Holy City. Revelation 22:3 mentions the last and most important thing—the <u>curse</u> is gone! When Adam and Eve first sinned, God placed a curse on creation. Because of it, women experience pain in childbirth, work is tiresome, and men and women suffer sickness, disease, and death. Once God throws Satan and his followers into hell and raises all believers into new bodies, the curse will be gone.

The Holy City will be the new place for God's throne. Believers will spend time here praising God and serving him. We aren't sure exactly what our tasks will be, but we have already been told that we will reign as priests. And best of all, believers can have total confidence that they won't be bored or sad, but will find <u>joy and fulfillment</u>.

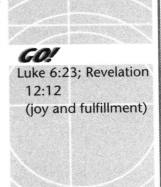

GO!
Luke 6:23; Revelation 12:12
(joy and fulfillment)

> **Revelation 22:4–5**
> They will see his face, and his name will be on their foreheads. There will be no more night. They will not need the light of a lamp or the light of the sun, for the Lord God will give them light. And they will reign for ever and ever.

Face-to-Face

In the Old Testament, <u>Moses</u> wanted to see the face of God. In the New Testament, <u>Philip</u> did too. God didn't allow either of these men to see his face because if they would have seen it, they would have died. When believers live in the Holy City, they will be able to <u>see God</u> and his Son, Jesus. They won't have to fear gazing at God's face because he will want us to see him. The name of God will be written on believers' foreheads to identify them as God's own. Along with God's name, we will have his godly character.

GO!
Exodus 33:18–23 (Moses)
John 14:8–9 (Philip)
1 John 3:2 (see God)

This is the second time we've been told that there will be no night in the Holy City. We won't need electricity to run this city and we'll be able to see for miles and miles by the light given off by God and his Son. Believers will have the privilege of ruling with God and Jesus for ever and ever. It will be a wonderful place to live.

J. Vernon McGee: *Who knows but what (God) will give to each saint—a world or a solar system or a galactic system to operate. Remember that Adam was given dominion over the old creation on this earth.*[1]

OUTSIDE CONNECTION

GO!
Colossians 1:9
(spiritual understanding)

behold: *take notice*

GO!
Revelation 1:3
(time is near)

> **Revelation 22:6**
> The angel said to me, "These words are trustworthy and true. The Lord, the God of the spirits of the prophets, sent his angel to show his servants the things that must soon take place."

Jesus Can Be Trusted

"The things that must soon take place" have already started. In fact, the first part of the prophecy of Revelation, the Church Age, is almost over. Everything from the Rapture to the Second Coming is still to come.

Jesus Christ is the true author of Revelation; John is just the messenger. Jesus sent his angel to give the prophets spiritual <u>understanding</u>. In other words, there is no "maybe" as far as these events are concerned. Everything written in Revelation will happen—it's just a matter of when! Jesus will do what he says.

> **Revelation 22:7**
> "**Behold**, I am coming soon! Blessed is he who keeps the words of the prophecy in this book."

Obedience with a Promise

Jesus will return as fast as you can blink your eyes. It's important that we are always ready. The <u>time is near</u>.

Many people wonder why prophecy is important. It's important not just because it tells the future, but because it can change lives! By knowing what will happen in the future, we can learn to care even more about people who don't know Jesus Christ as Savior. The fact is, God means for prophecy to be obeyed, and those who obey are promised a blessing.

> **Revelation 22:8–9**
> I, John, am the one who heard and saw these things. And when I had heard and seen them, I fell down to worship at the feet of the angel who had been showing them to me. But he said to me, "Do not do it! I am a fellow servant with you and with your brothers the prophets and of all who keep the words of this book. Worship God!"

Worship God Alone!

This is the <u>second</u> time an angel told John not to worship him. Only God is worthy of worship. The angel wanted John to know that he was just a fellow servant, similar to John, the prophets who came before him, and those who keep the words of Revelation.

 Don't worship or admire angels. Only God is worthy of worship.

GO!
Revelation 19:10 (second)

> **Revelation 22:10**
> Then he told me, "Do not seal up the words of the prophecy of this book, because the time is near."

DON'T SLAM THAT BOOK CLOSED

When Daniel wrote his prophecy several hundred years before Jesus was born, he did not understand some of the things God had shown him (check out LWBI, pages 101–102). He wanted an explanation, but the fulfillment of his prophecies were a long time away, so he was told to <u>seal up</u> his writings until the end time.

Revelation is different. When John wrote, his prophecy was already unfolding and the Church Age was beginning. For this reason the message was left unsealed. God wants people to hear these things now.

GO!
Daniel 12:4 (seal up)

> **Revelation 22:11**
> Let him who does wrong continue to do wrong; let him who is **vile** continue to be vile; let him who does right continue to do right; and let him who is holy continue to be holy."

vile: disgusting, evil

Eternal Destiny

The things people do right now, today, impact them for eternity. This verse doesn't mean that those who are sinners today have no hope for change. Jesus wants to give everyone an opportunity to believe in him and be saved. What this verse is

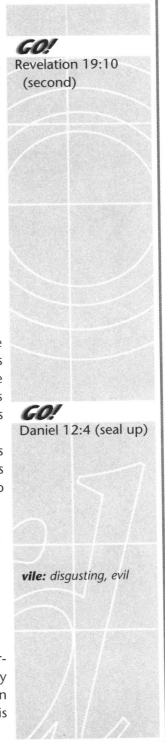

KEY POINT

The decisions people make in this life will determine their destiny and seal it forever.

saying is that a time will come when all unbelievers will be judged and thrown into the Lake of Fire forever. There will also be a time when those who do right and are holy because of Jesus Christ will be rewarded. So don't give up obeying God. The decisions people make in this life will determine their eternal destiny and seal it forever.

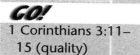

OUTSIDE CONNECTION

Kevin Johnson: *When Jesus comes back he'll bring peace to his friends—and judgment to his enemies.*[2]

> ### Revelation 22:12
> "Behold, I am coming soon! My reward is with me, and I will give to everyone according to what he has done."

KEY SYMBOLS

Rewards
Heaven or hell

Added Bonus

Christ will separate the non-Christians from the Christians, and everyone will receive rewards according to the <u>quality</u> of work they have done for Jesus Christ. This doesn't mean you can earn salvation. Salvation is a gift from God for those who put their faith in Jesus Christ's finished work on the cross. What's mentioned here is like an added bonus, above and beyond the great gift of eternal life.

GO!
1 Corinthians 3:11–15 (quality)

> ### Revelation 22:13
> "I am the Alpha and the Omega, the First and the Last, the Beginning and the End."

Mind-Boggling

We've heard this alpha-omega business <u>before</u>, so that means it's important. The idea that Jesus has always existed and will always exist blows people's minds. It's hard to understand this kind of existence because the only comparison we have is human life—birth, life, and death. Jesus is the first and last and the beginning and the end. Jesus uses all three of his titles to identify himself with the Father here. No one else can claim these truths. No one can explain this truth; it must be taken by faith.

GO!
Revelation 1:8, 17; 2:8; 21:6 (before)

224

How comfortable are you with the idea of being rewarded for the things you've done in your life?_____

_____

Do you think you are worthy of receiving rewards from God? Why or why not?

_____

_____

How might the idea of being rewarded by God someday make you want to live for him today?_____

_____

_____

Not much is said in church about rewards. For the most part it isn't something that many people feel comfortable discussing. No one deserves rewards, but we know they will be given because Revelation 12:12 says so. If we would let the goodness of God sink in, most of us would do more to honor him. We need to follow the advice of the apostle John: to watch out so that we will be *"rewarded fully"* (2 John 1:8).

Revelation 22:14

"Blessed are those who wash their robes, that they may have the right to the tree of life and may go through the gates into the city."

 HEAVENLY LAUNDRY

If your mom told you to do your laundry, that's good advice—especially if she was talking about this verse. People who choose to wash their robes do so by accepting Jesus as their Savior. They are blessed with two rewards: the opportunity to eat from the tree of life, and permission to go through the gates into the Holy City. Those who choose to leave their laundry undone refuse to accept Christ and reject his rewards as a result.

Check out these verses to see the other blessings mentioned in this book: Revelation 1:3; 14:13; 16:15; 19:9; 20:6; 22:7.

KEY SYMBOLS

Washed Robes
Those who accept Christ

Unwashed Robes
Those who reject Christ

> **Revelation 22:15**
> "Outside are the dogs, those who practice magic arts, the sexually immoral, the murderers, the idolaters, and everyone who loves and practices falsehood."

No Doggie Door for You!

The dogs mentioned here are people involved in the occult, sexual immorality, idol-worship, and lying. Instead of eating life-giving fruit, these "dogs" will be nosing through the rotting trash of hell. The sad truth is that no one will even throw them a bone.

> **Revelation 22:16**
> "I, Jesus, have sent my angels to give you this testimony for the churches. I am the Root and the Offspring of David, and the bright Morning Star."

Jesus—True Stardom

Jesus wants those who read Revelation to know that this testimony given to an angel is for the church. And Jesus wants us to know who he is. He is the promised Messiah called *"the Root and Offspring of David"* (see LWBI, page 52). He is Lord and God. The words *"bright Morning Star"* come from both the Old and New Testaments. Jesus is saying that he is the one who will appear near the end of earth's darkest hour (Tribulation). He alone will bring a brighter day to the world (Millennium).

> **Revelation 22:17**
> The Spirit and the bride say, "Come!" And let him who hears say, "Come!" Whoever is thirsty, let him come; and whoever wishes, let him take the free gift of the water of life.

Come On, Folks!

When God says "Come!" it is his final call. The Holy Spirit works in and through the bride of Christ (the church). Through the church all unbelievers are invited one last time to come to Jesus and drink of his salvation, the water of life.

GO!
Jeremiah 33:15
 (David)
Numbers 24:17;
 Revelation 2:28
 (Star)

Beware!

This is serious stuff. Anyone who adds to Revelation will have suffering added to him. It's really important when you read and try to understand this book that you don't take liberties with it by adding to its content.

There are religious groups today that teach God is love, but disagree with the message of salvation, God's anger, judgment, Tribulation, and hell. "Why would a loving God destroy the world?" they ask. "There can't be a hell! That's too cruel."

The truth is, God is just and his ways are perfect. Although we might not like everything in Revelation, we need to believe it is true and trust God with the future. And we need to check what others say against what is written in the Bible.

 Don't add words to the Bible or believe groups who use religious books, such as the Book of Mormon, as equal to the Bible. God <u>struck down</u> Ananias and Sapphira for introducing sin into the early church, and he could choose to do that again to those who do it today.

GO!
Acts 5:1–11
(struck down)

Nothin' More, Nothin' Less

Taking away from this important book brings on a second part to God's warning. Anyone who deletes anything from this book risks having his or her share of the tree of life and the Holy City erased. Those who delete something prove not only that they do not love God or believe in his Word, but that they are doomed to the Lake of Fire.

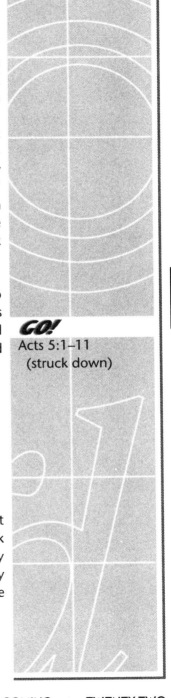

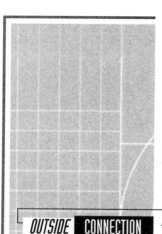

> **Revelation 22:20**
> He who testifies to these things says, "Yes, I am coming soon." Amen. Come, Lord Jesus.

You Betcha, Jesus Is Coming!

"I am coming soon" is Jesus' final promise. In answer to this promise of the Lord's return, John says, "So be it. Let it rip!" This is a statement of John's personal faith in Jesus, and his desire for Jesus to come back soon.

OUTSIDE CONNECTION

Max Lucado: *We can choose where we spend eternity. The big choice, God leaves to us. The critical decision is ours. What are you doing with God's invitation? What are you doing with his personal request that you live with him forever? That is the only decision which really matters.*[3]

> **Revelation 22:21**
> The grace of the Lord Jesus be with God's people. Amen.

A God of Grace

These final words of the Bible remind us that grace makes salvation possible. We can't earn salvation. It is a free gift. God's grace is what will keep us out of the Lake of Fire and let us pass through the gates of the Holy City.

Revelation ends similar to how it began, *"Grace and peace to you from him who is, and who was, and who is to come, and from the seven spirits before his throne"* (Revelation 1:4).

CHAPTER CHECKUP

1. What will believers have written on their foreheads in heaven?
2. How can a person be blessed by God?
3. How can we know that all of the words in Revelation are true?
4. Why did John get in trouble with the angel?
5. What is God's final promise to all who read Revelation?

▶ The River of Life will flow from the Throne of God through the Holy City. On each side of the river will be trees of life. (Revelation 22:1–2)

▶ The curse of the original sin caused by the fall of Adam and Eve will be lifted when God makes everything new. God will once again dwell among his people and be the light for their feet. (Revelation 22:3–5)

▶ The Spirit and bride call anyone who is thirsty to come and drink freely from the water of life. (Revelation 22:17)

▶ A final warning goes to anyone who adds to, or deletes from, Revelation. Those who don't follow this warning face the plagues and suffering that the book writes about. (Revelation 22:18–19)

▶ Jesus Christ has a final promise for all who read Revelation: He is coming soon. (Revelation 22:20)

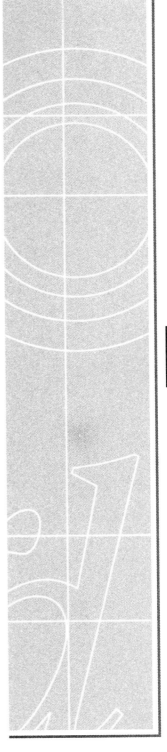

REVELATION 1: JOHN GOES DREAMING

1. Jesus got John's attention by having an angel deliver this message to John. (Revelation 1:1)
2. People might be afraid of Revelation because they don't understand it or feel it proclaims gloom and doom. Believers shouldn't be afraid of Revelation because it was given by the one who loves us and died for us. (Revelation 1:5)
3. Everyone alive, plus the dead who crucified him, will see Jesus when he returns to earth. (Revelation 1:7)
4. These seven churches are important today because the good and the bad qualities of each church are ideal for instructing all of God's people. (Revelation 1:11)
5. The high priest represents Jesus. Jesus is important because he intercedes on our behalf. (Revelation 1:13)

REVELATION 2: A REAL NEED FOR JESUS

1. The church in Ephesus messed up because they forgot their first love. (Revelation 2:4)
2. The church in Smyrna was physically poor and suffered greatly but they had treasures stored up in heaven that made them rich. (Revelation 2:9)
3. The church in Pergamum remained true to the gospel even though they were in a city with many pagan temples. (Revelation 2:13)
4. God was angry with the church in Thyatira because they put up with Jezebel, a false prophetess, who led many people into sexual sins. (Revelation 2:20)
5. The main message to Christians today is: Learn from these churches so you won't make the same mistakes they did. (Revelation 2:29)

REVELATION 3: YOU'RE EITHER HOT OR NOT

1. The church of Sardis had a reputation of being alive, but in reality, they were spiritually dead. (Revelation 3:1)
2. Some of the members at Philadelphia had rejected the name of Jesus. Instead, they were hanging out where Satan dwelled. (Revelation 3:9)
3. The church at Laodicea was neither cold nor hot, but lukewarm. To be in that middle state isn't good enough for Jesus. (Revelation 3:16)
4. The letter to the church at Laodicea probably applies to today's church. (Revelation 3:14–22)
5. In order to keep from being lukewarm Christians, we should be earnest, repent, and open the door to our hearts. (Revelation 3:19–20)

REVELATION 4: HOW IT'S GONNA BE

1. The three views of the Rapture are Pre-Tribulation, Mid-Tribulation, and Post-Tribulation.
2. The trumpet-like voice said, *"Come up here and I will show you what must take place after this."* After John heard the voice, his spirit was taken up to heaven. (Revelation 4:2)
3. The twenty-four elders in heaven will wear white. White symbolizes the righteousness of God. (Revelation 4:4)
4. The elders put their crowns before the throne and said that God is worthy. (Revelation 4:11)

REVELATION 5: TOTALLY WORTHY

1. This scroll is important because the future of all humankind will be affected by it. (Revelation 5:1–2)
2. The first time Jesus came to earth was as a sacrificial Lamb. He was gentle and loving and let himself be hung on a cross so he could

redeem the world. The second time Jesus will come as the Lion of the Tribe of Judah. This time he will rule and judge. (Revelation 5:5, 12)

3. The angels around the throne say this about Jesus: *"Worthy is the Lamb, who was slain, to receive power and wealth and wisdom and strength and honor and glory and praise."* (Revelation 5:11–12)

4. The church has been made a kingdom and each believer has become a priest whose purpose is to serve God. Believers today also have a purpose: to share Jesus' love with everyone. (Revelation 5:10)

5. Knowing that one day every creature will praise and bow before Jesus helps show that Jesus Christ is equal with God. The qualities of the Lamb in Revelation 5:11–14 are also attributes of God.

REVELATION 6: HORSES, DESPAIR, GORE, AND MORE

1. The person riding the white horse is the Antichrist. The Antichrist is carrying a bow, but no arrows. (Revelation 6:2)

2. The rider on the red horse was given power to take peace from the earth and make men kill each other. (Revelation 6:4)

3. A quart of wheat will cost a day's wage or pay during the Tribulation. (Revelation 6:6)

4. The rider on the pale horse is named Death. Hades or hell follows him. (Revelation 6:8)

REVELATION 7: MARKED MESSENGERS

1. The four angels held back the wind. They may have done this to prevent diseases from being spread around the world. (Revelation 7:1)

2. The 144,000 will cry out: *"Salvation belongs to our God, who sits on the throne, and to the Lamb."* Their message is important because many Jews who hear this message will finally believe that Jesus is the Messiah and will trust in him. (Revelation 7:10)

3. Those wearing white robes are the saved people who come out of the Tribulation. (Revelation 7:13–14)

4. When the martyrs get to heaven they will serve God. They will not be hungry or thirsty, and Jesus will take care of them and wipe every tear from their eyes.

REVELATION 8: TRUMPETS OF DOOM

1. Heaven was silent for thirty minutes because

God is very patient and wants to give the people on earth time to repent and turn from their sins. (Revelation 8:1, 4)

2. The golden censer is an incense burner that creates a fragrance. (Revelation 8:3) This censer symbolizes the sweet aroma of the prayers of the saints as they drift up to God. (Revelation 8:4)

3. At each of the first four trumpet blasts something different happened. The first angel brought hail, fire, and blood on the earth and a third of the earth was burned up. (Revelation 8:7) The second angel caused something like a huge mountain to fall into the sea and a third of the sea turned to blood, killing the creatures and ships in it. (Revelation 8:8) The third angel caused a star-like torch to fall into the water, turning a third of the water bitter and killing many who drank it. (Revelation 8:10–11) The fourth angel caused a third of the sky to become dark by striking the sun, moon, and stars. (Revelation 8:12)

4. The eagle was saying that more woes were coming and things were about to get worse. (Revelation 8:13)

REVELATION 9: TOUGH STUFF

1. The locusts came out of the Abyss. These locusts will torture people who do not have the seal of God on their foreheads. (Revelation 9:1–2, 4)

2. Those people who are suffering will wish to die, but God won't allow them to do so. (Revelation 9:6)

3. The release of the four angels will be requested by someone speaking for the martyred saints. (Revelation 9:11)

4. The four angels who are tied up by the Euphrates River will kill a third of the humans who are still left on earth. (Revelation 9:15)

5. The sins of the Tribulation are worship of false idols, demon worship, murder, black magic, sexual acts, and stealing. (Revelation 9:20–21)

REVELATION 10: JOHN GETS INVOLVED

1. The mighty angel wears a cloud with a rainbow above his head. His face will be like the sun and his legs will be like fiery pillars. (Revelation 10:1)

2. God has the voice of seven thunders. (Revelation 10:3)

3. When the Word of God is taken in, it is sweet, but also sour once the contents of it have been

digested and we understand God's judgments. Also it's sweet to know that Satan will be defeated, but sad to realize that many people won't come to know the Lord and will face punishment. (Revelation 10: 9–10)

4. God assigned John to prophesy about many peoples, nations, languages, and kings. (Revelation 10:11)

REVELATION 11: TWO WITNESSES AND AN ARK

1. John was told to measure the Temple but exclude the outer court because it had been given to the Gentiles, and they were trampling the holy city. (Revelation 11:2)
2. We aren't told who the two witnesses are, although one of them might be Elijah. These witnesses prophesy for 1,260 days and give testimony about Jesus and things to come. (Revelation 11:3, 7)
3. The death of the two witnesses will cause great rejoicing. (Revelation 11:10)
4. After three and a half days God raised the two witnesses up from the dead, and then took them up into heaven in a cloud. (Revelation 11:11–12)
5. Although Satan will try hard to fight against them, God and Jesus will soon rule the earth. Once this happens, things will never be the same. (Revelation 11:15–17)

REVELATION 12: THE GREATEST FALL OF ALL

1. The woman mentioned is Israel. She is important because she gave birth to a son—Jesus. (Revelation 12:1–2, 5)
2. The number of days equals three and a half years. This will be the last half of the Tribulation when the Jews will run from Satan to the place that God has prepared for them. (Revelation 12:7)
3. The angel that will cast Satan out of heaven is named Michael. He is the archangel. (Revelation 12:7)
4. Satan is angry because he will never be able to go to heaven again. He has been thrown out. Satan will now cause destruction on earth against the Jews and Gentiles who believe in Jesus. (Revelation 12:9–10, 13, 17)
5. Believers have three ways to overcome Satan: (1) trust in the blood of the Lamb, (2) have faith in Jesus, and (3) not fear death. (Revelation 12:11)

REVELATION 13: THE BEASTS ARRIVE

1. People will be saved during the Tribulation by trusting in Jesus Christ as their Savior and Lord. (Revelation 13:7)
2. The False Prophet will use miracles to get people to follow him. (Revelation 13:12–13)
3. The saints will need patience and faith to survive the Tribulation. Many people will be captured, killed, experience famine, and hardships. (Revelation 13:10)
4. No, the mark is none or these things. The mark is the number or name of the Antichrist. It will be 666. (Revelation 13:17–18)

REVELATION 14: ARMAGEDDON AND BABYLON

1. The 144,000 were pure because they did not participate in immoral activities or defile themselves with women. (Revelation 14:3–4)
2. People shouldn't have the Antichrist's mark put on their forehead or hand because those who have the mark will never have any rest. (Revelation 14:9, 11)
3. Jesus will reap the first harvest and the angels will reap the other one. During these harvests the wicked will be taken and thrown into the eternal fire. (Revelation 14:14–18)
4. The sinful nations will be trampled like grapes in the winepress of God's wrath. (Revelation 14:19–20)

REVELATION 15: SHORT, NOT SWEET

1. The three signs from heaven are (1) sun-clothed woman, Israel (Revelation 12:1); (2) the great red dragon, Satan (Revelation 12:3); and, (3) the seven angels with the seven last plagues. (Revelation 15:1)
2. The tribulation saints will be playing harps and will sing songs of worship to God. (Revelation 15:2–3)
3. The Bible says that Jesus is the only one who lived by all of God's standards. Jesus was the only sinless person to ever live. (Revelation 15:4)
4. The golden bowls will have the wrath of God in them. (Revelation 15:7)
5. Smoke will fill the Temple to keep everyone out. It symbolizes that those who choose not to believe in Jesus will no longer be shown mercy. (Revelation 15:8)

REVELATION 16: GOODNESS, GRACIOUS, GREAT BOWLS OF WRATH

1. The first bowl judgment is painful sores on the people who have the mark of the beast and worship his image. (Revelation 16:2)
2. The second bowl judgment turns the sea to blood and every living thing in the sea dies. (Revelation 16:3)
3. The third bowl judgment causes the rivers and springs of water to become like blood. (Revelation 16:4)
4. The fourth bowl judgment gives the sun power to scorch people with fire. (Revelation 16:8)
5. The fifth bowl judgment is total darkness. (Revelation 16:10)
6. The sixth bowl judgment dries up the Euphrates River, making way for the kings from the East. (Revelation 16:12)
7. During the seventh bowl judgment an angel cries out, saying, "It is done." There are flashes of lightning, rumblings, peals of thunder and a severe earthquake. All cities on earth, except for Babylon, are destroyed. Babylon is split into three parts. (Revelation 16:17–19)

REVELATION 17: BABYLON, MOTHER OF FALSE RELIGIONS

1. Babylon the mother refers to the false one-world religion that many people will follow. Babylon the city is an actual place where the one world government and all sorts of sinful practices will be allowed. (Revelation 17:1–5)
2. John was under the influence of the Holy Spirit when he saw this vision. (Revelation 17:3)
3. The ten horns are ten kings who have not yet received a kingdom. They will have power for a short time and will work along with the beast. (Revelation 17:12)
4. The Lamb who is the King of kings and Lord of Lords will overcome, along with his called, chosen, and faithful followers. (Revelation 17:14)
5. God will use the beast and the ten kings to destroy the false religions and to fulfill his prophecies. (Revelation 17:17)

REVELATION 18: BABYLON, CITY OF SIN

1. Babylon is a home to demons, every evil spirit, and every unclean bird. (Revelation 18:2)
2. A heavenly voice will call God's people out of Babylon so they will not share in Babylon's crimes or punishment (Revelation 18:4–7)
3. Babylon's sins are piled up to heaven. (Revelation 18:5)
4. Babylon will have plagues, death, mourning, and famine in the end. She will be consumed by fire (possibly a nuclear or atomic explosion) and will be judged by God. (Revelation 18:8)
5. Those who invested in Babylon or used her to make money will be sad because they will lose everything they invested and lose their source of income. (Revelation 18:11–19)
6. Heaven, the saints, and the apostles will rejoice because God has judged Babylon for the way she treated the righteous. (Revelation 18:20)

REVELATION 19: THE BEGINNING OF THE END

1. The multitude in heaven, the twenty-four elders, and the four living creatures will shout *"Amen, Hallelujah!"* (Revelation 19:1–6)
2. Jesus Christ is the wedding Lamb, and the church is his bride. (Revelation 19:7)
3. The saints will be wearing fine linen that is bright and clean. The garments represent the righteous acts of the saints made possible by God's righteousness. (Revelation 19:8)
4. John bowed down before an angel. The angel told him not to and insisted that he worship God instead. (Revelation 19:10)
5. The rider on the white horse will be called Faithful and True. (Revelation 19:11)
6. Those who followed the Antichrist will die by the Word of God that comes from Jesus' mouth and birds will eat their flesh. The Antichrist and False Prophet will be thrown into the fiery lake of burning sulfur or Lake of Fire. (Revelation 19:20–21).

REVELATION 20: A THOUSAND-YEAR REIGN

1. The angel will have the key to the Abyss and a great chain. (Revelation 20:1)
2. Satan will be tied up for a thousand years. (Revelation 20:2–3)
3. Those who had been beheaded because of their testimony for Jesus and because of the Word of God will be given authority to judge. Those who refuse to worship the beast or his image and don't receive his mark on their foreheads or hands will come to life and rule

with Christ for a thousand years. (Revelation 20:4)

4. After the thousand years Satan will go out and deceive the nations in the four corners of the earth and will gather them for battle. He will lead these followers of his to surround Jerusalem and attempt to conquer it. (Revelation 20:7–9)

5. God will send fire from heaven to destroy Satan's followers. Satan will then be thrown in the Lake of Fire where he will be tormented day and night. (Revelation 20:9–10)

6. The old earth and old heaven will be no more and a new heaven and new earth will take their place. All unbelievers will stand before God's throne and will be judged according to what God finds regarding them in the Book of Life. (Revelation 20:11–12)

REVELATION 21: OUT WITH OLD, IN WITH NEW

1. John was told to write this phrase because some may doubt the importance of Revelation. Some do not believe in the Rapture, Tribulation, Second Coming, or anger of God. These are the words of one who cannot lie and all humans would be wise to take God's words seriously. (Revelation 21:5)

2. Jesus can give the *"water of life"* because all authority belongs to him. He gained the authority and paid the price when he died on the cross. (Revelation 21:6)

3. The Holy City, the new Jerusalem, will come down out of heaven from God. It will be beautiful, and when it arrives everything on earth will be made new. This city will shine brightly and will have large walls, gates, and a street of gold. The foundation will be made of beautiful jewels. God and Jesus' light will shine so brightly that there will no longer be any need for the sun or moon. (Revelation 21:2, 4–5, 10–24)

4. The twelve names will be a reminder to all who enter the city that the Messiah, the words of the Bible, and salvation came through the Jews. (Revelation 21:12)

5. Only those whose names are written in the Lamb's Book of Life will enter into the Holy City. (Revelation 21:27)

REVELATION 22: JESUS IS COMING

1. Believers will have the name of God written on their foreheads. (Revelation 22:4)

2. A person can be blessed by God by keeping the words of Revelation and by obeying what this book says to do. (Revelation 22:7)

3. We can know that everything in Revelation is true because John was a witness to everything in this book and he wrote it down just as he saw it. (Revelation 22:8)

4. John got in trouble with the angel because he fell down to worship the angel and only God is to be worshiped. (Revelation 22:8)

5. God promises to all who read Revelation that he is coming soon. (Revelation 22:20)

235

George Barna is founder and president of Barna Research Group, Ltd., a marketing research company.

David Breese is the president of World Prophetic Ministry and a Bible teacher on *The King Is Coming* television program.

F. F. Bruce (1910–1990) was Rylands Professor of Biblical Criticism on Exegesis in the University of Manchester, England, and author of many Bible commentaries.

C. C. Carlson is the author or coauthor of nineteen books, including the best-selling *The Late Great Planet* with Hal Lindsey.

J. R. Church hosts the nationwide television program *Prophecy in the News*.

Dr. William R. Goetz, the former editor of *Personally Yours*, is currently vice president of sales and marketing for Christian Publications.

Billy Graham is a world famous evangelist and best-selling author.

Oliver B. Greene is a former director of the Gospel Hour, Inc., an author, and a radio show host.

Dr. Emory Griffin is the award-winning author of *The Mind Changers: The Art of Christian Persuasion.*

Nicky Gumbel, a former lawyer, is now ordained and on the staff of Trinity Brompton Church in London. He is also the author of *Why Jesus?, Why Christmas?, Searching Issues, A Life Worth Living,* and *Challenging Lifestyles.*

John Hagee is the founder and pastor of Cornerstone Church and president of Global Evangelism Television.

Ed Hindson is minister of biblical studies at Rehoboth Baptist Church in Atlanta, Georgia, vice president of *There's Hope*, adjunct professor at Liberty University in Virginia, and executive board member of the Pre-Trib Research Center in Washington, D.C.

David Hocking is a pastor, radio host, and director of Hope for Today Ministries.

Ron Hutchcraft is a thirty-year veteran of student and family work and president of Ron Hutchcraft Ministries. He writes books, speaks, conducts evangelistic outreaches, and hosts radio programs *A Word with You, Threshold,* and *Alive! with Ron Hutchcraft.*

William T. James has authored, compiled, and edited three books: *Storming toward Armageddon, The Triumphant Return of Christ,* and *The Earth's Final Days.*

David Jeremiah is president of Christian Heritage College, senior pastor of Scott Memorial Baptist Church in El Cajon, California, and radio host of *Turning Point.*

Greg Johnson, author of sixteen books, is the former editor of *Breakaway* magazine. Now he is a literary agent with Alive Communications.

Kevin Johnson pastored a group of more than 400 sixth through ninth graders in metro Milwaukee. He is now a full-time writer.

Tim LaHaye is a best-selling author, president and founder of Family Life Seminars, and husband to Beverly LaHaye, director of Concerned Women of America.

Hal Lindsey is often called the father of the modern-day prophecy movement. President of Hal Lindsey Ministries, he has written over a dozen books with a combined worldwide sale exceeding 36 million copies.

Jeanette Gardner Littleton is senior editor for Beacon Hill Press. She has over 1,500 articles printed in such publications as *Christian Single* and *Physician*.

Mark Littleton, a former youth pastor, is senior pastor at Westbridge Church in Des Moines, Iowa. He is the best-selling author of several books for teens, including *Beefin' Up: Real Feed for Amazin' Grazin'* and the *Truth about Rock*.

Max Lucado is a preacher with a weekly national radio program and author of many best-selling books.

Wim Malgo is the founder of Midnight Call, Inc., and the author of several books.

J. Vernon McGee is the former host of the popular *Thru the Bible* radio show.

Jim Petersen pioneered The Navigators ministry in Brazil. Jim is the author of *Living Proof* and *Church Without Walls*.

Larry Richards is the author of study Bibles and over 175 books on Christian education, theological study, and leadership.

Michael W. Smith is an award-winning Christian pop artist. He also launched his own recording label, Rocketown Records.

Greg Stier is executive director of Dare 2 Share Ministries International in Colorado. For information on street evangelism resources, call him at 800-462-8355.

Charles R. Swindoll is an internationally known writer, speaker, Bible teacher, and radio host.

Note: To the best of our knowledge, all of the above information is accurate and up to date. In some cases we were unable to obtain biographical information.
—THE STARBURST EDITORS

ENDNOTES

REVELATION 1: JOHN GOES DREAM-ING

1. Kevin Johnson, *Look Who's Toast Now!* (Minneapolis, MN: Bethany House, 1997), 16.
2. F. F. Bruce, *The Message of the New Testament* (Grand Rapids, MI: Eerdman's, 1972), 83.
3. Ron Hutchcraft, *The Battlefield for a Generation* (Chicago: Moody Press, 1996), 34.
4. George Barna, *Generation Next: What You Need to Know about Today's Youth* (Ventura, CA: Regal Books, 1995), 87.

REVELATION 2: A REAL NEED FOR JESUS

1. Tim LaHaye, *Revelation—Illustrated and Made Plain* (Grand Rapids, MI: Zondervan, 1975), 34–94.
2. Hal Lindsey, *There's a New World Coming* (Eugene, OR: Harvest House, 1984), 34–56.
3. J. Vernon McGee, *Thru the Bible with J. Vernon McGee,* vol. 5 (Nashville, TN: Thomas Nelson, 1981–1998), 901–915.
4. Emory A. Griffin, *The Mind Changers: The Art of Christian Persuasion* (Wheaton, IL: Tyndale, 1976), 192.
5. Barna, *Generation Next,* 19.
6. Nicky Gumbel, *Questions of Life* (Colorado Springs, CO and Paris, Ontario: David C. Cook, 1999), 78.

REVELATION 3: YOU'RE EITHER HOT OR NOT

1. Greg Johnson, *Like Is Like Driver's Ed* (Ann Arbor, MI: Servant, 1996), 16.

2. Michael W. Smith, "Michael W. Smith on Standing Alone," *Devo'Zine* (September/October 2000): 40.
3. George Barna, *Baby Busters: The Disillusioned Generation* (Chicago: Northfield, 1994), 52.
4. Johnson, *Life Is Like Driver's Ed* (Ann Arbor, MI: Servant, 1996), 177.

REVELATION 4: HOW IT'S GONNA BE

1. Johnson, *Look Who's Toast Now!* 98.
2. Max Lucado, *Six Hours One Friday* (Portland, OR: Multnomah, 1989), 174.

REVELATION 5: TOTALLY WORTHY

1. Lindsey, *There's a New World Coming* (Eugene, OR: Harvest House, 1984), 74.
2. Johnson, *Look Who's Toast Now!* 20.
3. Charles R. Swindoll, *Growing Deep in the Christian Life* (Portland, OR: Multnomah, 1986), 279.
4. Jim Petersen, *Lifestyle Discipleship: The Challenge of Following Jesus in Today's World* (Colorado Springs, CO: NavPress, 1993), 172.

REVELATION 6: HORSES, DESPAIR, GORE, AND MORE

1. John Hagee, *Beginning of the End* (Nashville, TN: Thomas Nelson, 1996), 117.
2. John Hagee, *Day of Deception* (Nashville, TN: Thomas Nelson, 1997), 49.
3. Hiroshi Nakajima, *The Jackson Sun,* May 20, 1996.
4. David Hocking, *The Vision of Heaven* (Portland, OR: Multnomah, 1988), 46.

REVELATION 7: MARKED MESSENGERS

1. Greg Stier, "Take It to the Streets," *Group* (September/October 2000): 59.

2. Max Lucado, *And the Angel's Were Silent* (Sisters, OR: Multnomah, 1992), 124.

REVELATION 8: TRUMPETS OF DOOM

1. Mark Littleton and Jeanette Gardner Littleton, *What's in the Bible for . . .™ Teens* (Lancaster, PA: Starburst Publishers, 2000), 121.
2. David Breese, *Earth's Final Days* (Green Forest, AR: New Leaf Press, 1994), 321.
3. Vince Aquilino, "Expect the Unexpected" (Syracuse, NY: To His Glory Ministries, 2000) <http://aplus-software.com/thglory/up091400.htm> (September, 14, 2000).
4. Lindsey, *There's a New World Coming,* 118.
5. William R. Goetz, *Apocalypse Next: The End of Civilization as We Know It?* (Camp Hill, PA: Horizon Books, 1996), 35.
6. Charles Smith, "Chinese Army Fires Super-Gun," *WorldNetDaily,* October 26, 2000, <http://www.worldnetdaily.com/news/article.asp?ARTICLE_ID=20650> (January 10, 2002).

REVELATION 9: TOUGH STUFF

1. David Jeremiah with C. C. Carlson, *Escape the Coming Night* (Dallas, TX: Word, 1990), 128–129.
2. *The World Book Encyclopedia 1990,* vol. 12, s.v. "locusts."
3. Oliver B. Greene, *The Revelation* (Greenville, SC: The Gospel Hour, 1963), 256.

REVELATION 10: JOHN GETS INVOLVED

1. David Hocking, *The Coming World Leader* (Portland, OR: Multnomah, 1988), 170.
2. Jeremiah with Carlson, *Escape the Coming Night,* 138.
3. Hocking, *The Coming World Leader,* 172.

REVELATION 11: TWO WITNESSES AND AN ARK

1. Jerrold Kessel, "Palestinian funerals, Israeli restrictions follow deadly day," CNN.com, December 9, 2000, <http://www.cnn.com/2000/WORLD/meast/12/09/mideast.02/index.html> (March 30, 2001).

2. Hal Lindsey, *Planet Earth-2000 A.D.* (Palos Verdes, CA: Western Front, Ltd., 1994), 156.
3. Steve Newman, "Earthweek," *Colorado Springs (Colorado) Gazette Telegraph,* December 9, 2000, A3.
4. William T. James, *Earth's Final Days* (Green Forest, AR: New Leaf Press, 1994), 15.
5. Hagee, *Beginning of the End,* 95.
6. Christian Jew Foundation, *Message of the Christian Jew* (San Antonio, TX: Christian Jew Foundation, November/December 1993), 6.

REVELATION 12: THE GREATEST FALL OF ALL

1. Hutchcraft, *The Battlefield for a Generation,* 11.
2. Billy Graham, *Angels* (Dallas: Word, 1995), 208.
3. Swindoll, *Growing Deep in the Christian Life,* 269.

REVELATION 13: THE BEASTS ARRIVE

1. Goetz, *Apocalypse Next,* 107.
2. Ibid., 201.
3. James, *Earth's Final Days,* 16.
4. LaHaye, *Revelation,* 258.

REVELATION 14: ARMAGEDDON AND BABYLON

1. LaHaye, *Revelation,* 267.
2. Daymond R. Duck, *On the Brink: Easy-to-Understand End-Time Bible Prophecy* (Lancaster, PA: Starburst Publishers, 1995), 118–120.
3. Graham, *Angels,* 233.
4. Wim Malgo, *The Wrath of Heaven on Earth* (West Columbia, SC: Midnight Call, Inc., 1985), 91.

REVELATION 15: SHORT, NOT SWEET

1. LaHaye, *Revelation,* 285.
2. Swindoll, *Growing Deep in the Christian Life,* 249.

REVELATION 16: GOODNESS, GRACIOUS, GREAT BOWLS OF WRATH

1. Malgo, *The Wrath of Heaven on Earth,* 116.
2. "Pollution Adding to Severe Global Warming," *CNN.com,* October 26, 2000 <http://www.cnn.com/2000/NATURE/

240

10/25/global.warming.ap/> (January 10, 2002).

3. CSIRO, "Burping Contributes to Global Warming," *Future Frame News*, July 24, 2000, <http://www.futureframe.de/news/000724-4.htm> (May 4, 2001). See also "Environment-Brazil: Cattle Contribute to Global Warming," *Inter Press Service*, November 28, 2000, <http://www.mycattle.com/2000/11/28/ip/0000-0868-KEYWORD.Missing.html> and Australian Greenhouse Office, "National Greenhouse Gas Inventory, 1999: Overview at a Glance," April 2001, <http://www.greenhouse.gov.au/inventory/facts/pdfs/nggifs1s.pdf>.

4. Goetz, *Apocalypse Next*, 129.

5. Newman, "Earthweek," A3.

6. Goetz, *Apocalypse Next*, 65.

REVELATION 17: BABYLON, MOTHER OF FALSE RELIGIONS

1. Ed Hindson, *Final Signs* (Eugene, OR: Harvest House, 1996), 103.

2. Hal Lindsey, "Revelation: The Mystery of Babylon," taped message #026A.

3. Goetz, *Apocalypse Next*, 233.

4. Duck, *On the Brink*, 118–120.

REVELATION 18: BABYLON, CITY OF SIN

1. Peter and Paul Lalonde, *301 Startling Proofs and Prophecies* (Niagara Falls, Canada: Prophecy Partners, Inc., 1996), 234.

2. Hindson, *Final Signs*, 107.

3. James, *Earth's Final Days*, 15.

4. Hocking, *The Coming World Leader*, 252.

5. Larry Richards, *The Bible—God's Word for the Biblically-Inept™* (Lancaster, PA: Starburst Publishers, 1998), 20.

REVELATION 19: THE BEGINNING OF THE END

1. J. Vernon McGee, *Thru the Bible with J. Vernon McGee*, vol. 5 (Nashville, TN: Thomas Nelson, 1981–1998), 1049.

2. Jeremiah with Carlson, *Escape the Coming Night*, 208.

3. J. R. Church, *Guardians of the Grail* (Oklahoma City, OK: Prophecy Publications, 1989), 312.

REVELATION 20: A THOUSAND-YEAR REIGN

1. Zach Arrington, *Confessions of a College Freshman* (Tulsa, OK: RiverOak, 2001), 42.

2. Swindoll, *Growing Deep in the Christian Life*, 299.

3. Hocking, *The Coming World Leader*, 290.

4. Ann-Margret Hovsepian, "Teenage Sisters Bring Gospel to Punks," *Christianweek*, January 2001, front page.

REVELATION 21: OUT WITH OLD, IN WITH NEW

1. Jim Petersen, *Lifestyle Discipleship—The Challenge of Following Jesus in Today's World* (Colorado Springs, CO: NavPress, 1993), 172.

2. Johnson, *Look Who's Toast Now!* 133–134.

3. Richards, *The Bible—God's Word for the Biblically Inept*, 322.

REVELATION 22: JESUS IS COMING

1. McGee, *Thru the Bible with J. Vernon McGee*, vol. 5, 1077.

2. Johnson, *Look Who's Toast Now!* 131.

3. Lucado, *And the Angels Were Silent*, 85.

INDEX

Boldface numbers refer to defined (What?) terms in the sidebar.

243

Chemical weapons, 84
  (*See also* Weapons)
Cherubim, **51**
Child of God, 37
China:
  army of, 155
  communist, 66
  Taiwan rocket gun, 84
Christ (*see* Jesus Christ)
Christian Era, 47
Christians:
  backsliding, 20, 21
  courage, need for, 35
  indifferent, 33, 39
  Jesus never leaving, 29–30
  judgment of (*see* Judgment)
  living for God, 35
  martyrdom (*see* Martyrs)
  overcomers (*see* Overcom-
    ers)
  qualities of, 27
  at Rapture, 34, 37
  rewards of, 30
  Satan, overcoming, 121–122
  Satan's rampage against, 123
  sin, overcoming, 20
  and spiritual adultery, 29
  at Tribulation, 68–70
  tribulation saints (*see*
    Tribulation saints)
  true and false, 36, 37, 39–40
  (*See also* Born again;
    Overcomers; specific
    topics)
Christian witness (*see*
  Witness, Christian)
Church:
  bride of Christ, 186–189,
    210, 226
  John as representing, 48
  peace to come, 51
  resurrection of, 202 (*See
    also* Rapture)
  (*See also* Christians; specific
    churches)
Church, J. R., on the Millennium, 194

Church Age, **10**, 14, 18
  Christian Era, 47
  Laodicea period as last of,
    39
  as nearly over, 45, 222
Churches, seven (*see* Seven
  churches)
Cloud(s), 95–96, 140
Colors, symbolism of (*see*
  specific colors)
Commission, **100**
Commissioned, **59**
Communism, **66**
Consuming, **204**
Convicts, **25**
Correspondents, **3**
Counsel, spirit of, 7
Covenant, **65**
Covenant, ark of (*see* Ark of
  the covenant)
Cowardice, 212
Creatures, four living, 51–52,
    56–58, 60, 76
  and Babylon's destruction,
    186
  first, 64–65
  fourth, 67–68, 68
  second, 66–67
  and seven golden bowls,
    147–148 (*See also* Seven
    bowl judgments)
  silencing of, 79–80
  third, 67
Crown of life, **23**
Crown(s):
  of Antichrist, 64–65
  Christians receiving, 206
  of Jesus, 140, 191
  seven, 116
  of twelve stars, 115–116
Crucified, **7**
Crying, end of, 77–78, 210–
    211
Cults, **xii**

D

Daniel, prophecy of, 133, 223

Darkness, 64, 87–88
  fifth plague, 154–155
  nuclear winter, 85
Dates:
  "No man knows...that day
    or hour," xii
  predicting, xii
  (*See also* Future events)
Daughters of Babylon,
    163–164
David, key of, 35–36
David, Root of, 56–57, 226
Day of Atonement, 148
Death, 64, 206
  for believers/unbelievers,
    206–207
  eternal, 137
  fearing/not fearing,
    121–122, 140, 141
  first and second, 212
  "I was dead," 13
  Jesus as overcoming, 82
  pale horse, 67–68
  physical and spiritual, 23
  (*See also* individual names)
Deceiving spirits, **165**
Deeds, judgment of, 27
  (*See also* Judgment)
Deluded, **194**
Demon(s), 155–156
  in Babylon, 175–176
  "deceiving spirits," 165
  worship of (*see* Idol
    worship)
  (*see* Abyss; Satan)
Deny, **9**
Desert:
  Israel protected in, 118,
    122–124
  Jordan, 118
Destruction, mass, 64
  seventh plague, 158–159
Detestable, **175**
Devil (*see* Satan)
Devil's Millennium, 28
Devours, **106**
Dictators, 170

Difficulties, 40
Disciples, **5**
  (*See also* Apostles)
Discipline, by Jesus, 40–41
Disease(s), 68, 220–221
  sores (first plague), 151–152
Dogs, 226
Dome of the Rock, 103–105
  illustration of, 106
Domitian, the emperor, 8
Donkey, 85
Dragon:
  Antichrist as, 125 (*See also*
    Antichrist)
  evil spirit from mouth, 155
  False Prophet speaking like,
    131
  red, 116–120
  Satan as, 133, 145
  (*See also* Satan)
Dreams, of Joseph, 115–116
Drugs, 93
Duck, Daymond R., on the
    Church Age, 18

E
Eagle, 51–52
  talking, 85
  woman given wings of, 122
  (*See also* Creatures, four
    living)
Earth:
  burning of one-third, 64, 83
  destruction of, 205
  future events (*see* Future
    events; specific topics)
  God to rule, 110–111
  Israel as, 130
  judgment on, 83
  new, 209–210
  repopulation of (post-
    Tribulation), 201
  Satan inhabiting, 111, 120
  second beast from, 130
  seven trumpets, results of
    (*see* Seven trumpets)
  wickedness, peak of, 142

Earthquake(s), 64, 69, 82,
    110
  at Armageddon, 159–160
  in Jerusalem, 109–110
  Satan's troops swallowed,
    123–124
  two witnesses, raising of,
    109–110
East, angel from, 73–74
Economic collapse, 64
  of Babylon (*see* Babylon,
    destruction of)
Eden, Garden of, 20, 51, 220
Egypt, 117, 146
  Sodom and, 108
Elders, twenty-four, 50, 53,
    56–58, 60, 76
  and Babylon's destruction,
    186
  at seventh trumpet, 110–111
  two questions, 77
Elijah, 48, 106
Elude, **89**
Emperor, Domitian as, 8
End-time events (*see* Future
    events)
Enoch, 48
Ephesians, Book of, 214
Ephesus, church at, 18–19
  (*See also* Seven churches)
Ephesus period, 18
  (*See also* Church Age)
Esdralon, 158
Eternal life, 49, 217, 228
  choices regarding, 71
  gaining, x
  (*See also* Heaven)
Euphrates River, 64
  angels, four bound at, 91
  sixth plague, 155
Europe, 126, 133, 169
Evangelism (*see* Witness,
    Christian)
Evangelistic, **36**
Eve, 220
Events, future (*see* Future
    events)

Evil (*see* Satan; Sin)
Evil spirits (*see* Demons)
Eyes, seven, 57
Ezekiel, prophecy of, 66, 108

F
Faith, x, 27, 112
False Prophet, 58, 130–132,
    131
  Antichrist, as helping, 130
  Babylon, headquartered in,
    183
  as beast, 108
  evil spirit from mouth, 155
  fate of, 194
  top religious leader, 125
Fame, 93
Famine, 64, 67, 85
Fear:
  of Jesus, 147
  of the Lord, spirit of, 7
Fear God, **137**
Fire, 83
  Babylon consumed by,
    178–179
  earth burning, 64, 83
  God's judgment, symboliz-
    ing, 146
  from heaven, 130
  lake of (*see* Lake of Fire)
  pillars of (angel's legs),
    95–96
  plague of, 92–93
Flesh, **25**
Flood, the, 56
Food:
  manna from heaven, 26
  in new Jerusalem, 220
Forerunner, **28**
Four angels, 73–74
Four living creatures (*see*
    Creatures, four living)
Friends, friendships, 34, 93
Frogs, 155
Fruit, from the Tree of Life,
    220
Future events, 47, 58, 222

on earth, 63
order of, 45
Revelation as about, x, xi
"what must soon take
place," 5
(*See also* Dates; specific
topics and events)

G
Garden of Eden, 20, 51, 220
Generations, 8
Genesis, Book of, 115
Genre, **7**
Gentile(s), **75, 168**
believers among (*see*
Christians)
governments, 116, 168–169
Jerusalem, controlling, 105
144,000, excluded from, 75
Gethsemane, Garden of, 21, 81
Glass:
sea of, 51
sea of, second, 146
Globalism, 163
Global warming, 154
Glorified bodies, **69**
Gnashing, **188**
God:
attributes of, 29
face of, 221
relationship with, 34 (*See
also* Christians; Faith)
Trinity, the (*see* Trinity)
wisdom of, 99
Godliness, 99
God's Word (*see* Bible; Word
of God)
Goetz, Dr. William R.:
on the Antichrist, 128
on Antichrist and the
prostitute, 171
on Armageddon, 158
on the Chinese army, 155
on Tribulation government,
126
on weapons, nuclear and
chemical, 84

Gog, **203**
Gold, 165
city of, 215
golden cup, 165
Golden altar, 91, 104
illustration of, 81
Golden bowls, 57–58
(*See also* Seven bowl
judgments)
Golden censer, 80–82
illustration of, 81
Golden lampstands, seven,
10, 14
(*See also* Seven churches)
Gomorrah, Sodom and, 56,
108
Gospel, 73
and eternal life, 137
last chance to accept, 137
spreading, 76 (*See also*
Witness, Christian)
Government:
Antichrist as leader, 116,
125–128, 139, 169
dictators, 170
Gentile, 116, 168–169
satanic (*see* Antichrist)
seven heads, 116
seven hills, 168
ten kings, 169–170, 193–194
Tribulation, 125–126
world, 116, 126, 164, 176
chart of seven, 127
Grace, **64,** 228
Graham, Billy:
on death, 140
on Satan's last stand, 119
Grapes, 142
Great Tribulation (*see*
Tribulation, the Great)
Great White Throne Judg-
ment, **27,** 204–208
Greek alphabet, 8
Greene, Oliver B., on locusts,
90
Griffin, Dr. Emory, on loving
sinner but hating sin, 20

Gumbel, Nicky, on the Bible,
25

H
Hades, 13, **13, 206**–207
(*See also* Hell)
Hagee, John:
on Antichrist, 65
on financial collapse in
America, 67
on two witnesses, death of,
109
Hail, hailstones, 83, 111,
159–160
Hallelujah, **184**
Happenings:
Babylon, rebuilding,
172–173
dictators, 170
diseases, 68
earthquakes, 110, 160
frogs in Hawaii, 156
global warming, 154
Iranian bird migration, 107
Israel, Christians driven
from, 177
locusts, 88, 90
the mark of the beast, 132
moon landing, 97
Muslims in Jerusalem, 104
the Reformation, 34
slavery, 180
Taiwan rocket gun, 84
war, 66
world council of religions,
176
Harlot, **28**
Babylon as (*see* Babylon
("the prostitute"))
Harp(s), 57–58, 136, 182
Harvest, **140**–143
Healing, 220
Heart, Jesus as seeing, 22, 29
Heaven, 78, 207
destruction of, 205
glorified bodies, 69
Jesus as way to, 76–77

S

Sackcloth, **105**
Sacrifice, 104, 147–148
Saints:
  prayers of, censer symboliz-
    ing, 80–82
  resurrection of (Old
    Testament), 202
  tribulation (*see* Tribulation
    saints)
Salvation, 76–77, 223–224
  (*see* Born again; Witness,
    Christian)
Sapphira, 227
Sardis, church in, 33–35
  (*See also* Seven churches)
Sardis period, 18
  (*See also* Church Age)
Satan, 64, 120
  angels and, 73–74, 117–119
  city of, 138
  defeat of, 58, 146
  on earth, 111
  falling star as, 87–88
  final judgment of, 204
  final release of, 201
  Jesus, efforts against,
    117–118
  Michael, war with, 118–119
  Millennium, bound during,
    199–201
  second rebellion of, 203–
    204
  synagogue of, 22, 36
  at Tribulation, 63
  ways to overcome, 121–122
  world of, 91
  (*See also* Abyss; specific
    topics and events)
Satanic government (*See
  under* Antichrist)
Satanism, 117, 129, 163
Saved (*see* Born again)
Savior, Jesus Christ as:
  trusting, 20 (*See also* Jesus
    Christ)
Scepter, iron, 192

Scripture (*see* Bible)
Scroll:
  angel with, 96
  Jesus as opening, 57–58
  John as eating, 99–101
  seven seals, 55–56 (*See also*
    Seven seal judgments)
Sea, 164
  Antichrist as from,
    125–126, 130
  clear as crystal, 146
  creatures, ships destroyed,
    83
  of glass, 51
  of glass, second, 146
  in heaven, 146
  judgment on, 83
  object thrown into, 83
  polluting of one-third, 64,
    83, 152
  second trumpet, 83
  tribulation saints coming
    from, 146
  (*See also* Water)
Seals, seven (*see* Seven seal
  judgments)
Second Coming, 13, 37, 58,
  190–194
  "I am coming soon," 228
  still to come, 222
  Tribulation, at end of, 59
Seraphim, **51**
Serpent:
  Satan as, 120
  (*See also* Satan)
Servant(s), servanthood, 5
  Angels as, 189–190,
    222–223
  Christians and, 27
  Jesus as, 5
  "Servant John," 5
Seven, the number, 10, 133
Seven angels, 79–80, 146–
  147 (*See under* Angels)
Seven bowl judgments
  (plagues), 63–64,
  145–148, 151–161, 213

  as wrath of God, 147–148,
    151–161
Seven churches, xi, 3, 18
  angels of, 12–14
  golden lampstands as, 10,
    14
  letters to, 17
  map of, 9
  Revelation written to, 6
  Son of man amidst, 10–11
  (*See also* specific names and
    topics)
Seven crowns, 116
Seven eyes, 57
Seven golden lampstands, 10,
  14, 18
Seven horns, 57
Seven lamps, 50
Seven letters, 17
Seven parallels, 4
Seven seal judgments, 38,
  55–56, 63–64, 79–80
  fifth, 68–69, 153
  first, 65–66
  first four, 66
  fourth, 67–68, 68
  of Jews, 74–75
  last three, 68
  second, 66
  seventh, 79–80
  seventh opened, 99
  sixth, 69–70
  third, 67
Seven spirits, 6–7
Seven stars, 12–14, 18
Seven thunders, 96–**97**
Seven trumpet judgments,
  63–64, 79–80, 83–87, 91,
  94, 99, 110
  seventh trumpet, 110–111
Seven virtues, 6–7
Sexual immorality, 28–29,
  212, 226
Sexual purity, 136
Sickle, 140–143
Sickness (*see* Diseases)
Sign(s), **115**

first sign in heaven, 116
second sign in heaven, 117
watching for, x
Silence, thirty minutes of,
79–80
Sin(s), **7**
backsliding, 19
church, brought into, 28
hating, but loving the
sinner, 19–20
Holy Spirit convicting of,
207
Jesus as solution, 104
Jesus paying for, 13, 59
justification, 121
Lake of Fire, 212
original, 20, 220–221
overcoming, 20
repenting, 41
(*See also* Judgment)
Slavery, 180
Smith, Michael W., on living
for God, 35
Smyrna, church in, 21–23
Smyrna period, 18
(*See also* Church Age)
Sodom, 56, 108
Song(s):
of the 144,000, 136
of the Lamb, 146–147
of Moses, 146
new, 58–59
Son of God (*see* Jesus Christ)
Son of man, 10–11
(*See also* Jesus Christ)
Sores, 64
Soviet Union (*see* Russia)
Spirit, **25**
Spiritual adultery, **29**
Splendor, **217**
Stadia, **142**
Star(s):
angels, 117
Bright and Morning Star,
29–30
darkening of, 85
falling, 69–70

falling, Satan as, 87–88
morning star, 88, 226
seven (*see* Seven stars)
twelve, crown of, 115–116
Stier, Greg, on witnessing, 76
Stone(s)
boulder, 182
precious, 49, 165, 215–216
white and black, 26
Stop (feature) (*see* Warnings)
Sudan, 180
Suffering, 40
Sulfur, 139, 204
Sun:
darkening of, 69, 85, 87–88
dimmed, 64
not needed in new Jerusa-
lem, 216–217, 221
scorching, 64, 153–154
"shone like the sun," 95–96
woman clothed with (*see*
Pregnant woman
(Israel))
Sunday, Holy Spirit coming to
John, 9
Swindoll, Charles R.:
on death, 206
on sacrifice, 148
on the Second Coming, 58,
121
Sword:
Bible (Word of God) as,
24–25
sharp, 192
Symbolic, **4**
Symbolism in Revelation, xii,
14, 87
Symbols, key (*see* Key
symbols)
Synagogue, **22**
Synagogue of Satan, 21–22

T
Taiwan rocket gun, 84
Teachers, false and true (*see*
Leaders)
Tears, end of, 77–78, 210–211

Teens:
beliefs of, 22
spirituality of, 10
Temple:
absent, in new Jerusalem, 216
destruction of, 133
Temple, heavenly, 147
Temple in Jerusalem, 81
Antichrist entering, 171
conflict over control,
103–105
layout of, illustration, 104
(*See also* Ark of the Cov-
enant)
Temptation:
absence during Millennium,
201
after Millennium, 203–204
of Jesus, 117
Ten Commandments, 147
Ten thousand times ten
thousand, **60**
Ten virgins, parable of, 188
Testimony, 189
(*See also* Christian witness)
Thirst, **212**
Throne
Great White (*see* Great
White Throne Judgment)
seven spirits before God's,
6–7
Thunder, thunderstorms, 50,
111, 159
seven thunders, 96–**97**
Thyatira, church in, 26–29
(*See also* Seven churches)
Thyatira period, 18
(*See also* Church Age)
Torture, 64
Tower of Babel, 166, 173, 177
Tree of life, fruit from, 220
Trials, 40
Tribulation, the Great, **14,**
37, 63, 77, 108, 226
Babylon in timetable of, 138
Believers, removal of before,
30

256

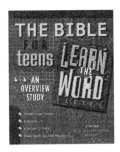   

• **Learn more at www.learntheword.com** •

The Bible for Teens—Learn the Word™ Series
Who says Bible study has to be boring? Finally, there is a Bible commentary that meets the needs of today's teens by explaining biblical principles and Scripture in a fun, informative, and entertaining format. Adapted from *The Bible—God's Word for the Biblically-Inept™*.
(trade paper)   ISBN 1892016516   **$14.99**

Revelation for Teens—Learn the Word™ Series
Don't sweat the future. Learn everything God wants you to know about what's going to happen, including the Rapture, the Tribulation, the Antichrist, and the new heaven and earth. Study one of the most exciting books of the Bible in this series of commentaries for teens adapted from *Revelation—God's Word for the Biblically-Inept™*.
(trade paper)   ISBN 1892016559   **$14.99**

Bible Bytes for Teens: A Study-Devotional for Logging In to God's Word
Teens can focus on byte-sized Scripture passages and related teaching to get clear spiritual direction for their day. Also included are reflective study questions and a power-packed design that teens will love.
(trade paper)   ISBN 1892016494   **$13.99**

What's in the Bible for . . .™ Teens
By Mark Littleton and Jeanette Gardner Littleton
Written to teens, this book explores biblical themes that speak to the challenges and pressures of today's adolescents, such as relationships and peer pressure. Helpful and eye-catching "WWJD?" icons, illustrations, and sidebars are included.
(trade paper)   ISBN 1892016052   **$16.95**

IT'S THE BIBLE MADE EASY!

The *God's Word for the Biblically-Inept™* series is already a best-seller with over 300,000 books sold! Designed to make reading the Bible easy, educational, and fun, this series of verse-by-verse Bible studies, topical studies, and overviews mixes scholarly information from experts with helpful icons, illustrations, sidebars, and timelines. It's the Bible made easy!

God's Word for the Biblically-Inept™ Series

TITLE	ISBN	TITLE CODE	PRICE
Acts *by Robert C. Girard*	ISBN 189201646X	**GWAC**	**$17.99**
The Bible *by Larry Richards*	ISBN 0914984551	**GWBI**	**$16.95**
Daniel *by Daymond R. Duck*	ISBN 0914984489	**GWDN**	**$16.95**
Genesis *by Joyce L. Gibson*	ISBN 1892016125	**GWGN**	**$16.95**
Health & Nutrition *by Kathleen O'Bannon Baldinger*	ISBN 0914984055	**GWHN**	**$16.95**
John *by Lin Johnson*	ISBN 1892016435	**GWJN**	**$16.95**
Life of Christ, Volume 1 *by Robert C. Girard*	ISBN 1892016230	**GWLC**	**$16.95**
Life of Christ, Volume 2 *by Robert C. Girard*	ISBN 1892016397	**GWLC2**	**$16.95**
Luke *by Joyce L. Gibson*	ISBN 1892016478	**GWLK**	**$17.99**
Mark *by Scott Pinzon*	ISBN 1892016362	**GWMK**	**$17.99**
Men of the Bible *by D. Larry Miller*	ISBN 1892016079	**GWMB**	**$16.95**
Prophecies of the Bible *by Daymond R. Duck*	ISBN 1892016222	**GWPB**	**$16.95**
Revelation *by Daymond R. Duck*	ISBN 0914984985	**GWRV**	**$16.95**
Romans *by Gib Martin*	ISBN 1892016273	**GWRM**	**$16.95**
Women of the Bible *by Kathy Collard Miller*	ISBN 0914984063	**GWWB**	**$16.95**

For purchasing information see page 259   •   Learn more at **www.biblicallyinept.com**

WHAT'S IN THE BIBLE FOR YOU!!!

From the creators of the *God's Word for the Biblically-Inept™* series comes the innovative *What's in the Bible for . . .™* series. Scripture has certain things to say to certain people, but without a guide, hunting down *all* of what the Bible has to say to you can be overwhelming. Borrowing the user-friendly format of the *God's Word for the Biblically-Inept™* series, this new series spotlights those passages and themes of Scripture that are relevant to particular groups of people. Whether you're young or old, married or single, male or female, this series will simplify the very important process of applying the Bible to your life.

What's in the Bible for . . .™ Couples *Kathy Collard Miller and D. Larry Miller*   WBFC
(trade paper)   ISBN 1892016028   **$16.95**

What's in the Bible for . . .™ Women *Georgia Curtis Ling*   WBFW
(trade paper)   ISBN 1892016109   **$16.95**

What's in the Bible for . . .™ Mothers *Judy Bodmer*   WBFM
(trade paper)   ISBN 1892016265   **$16.95**

What's in the Bible for . . .™ Teens *Mark Littleton and Jeanette Gardner Littleton*   WBFT
(trade paper)   ISBN 1892016052   **$16.95**

● **Learn more at www.biblicallyinept.com** ●

Purchasing Information

www.starburstpublishers.com

Books are available from your favorite bookstore, either from current stock or special order. To assist bookstores in locating your selection, be sure to give title, author, and ISBN. If unable to purchase from a bookstore, you may order direct from STARBURST PUBLISHERS®. When ordering please enclose full payment plus shipping and handling as follows:

Post Office (4th class)
$3.00 with a purchase of up
   to $20.00
$4.00 ($20.01–$50.00)
8% of purchase price for
   purchases of $50.01 and up

United Parcel Service (UPS)
$5.00 (up to $20.00)
$7.00 ($20.01–$50.00)
12% ($50.01 and up)

Canada
$5.00 (up to $35.00)
15% ($35.01 and up)

Overseas
$5.00 (up to $25.00)
20% ($25.01 and up)

Payment in U.S. funds only. Please allow two to four weeks minimum for delivery by USPS (longer for overseas and Canada). Allow two to seven working days for delivery by UPS. Make checks payable to and mail to:

Starburst Publishers®
P.O. Box 4123
Lancaster, PA 17604

Credit card orders may be placed by calling 1-800-441-1456, Mon–Fri, 8:30 A.M. to 5:30 P.M. Eastern Standard Time. Prices are subject to change without notice. Catalogs are available for a 9 x 12 self-addressed envelope with four first-class stamps.